WORMS

IN THE

APPLE

Joe DeCicco

Award winning author of Angel with a Gun

This book is a work of fiction. All names, characters, organizations and incidents are either a product of the author's imagination, or, if real, are used fictionally without any intent to describe their actual account.

Contact the author by E-mail at romanonovels@yahoo.com

Printed in the United State of America
Charleston, North Carolina
for

JNJ Associates Publishing Co

JNJ Associates Inc.
PO Box 237, Hampstead, N.C. 28443

First Published: August 13, 2010

ISBN 10:0-9897227-1-6
ISBM 13: 978-0-9897227-1-1

Dedication

To the hardworking, honest, police officers in our society, especially those who paid the ultimate price for the privilege of serving others.

Special homage is paid to the 404 valiant public servants who perished on September 11, 2001 including 60 police officers, the visible guardians of our precious liberties.

An individual thank you is extended to my loving wife Judy who has never discouraged my efforts to put some of my "stories" down on paper and for graciously acting as my editor.

Prologue

This work is based on real police incidents and personalities. Names have been changed to protect the dignity of family members who may identify similarities of relatives depicted in this accounting.

Follow along as another chapter in the career of Michael Romano, a New York City cop unfolds.

When Michael was young, his parish priest explained that when Saint Michael slew Satan, usually depicted as a serpent, to keep the world safe, he acted as God's policeman. From that moment on, Mike identified with Saint Michael, who happens to be the patron saint of police officers. In Michael's mind, he is society's guardian, an angel who happens to wear a gun. Romano adheres to his own unwavering moral code as he does what he feels he must, to protect the public from the miscreants of society, to rid his world of the worms in the apple.

While assigned to his former command, Michael became almost obsessed about apprehending a child rapist. Aided by Providence, he finally brought that child molester to a final justice. The perpetrator died of gunshot wounds.

Romano also wanted to bring a corrupt high ranking officer, Dennis Bryan, to justice for protecting the rapist. Mike was transferred to a new command. His new Commander will be the very same corrupt cop, Dennis Bryan.

While not perfect, Michael Romano does his job, always mindful of his ultimate goal, bringing the corrupt boss to justice, to remove that particular worm from the apple.

Chapter One

Finally cleared after six weeks by the Medical Section for full active duty, Mike would begin his new command assignment. Tomorrow morning, he would report to the command of Deputy Inspector Dennis Bryan, brother- in-law and protector of that very same child molester. Michael spent many hours in thought, trying to determine if chance, providence, or Saint Michael himself, stepped in and sent him to that command.

Betty Romano, Mike's wife of 11 years, went bug eyed the moment he had told her he was being transferred to the precinct that Bryan commanded.

"Michael, by now he must know who you are," she chided him. "He knows you shot and killed Brian Wilkey during the 1977 Blackout. It has to be in your personnel folder. After all you killed his brother-in-law. The guy was family." Betty had no way of knowing that Dennis actually loathed the man and only protected him because he had feared his own wife, Elizabeth, who was Brian's sister.

"Sure", he responded. "Dennis knows I'm the guy that shot his brother-in-law and hopefully sent him to Hell like he deserved." Without taking a breath, Mike continued, "But he has no idea that I made any connection between him and that pervert, no idea at all."

Betty responded with, "Bu buubttt…"

Mike promptly cut her off with, "Don't worry, I'll be fine. I survived in the 32nd precinct and survived a couple of gunfights. Didn't I?"

In a voice resounding with a mixture of pride and worry, Betty quickly answered with, "Sure Mike, but I know you. If you think you're right, you go ahead full force. "

Mike thought carefully before answering her. "Look Betty, I know that I can run away with myself at times.

But, what better way to learn about Bryan then to work in his command. Maybe someday he'll get what's coming to him and I'll be able to help deliver the gift. Anyway, it's a busy command and there's a lot to learn. My expertise and career can grow there."

"You just be careful. You are not Saint Michael." Betty answered as she reached out and gave him a little light tap on his arm. Realizing she hit the old wound, she smiled and kissed him. "I love you crazy man."

Mike went into their bedroom and packed a duffle bag with necessary equipment and gathered some uniform shirts and pants for the following day.

Now alone in their bedroom Michael's head began to pound as he vividly recalled the circumstances of the night he was wounded.

Romano had been on a smoky rooftop of a burning building during the blackout of 1977. He heard a child whimpering. When he found the child, he came upon a pedophile about to satisfy his lust with another young girl. The man ran. As

Mike pursued his quarry into an elevator machine room, *without warning, just outside the beam of his flashlight, was the flash of a gunshot. Mike instinctively jumped back. He heard the bullet ricochet. Something hit him ; was it just paint or concrete chips perhaps. But his hand and arm stung viciously. His right hand extended into the doorway. His gun barked twice, lighting up the room for a split second. The would-be archangel saw what looked like the prone figure of a man bounce at the impacts.*

Brian Wilkey died slowly and in great pain. It was, as it should have been.

Mike Romano touched the visible remains of his wound on his arm, a badge of merit. He certainly felt like an avenging angel, a soldier of the Almighty and he had the scar to prove it.

Tomorrow another battle would begin.

Chapter Two

Dennis Bryan commanded the police precinct known as Midtown South. The building itself was located at 350 W. 35th street in Manhattan, between 8th and 9th Avenues, the heart of New York City, known around the world as The Big Apple. The building ran thru the block exiting onto W.36th Street. There were almost six hundred police officers in that command, making it the largest in the City. Roll calls were complicated. There was; the 0600 x 1400, 0800 x 1600, 1000 x 1800, 1600 x 2400, 2200 x 0600 and of course the midnight tour, 2400 x 0800 hours

***

It was a sunny Tuesday morning when Mike Romano approached his new command. The actual Department designation was the 14th Precinct. It was also known as Midtown South Precinct, MTS or more fondly as, The South. Before entering the front doors, he stopped a moment to look at the building.

Tan glazed brick façade, double glass doors, a small vestibule and another set of glass doors. To the right of the entrance, a small barren plant area composed of the same bricks as the building. The building was three stories high and looked similar in design to the Police Academy.

Mike was nervous. His mind raced. *Would Dennis Bryan be there? Would he try to talk to me? Could I control myself and not respond with a smartass remark?* Romano entered the building and stood in the lobby. The commander's office was directly to the right of the main entrance. Mike deduced that the planter area he saw was positioned directly outside the CO's window. He filed the information in a corner of his brain for possible future use.

Lady Luck was with Mike. Bryan was not working that day. It would be some time before Romano would have any contact with his new boss. When Mike first saw Bryan in a photo, he thought that the man looked like a large pumpkin. Bryan had a ruddy complexion, red hair, big protruding ears and large eyes, was overweight and stood over six feet tall. From that moment, Mike always thought of him as The Great Pumpkin. Seeing him in person at Wilkey's funeral only confirmed the less then flattering nickname.

Mike entered and continued to absorb his surroundings. Directly across from the building entrance was an elevator. *This place is modern, not like that ancient bastion of justice, the old 32,* he thought. He saw "The Desk" on the left. On each side of "The Desk" were small vestibules that lead to some offices. Mike was to learn what offices were back there as his career unfolded. Directly opposite the desk, on Michael's right, was a large room separated from the main area by a floor to ceiling folding partition. It was the muster or roll call room.

Striding up to the desk officer, Mike stood still and waited for the occupant, whose back was turned and looking down at a wall shelf lined with papers to turn around. As the man turned, Mike observed his rank. He was a Lieutenant. Mike snapped a quick salute as was customary. As he lowered his hand, he recognized a friendly face. It was Lieutenant Fondalar; formerly of the 32nd Precinct . Mike was elated.

"Hello Romano. What brings you here?" the Lieutenant asked with a cheery smile.

Mike was pleased to be remembered and quickly replied, "I've been assigned here sir. Career path or something, I guess."

Fondalar smiled, "When I saw your name on the teletype yesterday, I didn't know it was the Romano I knew. Happy to have you here kid. Your papers should be here sometime today.

Go downstairs and find yourself a locker and suit up. Report back to me in about thirty minutes."

Mike grinned and snapped another salute. "Yes sir." He then found his way to the basement locker rooms. After finding himself a locker, he put on his uniform, stored his remaining gear and snapped on his old combination lock and went up to the muster room. It was now about 0830 hours, 8:30 a.m. in civilian time.

The muster room began to fill up. There were people coming and going, mostly in uniform. Mike was amazed at the activity. He heard that the command had 600 officers, give or take, with six roll calls per day. Actually seeing it live and in person was something else.

By approximately 0920 hours the room was filled with cops of every shape, size and ethnicity. However, Mike did not notice any supervisors. He negotiated his way out of the room and returned to "The Desk" and asked, "Hey Loo, where do I fit in? What's my tour going to be?"

The desk officer responded with, "Today you're going to get posted with a patrol car team from the ten to six roll call. They'll show you around our command. Go on calls with them. It's a little different than the 'Three Two.' Consider it an orientation. Tomorrow you come in with the 15th squad working their day tour."

"Ok Boss", was the reply. Mike returned to the muster room, weaved his way thru the mass of humanity and took a seat on a window sill in the rear of the room.

Shortly thereafter, two Sergeants strode in. One was one of the biggest men Mike had ever seen. Their name tags were Holbrook and Halft, respectively. Halft spoke, "Roll Call. Listen up," and proceeded to call assignments by foot post and sector. One of the foot posts had an odd name, The Apple. Mike thought, *what's the Apple? Where is it? The boss gave no location.* Halft continued, "Sector King, Pinto and Lowery. You guys have a ride along today, Romano, who came here from the

Three Two. Show him what we have here" Strictly for the new man he added, "It's not like Harlem, but we sure have enough to do. Mike, raise your hand so they can find you. You go off duty at 1600 hours See you again in the a.m. tomorrow."

Two cops walked up to Mike. One of them looked familiar. The man smiled and asked, "Mike Romano? Is that you? I haven't seen you in years. Uncle Bob told me you joined the force. When did you get here?"

Romano was raised as a Catholic. Uncle Bob was Mike's godfather. Bob actually stood up for him at his Confirmation, one of the church rituals, signifying a right into responsible manhood, many years before.

"Joe?" Mike asked as his memory cells jogged into play, "I didn't know you worked here. What a small world."

Joe's full name was Joseph Pollo. When the men were younger, up until they were in their late teens, Mike would see his cousin Joe about four times a year.

When the north eastern section of the Bronx was still not completely developed, Mike and Uncle Bob would visit the little ten acre farm where Joe's parents' lived. The Pollo family had originally settled there in 1921 when they emigrated from their native Italy. Grandpa Antonio Pollo still raised chickens, goats, rabbits and ducks, along with various produce. Joe had lived there with his parents and his grandfather. The farm had been in the family for years. Grandpa's wine making skills were well known among all the relatives. Developers bought the land in the early 60's. Mike hadn't seen the Pollos in at least ten years.

"Hey Joe, what's with Pinto? Did you change your name?"

"No Mike, I got the name because of the large white birth marks I have on my hands since we were kids. You know like a pony. It kind of stuck."

"Sorry Joe, I didn't mean anything by it. Didn't mean to insult you and no, I don't remember them."

"It's all good Mike, no insult taken, I kind of like it. Pinto, that is. When we were kids, I was often called Marco Polo, Pinto has a better ring."

Mike looked at his cousin's hands. Joe's dark Italian skin was broken up with very pale irregularly shaped areas of two to four inches in size. They did look like the markings of a pinto pony, but in reverse. Mike was curious if the marks were over his entire body but didn't have the courage to ask.

The two men exchanged news as they all walked to Joe's assigned patrol car.

Once in the auto, with Joe driving, the tour began. As Pinto entered traffic, Mike's indoctrination began. Joe and Lowery took turns answering any questions.

***

The precinct encompassed an area known to native New Yorkers as the Garment Center, basically, Sixth Avenue from 28th Street to 34th Street; the Theater District, 42nd Street up to 48th Street along Sixth Avenue and Broadway crossing at Times Square. It also included the Port Authority Bus Terminal. It was a large parcel of land, extending from 42nd Street on Eight Avenue thru to Ninth Avenue and from 42nd to 40th Street.

At the center of Times Square was a MTS Police Substation, a rather small building, slightly larger than a military recruiting office. The building sat on a traffic island in the center of the intersection of 7th Avenue, Broadway and 42nd Street directly across from the famed Times Tower.

The Substation was manned twenty four seven. An officer was always on duty. Citizens could walk in to report any complaints or observations regarding the area. Naturally, the officers on duty also took crime reports and forwarded them to the command.

During his narration, Joe Pinto explained that "The Apple" was only on 42nd Street from 8th Avenue on to 6th Avenue.

Inside, on the counters, were theater programs and brochures alerting tourists to the attractions of the area. Included in the plethora of printed material were also somewhat more interesting booklets and flyers cautioning them about the area's pitfalls.

Further east on 42nd and 5th Avenue was the New York Public Library and Bryant Park. Continuing along 42nd Street was New York's famed Grand Central Station on the corner of Park Avenue, an ornate edifice from a bygone era. The interior of that landmark building was all granite and marble. Between 5th Avenue and Park on the South side of 42nd was the New York Daily News building.

After touring the Apple and the surrounding area, Joe and his partner brought Mike down to 34th Street. Macy's Department Store smothered a whole block from 34th Street thru 33rd Street between 6th and 7th Avenues. Between 33rd and 31st on 7th Avenue sat Penn Station. Penn Station itself was now below street level, under a giant office building, One Penn Plaza. Upon climbing the terraced stairway into the lobby of Penn Plaza, one would also find the main entrance to Madison Square Garden. The Garden itself encompassed the acreage behind Penn Plaza and spilled out onto 8th Avenue.

Over on the western border of the command was Hell's Kitchen and old freight yards that ran adjacent to the Hudson River, covering about one hundred acres. Touring the command, Mike was basically silent. He was taking it all in.

Mike asked, "Hey guys, I see lots of sex shops and porn type theaters, especially on and near 42nd Street. Get any calls in those things?"

Pinto was concentrating on Midtown traffic as he drove. Lowery answered. "Yeah Mike, we get our share of calls. Usually they're handled by the local foot post. You must have noticed there are men on almost every block, two on each block of the Apple."

Mike responded, "There sure must be a lot to do. How come we haven't gotten any calls, by the way?"

Joe Pinto answered, "Fondalar probably put us out of service with Central so we could have some time to show you around. We'll fix that now."

Hearing his partner, "Lowery picked up the mike. "South King to central, K". ("K" was the equivalent of "over", designating that the transmission was ended and a response expected.)

"Ten-four South King, back in service. King, handle parking condition on 47th and Broadway. Dispute in progress. Please notify if backup needed."

Lowery responded, "King, ten four, Central. On the way."

***

Arriving at the intersection of 47th Street and Broadway, the trio observed the driver of a UPS delivery in a heated exchange with a Parking Enforcement Agent (Meter Maid as they were referred to). It seemed that the driver double parked his truck to make several deliveries inside a building. When he returned to his truck he found a summons on the windshield. His claim was that the meter maid was present when he stopped and should have asked him to move if she felt it necessary. He was incensed the she waited until after he loaded his hand truck and went inside to tag the truck. The UPS man was articulating his feelings with gusto, in no uncertain terms. The two of them were locked in an intense verbal battle. All three cops exited the car.

"What do you think Mike?" Lowery asked, trying out the new man.

Mike quickly answered, "The NYC Traffic regulations state that a delivery truck can double park when making a delivery if no other legal parking space is within 50 feet of that delivery. Looking at the curb here I would say the guy is right and the Meter Maid is wrong."

At that point, the UPS driver said, "You're in for it now woman. The cops are gonna burn you."

Pinto took over, "Easy guy. We aren't going to burn anyone."

After asking the driver for his copy of the summons, he wrote across the face and in the borders of the form, This summons was written in error, truck was legal. It was followed by, a signature, Officer Pollo, MTS # 29345".

The traffic agent was visibly upset but said nothing. Mike asked to look at the summons and mentally recorded what Pinto had written on it.

Joe explained to the UPS man that he should plead not guilty on the reverse side of the summons form and mail it in to the address that was listed. He would not have to pay the fine. The meter maid was less than happy and tried to get the officers to charge the driver with disorderly conduct. They would not.

Lowery picked up the conversation at that point and spoke directly to the meter maid," We are the police. On the street we supersede the traffic signs and all traffic regulations. We are over you. Now please go before it gets too involved and we have to take other action." It was a veiled threat and the woman didn't stay around to find out what was meant.

Mike was impressed. He had just learned something.

Back in the car, Mike remarked, "Hey guys that was cool. I never used that one before. Does that happen often around here?"

Pinto answered, Yeah Mike. But sometimes those confrontations result in a collar, someone goes to Central Booking. In those cases, it's usually the drivers that escalate the argument into an arm waving confrontation. From that, it usually escalates into a pushing and shoving altercation. The 'Meter Maids' then try to have the guys locked up for assault. Most often we can explain that he or she, the parking enforcement agent, can also be arrested on an assault complaint filed by the driver. That knowledge usually ends it right on the spot. If the parties are insistent, we start to scratch out a cross complaint. When the bigger mouth sees what we are doing, they stop insisting on an arrest. However, if one of them is injured we have to make a collar. That's pretty rare though. What you just saw are how most of those runs are handled."

"It was interesting", Mike replied, "thanks".

The rest of the tour was relatively non eventful. They handled a traffic accident and two aided cases (sick or injured). By 1600 hours, Mike was returned to the command. "Hey Joe," he shouted as he got out of the car, is there any way to get steady tours for a new guy. I'd like ten to six if possible."

Pinto replied, "Tomorrow ask for Lieutenant Armini. He's in charge of the day tour guys. He's a real good guy, you'll like him. Maybe he can hook you up."

"From the Three Two?" Mike asked.

"Maybe, don't know. He's been here about 8 months. Tell him we're cousins and that I recommend you. See you around. It's been fun."

That night at dinner, Mike told Betty about meeting his cousin Joe at the station house. She had never met Joe but knew Uncle Bob and had been to the small farm that his folks had in the upper Bronx. Betty smiled as she remembered one of her husband's favorite family stories.

One Thanksgiving when Mike still lived at home as a teenager, several family members had gathered at his apartment to celebrate the holiday. While the women prepared the meal, Uncle Bob, asked Mike if he wanted to visit the Pollo farm to kill some time. Bob had also wanted to get some of the family's home made wine for the holiday dinner. Mike jumped at the chance.

While walking around the Pollo property, Mike remarked that the droppings from the goats looked like olives. That gave Bob, always a jokester, an idea. When the time to depart was near, the senior Pollo gave them two gallons of homemade wine to take back with them. Bob then explained his idea for a joke to Mike. As they left the farm, Bob and Mike stopped at the goat sheds and assisted by Joe Pollo, scooped up some droppings into a small paper sack to take with them. On the way home Bob further explained that they would stop in an old Italian neighborhood to buy some olives and other holiday delicacies. Once at home they would hide the real olives and substitute the droppings. The plan was to see if anyone noticed the gag. Naturally they would not allow the bogus olives to be served on the dinner table.

Back home, Mike's mom put the "olives" in a small crystal serving boat remarking, "These look old and dried out. Where did you guys get them?"

"Yeah, they do", was echoed by Bob's wife, Connie. The server was handed off to the family matriarch, Mary, Mike's grandmother. Bob and Mike were bursting at the seams at that point. They could hardly hold a straight face.

Not one to mince words, Mary said," My word, these olives look like shit. They smell like it too."

Mike and his uncle burst out with riotous laughter saying, "That's because they are. The Billie goats gave them to us."

Mike, managed," Grandma, you're the only one who could tell." Still laughing he begged forgiveness. Uncle Bob was doubled over and holding his side.

"You guys are gonna get it", Mary said with a smile on her face. She promptly threw the "olives" out and made Mike wash the server. The rest of the day went off without incident. Everyone ate too much.

After reviewing the "Thanksgiving olive" story in her mind and still smiling, Betty turned to her husband, "Michael

Romano, you ever bring home any olives in a paper sack to me and I'll find some goats for you to sleep with."

"Wow, Betty, you have some memory. You still remember the story I told you about Joey, Uncle Bob and the goats. That was years ago."

The Romano children, Anne, now eight years old and Donald almost six wanted to know why their parents found olives so funny. Mike answered that it was a grownup joke. Later that evening, with the children in their beds, Betty took the opportunity to once again bring up her concern regarding Mike working in the command lead by Dennis Bryan.

"Michael, you know that I'm still concerned about any possible interaction with you and Bryan. I know that you honestly feel that you can handle anything, but he is now your commanding officer."

Mike responded by pulling his wife close to him, turning her around, hugging her and answered, "Betty, cops working in a station house may see their boss maybe once a month. They deal with the desk officers and their own sergeants, not their commanders."

Betty wasn't buying his explanation, broke free and turned to face Mike. She knew her husband's sense of right. He would try to go after Bryan if he thought that the man was engaged in improper activity. "Michael Romano, if you jeopardize the stability of this family, I'll hang you myself. Be careful of that man, please."

"Don't worry your pretty little self about it. I'm there to do my job, not save the world from crooked cops. That's the job of Internal Affairs, not patrol officers like me."

"Michael, I know you can get carried away with an idea sometimes. Try not to poke around Bryan too much. Remember, you already know he's crooked, let IAD deal with him. Stay out of it. He's not the serpent in the church stained glass window. And you're not Saint Michael."

Seeing the look of a chastised puppy on Michael's face, she quickly added, but you're my Saint Michael, you always watch over me and the children."

Betty took a few steps backward. As she began loosening her clothing, she asked, "Do you think the kids are sleeping?"

Mike smiled, "I sure hope so."

***

Mike's second day at MTS was a Wednesday. He was up and about at 6:00 a.m. and anxious to meet with Lieutenant Armini. The last time he saw Louie Armini, the Loo was only a sergeant. Mike was happy to learn that Armini had risen in rank and was in charge of over 100 men of the Day Squad consisting of, the 8 x 4 and 10 x 6 tours. Romano couldn't wait to see one of his old supervisors and excitedly prepared to leave for work.

Mike's anticipation at seeing his old boss was peaked. As often happened when he got righteous or excited about the job, Mike heard the rustle of large feathered wings in his mind. *There I go again. I must be crazy,* he thought.

Betty heard him crashing around as he hurriedly showered and dressed. She crawled out of bed and asked him to "keep it down" and not wake up the kids. After gulping down some coffee and two slices of buttered toast Betty prepared for him, Mike gave his wife a quick peck on the cheek, slapped her on the butt and rushed off.

Romano entered the station house at 8:50 a.m. Rapidly entering the building, he quickly saluted the desk officer and went downstairs to change into his uniform. As others entered the locker room, he nodded to some of men he remembered from the previous day. By 9:10 a.m., Mike was in the muster room waiting. He spotted Armini as the Lieutenant entered the room.

Quickly striding up to the man, Mike almost shouted, "Hey Loo", what a pleasant surprise seeing you here. Didn't know you made Lieutenant. Let alone assigned here." Mike was on a roll now. "I'm assigned to rotating tours and would like steady ten to six." Armini smiled. Mike continued almost without taking a breath, "My cousin

Joe Pinto, really Joe Pollo, told me to see you. Do you think there's an opening for me? What do you say?"

Armini smiled again. He had always liked Romano and fondly remembered the day Mike was shot at as he drove home. He remembered patting Mike on the back and saying, "Welcome to the Three Two".

"Mike, it's good to see you here. You're a worker. Sure, we can squeeze you into the ten to six detail, but not until you swing out and come back in. I'll set it up with Sergeant Holbrook. He has the squad that does the Apple. See him when you swing back in. Meanwhile go stand roll call."

***

Mike was assigned a foot post in front of the New York Times Building just off Broadway and 45th Street for the day. He was told not to leave the post except for meal. He would be relieved for that hour. It was a priority post as there were some union rumblings. His assignment was some distance away, 10 blocks north and 3 blocks east from the station. Not wanting to walk, Mike went outside to look for a patrol car team to drive him. He found his cousin Joe and Lowery.

"Sure Mike, we'll drop you off. Climb in." They drove toward the Times Building.

Mike asked, "Hey guys, why are you cruising 42nd and 8th Ave? I gotta get to post." He was nervous because he was new and trying to get into a detail.

The response came from Lowery, “Don’t worry, nothing happens there anyway. We’ll get you there in a few minutes. First we have to find someone.”

As Joe slowed the car, Lowery hung out the opened window. “Hey, Lorraine. Come on over,” he shouted.

Mike saw a good looking young woman with long black tresses halfway to her ample, perfectly formed ass. She was wearing shiny black tights and a short gray skirt. She looked like a hooker. He thought, *Sure I’m on 42nd street and a nice looking woman comes by and I call her a hooker. She’s walking in plain sight on a busy street, can’t be.*

Lorraine came over as Pinto stopped the car. Lowery exchanged some words with her. “How’s business? Everyone treating you well? Anybody breaking your balls? I heard you only work by appointment now and only in the Garment District.”

Lorraine answered, “Yeah. My boyfriend in Jersey doesn’t want me to be locked up or hurt because of the strange people around here. I only work with my regulars who have my pager number. If I don’t recognize the number, I don’t call back. Someone new has to reach me from the office of a known customer. Once in a while I’ll come up here to see an old client. Sometimes I even visit a cop or two in a week.”

Mike didn’t believe the conversation. She was a hooker. She was not a street walker but a call girl, and serviced cops too. He wondered if they paid her and what she charged.

Lowery continued the conversation as he waved his hand towards Romano,” This here is Mike, he’s Joey’s cousin.” Turning around to Romano he ordered, “Say hi to Lorraine, Mike.”

Dumbfounded, Mike could only reply, “Hi Lorraine.”

Lowery added, "Well, we have to go now Lorraine, see you later."

Lowery tapped Joe's arm and he piloted the car to up to the Times Building.

As Mike got out, Joe asked, "Mike, when is your meal? We may come back to give you a ride in. By the way, do you like hamburgers, hot dogs and maybe a beer?"

"Sure Joe, 1300 hours, why?"

"Ok. See you later." It was 1010 when they rode off.

The foot post was boring. Nothing happened at all. There weren't even any people on the sidewalk to look at except for the occasional person entering or exiting the building. Once every ten minutes or so, a Times truck would pass without stopping. At 1250 hours Joe Pinto and Lowery pulled up with Lorraine in the back seat of the car. Mike could not believe it. *Lorraine, was she arrested or a complaining witness?*

"Jump in Mike," Lowery said. "We're taking you to meal."

"Where?"

"To a cookout party. We have hamburgers and some drinks." Lower y replied. "First we have to stop and pick up one of Lorraine's friends and some Pina Coladas."

Romano was both nervous and excited. *I'm going to a daytime party complete with prostitutes and booze.* As Mike climbed in the rear seat, he vowed silently to only watch and not participate should there be any activities involving the girls. He was uncomfortable sitting next to Lorraine. He thought of Betty. She could never understand why he even got into the car.

Pinto stopped the patrol car just past a bar on Ninth Avenue and 42nd Street, two uniformed cops and a girl came out, each carrying paper sacks. They walked over to the vehicle, nodded to the group and climbed in. Each of the cops took a girl onto his lap. Mike was forced into a corner. The rear seat of the patrol car looked as if it belonged in a circus.

"Got the drinks guys," one of the men said. "This here's Linda. Say hello Linda"

"Hello", was a squeaky voice response. The girl sounded like a cartoon mouse.

There was no further conversation as the car proceeded south. However, at a stop light, several pedestrians were looking at the crowded rear seat. One of the cops said, "Hey girls, let's moon them."

Mike was stunned. The girls dropped their pants and the other cops followed. The mooners struggled a moment but managed to get their collective asses up towards the glass. The girls were sprawled across Mike with their butts plastered against the windows in the rear of the car. Joey Pinto even had his butt against the front side window. Lower y honked the horn and stepped on the gas and they shot off. It all took about 20 seconds. By the time Mike got his composure, everyone's clothing was on with the girls again sitting on the two cops' laps. It happened so fast that Mike, in the confusion, didn't even get a good look at the half naked women. He was mildly disappointed.

The rest of the ride was riddled with giggles and laughter. Everyone was sipping Pina Coladas, even Mike. The overstuffed patrol car pulled up to a once gated entrance at W.33rd St. and 10th Avenue at 1305 hrs, 5 minutes into Romano's meal time. He had less than an hour to get back to his post and began to get nervous.

As the car bumped over the curb and onto an old dusty gravel covered access road, Mike took stock of his surroundings.

They had just entered the seldom used railroad freight yards that bordered the Hudson River. Mike scanned the view. The area was huge. It ran from 40th street, adjacent to the Lincoln Tunnel down to 30th Street, from 10th Ave. and on westward to the river. Here and there scattered throughout the area were metal buildings and rat's nest of railroad tracks. Most of the buildings were in disrepair. The yards were being phased out.

Lowery drove into the acreage about one quarter mile. As the car advanced, Mike saw at least 4 patrol cars and a dozen cops. The 75 degree temperature and strong sun accounted for the fact that some of the men had their uniform shirts off and left them hanging in helter skelter fashion on patrol car dome light racks, folding chairs and the branches of shrubbery that was scattered about. They were now on a hard packed dirt road. Lowery piloted the car just past an old brick pad that held a 55 gallon drum, cut lengthwise, sitting on a stand. There he stopped and announced,

"Every one out, let's eat and whatever."

The top of the drum was covered with a makeshift cooking grate littered with hot dogs and hamburgers. The drum's interior glowed with hot coals that flared up into spiked tongues of flame as fat dripped down.

Sitting next to the "grill" were two ice chests loaded with canned soft drinks and beer. By this time, Mike and his crew had finished the Pina Coladas and threw the white paper drink containers into another oil drum that acted as a trash receptacle. Joe Pinto pushed Mike along and introduced him around to some of the other cops.

"This is my cousin Mike, he's cool. Mike is one of us, a straight and square guy, someone who'll cover your back."

Mike's mind raced, *I can't believe all this, barbeques in the middle of the day. We're picking up call girls in a patrol car to party with cops. And I'm instantly accepted because of my cousin. What's going to happen with those girls?* Curiosity was beginning to invade his mind.

While still digesting the entire scene, and wanting to think of something besides what kind of trouble he could get into, Romano walked over to the cop tending the grill. "You guys have buns to go with that burger. I could sure use one."

drum looked at Mike's name tag, "Sure Romano. You got it."

Mike thanked him and after squirting some ketchup on it, moved off to the side to eat the burger and watch the cops and the two hookers milling around. After scanning the area for any other females, Mike realized that Lorraine and Linda were the only women present. He guessed that there were at least a dozen cops and at least police cars there.

The burger was moist and juicy. Mike moved over to a patrol car, pulled his memo book out and placed it on the fender of the vehicle. He then placed the burger on top of the book. Now he was getting warm. Mike decided that it was a result of the effects of the drinks, his bullet resistant vest, the midday sun and the increase of his blood pressure because of nervous energy at the goings on.

Romano began to think, *this equipment belt is getting heavy. Damn thing must weigh at least 10 to 15 pounds. Gotta take it off. Lots of the other guys have their belts off and even shirts. No, I'm not going that far.* In an uncharacteristic move, Mike hung his belt and uniform cap on the light rack of the car in front of him. As he picked up the burger, he placed his memo book into his rear pocket. Mike then walked off only a few feet. His was determined not to let his cap and firearm out of his sight.

Lorraine and Linda came walking slowly past Mike. Now he had time to take a good look at the two women. Lorraine was built like the proverbial brick shit house. Not an ounce of fat could be seen thru her tight pants. Her posterior assets were accented by the high heeled ankle boots she wore. Her white blouse was slightly opened. She obviously was not wearing a bar. Her breasts stood out like two ski slopes. Linda's body was an almost carbon copy of Lorraine's, but with short blonde hair. She wore a tight grey skirt and red heels. Her tan colored tailored blouse was unbuttoned to her navel. Even though her breasts peaked out as she moved, she almost looked like a business woman.

"Hey Mike," asked Linda, "Anything we can get you or do for you?", as she gently ran her right hand across her breasts, allowing a quick peek at one nipple, then the other. Romano almost choked on the burger in his mouth." *My god, I've just been propositioned by call girls while I'm working. Well sort of."*

"No thanks ladies. I'm fine right now. Just enjoying the day. Happy to be here."

"Ok Mikey," was the response from Lorraine. "Anytime you need something, just ask. Anything, anytime, see you," as they walked off swinging their magnificent derrieres.

Time was passing quickly as Mike realized that he was due back at his foot post in 20 minutes. He knew that it would take at least 5-10 minutes to secure a ride. He didn't know where Joe and Lowery were. He was upset that he never noted the number on the side of their patrol car.

"Holy shit, IAD" (internal affairs) someone shouted. "On the far end, coming from the river, a black car, coming fast."

Cops started running in every direction. A couple of the cars began driving off shooting gravel behind them as they fled away. Mike looked across the vast expanse to see a large black unmarked police type vehicle roaring down on them from the river side. The dust trail looked like The Lone Ranger was coming. He spit out the last bit of his hamburger and bolted.

Mike ran into a long rusty steel building that was behind him.

Once inside he looked around and thought, *At least 100 feet long and was either an old maintenance shop or something like that. Tracks lead into it and apparently exiting the half closed rear doors. I can run out the back.*

It took another few seconds before Mike realized that he had left his cap and gun belt hanging on a car's roof lights. His stomach twitched simultaneously with his sphincter muscle. He almost soiled himself.

Holy crap. What an idiot I am. Those items are traceable. My shield number is on my hat and the serial number on my weapon comes back to me. Maybe if I can make the street, I can concoct a story. Like I was jumped and held up at gunpoint. If I mess up my clothes, maybe they'll buy it and I can save my job.

Mike's mind was racing as fast as his heart. He began bracing for the long run to the rear exit of the building.

One last look back to where he left his equipment made him freeze. He spotted Lowery who began laughing loudly, *Is he crazy?* and saw Lowery slapping five with Pinto and heard them shouting, "All a joke guys. Come on back."

After his heart stopped beating like a marching band at a football game, Mike approached Pinto, and learned that his cousin and Lowery, always ready for a laugh, had set the whole thing up. Apparently cookouts at the yard were fairly common events. They explained to Mike that earlier that same day, Lowery had been approached by a Conrail Police Officer he knew from the yards. The railroad cop wanted to know if the men were going to have a cookout anytime soon. The Conrail cop wanted to attend. Lowery had told him that one was scheduled for that very same day.

Lowery and Pinto thought it would be funny if the Conrail officer would come zooming in like IAD trying to catch cops in the wrong and to watch the result.

As the men explained their gag to Mike, Lowery was almost peeing in his pants he was laughing so hard. Pinto couldn't breathe. The gag had worked real well. Once things calmed down, Mike retrieved his belongings and began making an attempt to secure a ride back to his post. It took almost another hour to convince a team to drive him back to the

Times building. Joe Pinto and Lowery would not drive him. They were having too good a time.

Back at his post, Mike learned that he was never missed and nobody was even looking for him, not even a supervising sergeant. At 1530 hours Mike, still bored at his post, called for transportation to MTS. Patrol sector David answered the call and brought him in. There was no mention of the earlier incident. Mike did not know if the transport team were present in the yards or even knew about it. He didn't care. Mike consciously thought, *Thank you Saint Michael, you got me through that one.*

Chapter Three

Two days after the freight yard incident, during roll call, Mike was notified that he was re-assigned the ten to six Apple detail when he returned from his RDO's (regular days off). Roll call for that tour would be at 0930 hours He would work Monday thru Friday with weekends off. He could hardly wait.

***

"Romano," the huge Sergeant Holbrook bellowed, during Mike's first ten to six roll call. "You and Deluca have post ten on the Apple. Meals are at 1300 and 1400 hours; work out who goes first. Romano, raise your hand."

After the usual notifications, Holbrook shouted, "Dismissed. Take your posts."

Approaching Mike was a very distinguished looking cop. He was basically the same height as Romano, only slightly heavier. He looked like an old time sea captain, "Commander Schweppes", who used to advertise a line of soft drinks. It was Deluca. He wore a salt and pepper goatee with a small mustache, capped by dark eyebrows and grey hair. He also had a ready smile and he looked very friendly.

"Hi, Romano, I'm Deluca. Eugene Deluca, Gino to my friends. Pinto spoke highly of you. We'll do the job and have fun too. You're gonna like the post. It's mine, steady. I didn't know a new man had such a big hook." (hook was one of the terms used to designate a person who could get you preferential treatment in the job.)

"Hey Gino, Neither did I." How do we get to post today?"

"We walk Mike. It's the best way. You'll see."

"OK then let's go. Lead the way."

Each of the new partners signed out a radio and left the station house through the front door. They swung west on 35th street to Ninth then north, remaining on the east side of the avenue.

Walking gave Mike time to absorb the flavor of the area. The neighborhood was a cornucopia of sights, smells and sounds. Directly around the corner from the station house was an old fashioned butcher. In the window, whole lambs were hanging. Along with them were chickens and some smaller birds, unknown to Mike. Two doors down was an old time Italian grocery/deli. The window was chock full of aged cheeses and the like. Just walking past that place made Romano's mouth water. *You can almost smell them thru the glass, maybe I could get a good sandwich there some day*, he thought.

Crossing the corner of 36th Street, the team passed a makeshift fence surrounding an open plant/flower shop. There were various shrubs, trees and flowering plants within the enclosure. Romano tried to imagine where the gardens were. *Rooftops*, was all he could think of.

The next block brought more meat shops. There were even whole pigs in two of the windows. Scattered among this slightly grotesque array of shops were entrances to apartments that were above most of the stores. Mike took it all in. Glancing across to the west side of the avenue, Mike saw old tenements scattered between a plethora of more small shops. As they got closer to 40th Street, Mike could see the bus ramps to the Port Authority building on the west side of the avenue. *Boy, it sure is crowded here,* he thought.

The intersection of 42nd Street and Ninth Avenue was nothing but bus ramps for the Port Authority building on the south west side. The east side of the street housed the building itself. On the north east side was a parking lot, adjacent to an old hotel sitting next to a seedy looking bar. The North West side to 42nd had another parking lot and what appeared to be commercial lofts. There was nothing of any interest except women; lots of women. All shapes and sizes. They were constantly moving.

Hookers. I finally see Times Square hookers. Not very pretty. Kind of raunchy. Not at all like Lorraine and Linda, Mike thought.

Mike thought he heard Gino say, “Lorraine parks her Caddy here.”

Gino guided them to the corner of 8th Avenue and 42nd. They now stood on the North West corner, just across the street from the official beginning of their post. The new partners were standing under the marquee of Sex World. The second line read, “The Best Live Shows in Town.” Mike had heard about the openness of porn in the area, but never saw it in person. He was slightly surprised.

“Take note Mike,” Gino said, “even though it’s not officially our post, we will probably be in here from time to time. When we go in, don’t forget to come out.” He said laughingly.

“Come on, there are people to meet.”

Now, officially on The Apple, Romano tried to take it all in.

***

Directly on the corner was an angled entrance to something called ‘Under 21.’ Gino explained that it was a haven for young kids. Runaways, kids “stranded” at the bus terminal or kids with other problems could go there for help or a meal. There were games and activities inside also. The place was supported by donations and the Catholic Church.

“Some priest named, Rickter runs the place. Careful if you go in there Mike. He doesn’t like cops.”

Just off the north east corner was an Orange Julius, kind of like a Nedicks. Their bill of fare was cheap breakfasts and sandwiches, soft drinks, and stale doughnuts. Adjacent to the shop was a white tiled entrance reminiscent of days gone by that lead to the subway. Next to that was a small storefront. The place sold smoking paraphernalia, holsters, cameras and other electronic sundries. It also catered to the people who bought porn magazines, sex toys and films.

Gino said, "We watch the place from time to time, it's reported to be selling pot and possibly other drugs too. Never could prove it though. Every few weeks, I toss (search) people leaving the store and always have negative results."

On the right side of the doorway to the smoke shop was the street level entrance to Cu-Lei Garden, a Chinese restaurant spanning the lofts above four other street level shops.

Let's make our first tour of the post," Gino said as he gently guided Mike eastward.

The balance of the block between 8th Ave. and Broadway was littered with similar establishments, some of which had dubious claims to legitimate enterprise, interspaced with three movie theaters. Two of the theaters featured what was known as "art films" at the time. The other blatantly advertised outright hardcore porn flicks. The sidewalk was alive with a mass of humanity. Some were apparent drug dealers, interspaced with obvious wide eyed tourists with a sprinkling of legitimate, working class people thrown into the mix along with an assortment of various other miscreants. It sure was a wormy Apple.

Once they had reached Broadway, Gino directed Mike across the street to the south side. On that corner was another orange juice and fast food business. Next door, going west, was a pizza shop, King of Pizza. Gino explained that Tony, the owner, loved cops and they could take breaks there. He would introduce him later. The team continued past two more sleazy businesses.

Stopping in front of the third one, Mike looked at the blackened windows and asked, "Gino, what goes on in there? Is it like the sign says? Sex shows. Is it like the big place on the other corner? "

The answer came , "Yeah Mike, it is, only much dirtier, I mean dirt and germ wise. Add to the fact that it's even more perverted then Show World. You'll eventually see what goes on there. I'm sure we'll have cause to go inside before the month is out. If and when we go inside, never sit down, not even in the manager's office. The place is a breeding ground for bacteria. I don't think the place ever gets cleaned. They keep it pretty dark, so if you go in there, be careful. Remember, don't even touch the walls. No telling what's on them."

Mid- block on the south side was an old theater, The Amsterdam Theater. Properly maintained, it still retained some of its former ambiance from earlier days, before 42nd street's decline. The Amsterdam was built in the beginning of the 20th century. Once it was the entertainment capital of New York. The famed Ziegfeld Follies performed there from 1913 to 1936. The Amsterdam continued to show only legitimate Hollywood films.

Gino kept the tour going, ending up at an open parking lot on the corner.

"I can't believe the various people and all the porn here Gino. It seems that every second store is an all-around camera/electronics/junk tourist trap kind of place and the ones in between are peep shows or sex palaces."

All Mike heard was, "Welcome to The Apple."

***

As the weeks passed, Mike found that he enjoyed working with Gino. He especially enjoyed "The Apple". Several weeks into his tenure at MTS Mike had occasion to work alone. Gino had to use one of his vacation days. He had called Mike the night before and apologized for the short notice. Something unexpected came up. Luca asked if Mike had a preference for a partner while he was gone, offering to set it up with roll call. Mike told him that it didn't matter because there were always men on Broadway and the block on 42nd between and 7th Avenue. He thanked Gino for the offer, and told his partner that he was sure that he could manage one day alone.

While Romano was walking to his post, his portable radio crackled, "A ten-twenty, past robbery on The Apple", the dispatcher continued, "Fifteen minutes in the past. No perps on the scene. Request unit to respond, K". The transmission momentarily ended before announcing the location of the job.

When the address was given, Mike recognized it as the Chinese restaurant above the stores on the corner of 42nd and 8th. The call was answered by a foot cop on the adjacent post. Mike knew he would stop in to give assistance when he arrived.

As Romano approached the corner of 42nd and 8th, the radio squawked again and gave out an aided (sick or injured) case just off the corner of 42nd and 8th Avenue in one of the live sex shows. It was a small place across from Sex World.

Mike acknowledged the call, "Apple post ten will handle Central. Will check and advise, K"

"Ten four, post ten," the response came.

Once inside the shop Mike was ushered past a row of booths. He had seen similar booths many times since being assigned to post ten. Often he and his partner would chase marijuana salesmen into one of the area's sex shops. The layouts were always the same.

At the entrance of each booth was a black curtain. Inside the booths were large glass windows with a solid opaque plastic sheet on the inside of the window. The panel would rise after a customer would insert tokens into a control box. The tokens were bought from a man near the shop's entrance. When the glass was up, the customer could view the show. Usually it was a nude dancer but sometimes, there were couples performing. It could be distracting to a cop trying to do his job.

However, Mike and Gino would usually get their man. The perps would act as if they were there watching the show. Only problem was that they never had time to get coins necessary to view the show. The team would push curtains aside as they looked for their man sometimes embarrassing patrons. The man they sought was always found with the screen down and no tokens in his hand because he didn't have the chance to buy any with the cops on his tail. The two cops would make their collar. In the rear of that particular shop, Mike was greeted by someone claiming to be the manager as he exited a small office. He told Romano that one of his girls was sick and ushered Mike to a stairway alongside of the office. It descended into the basement.

At the bottom of the steps Mike entered a large open room. The place was filled with small dressing tables and women, lots of women, most of them almost naked, clad only in G-strings. The place smelled like a locker room at the Police Academy. On the floor was a totally naked girl with a large cut on her head. Mike thought, *Wow. It's fun being around all these women. This little nudie is cute, boy is she put together, but she's naked and hurt. Why isn't she covered with a sheet or something?* She was not conscious.

Mike directed an order at no one in particular, "Someone get me a sheet to keep her warm, she could be in shock."

While waiting for some sort of cover, Mike looked around at the other people in the room. There were only two men, wearing nothing but red jock straps.

Mike was about to again ask for a cover for the girl when a voice spoke from behind him, "Romano, this is my post and the robbery is on yours. Do you have any complaints if we switch? I'll stay here and handle this, you take the robbery. Besides you're married and I'm not." It was the man who was actually assigned to the post.

Mike turned around. He was not exactly comfortable down there among all those naked women. He felt a loyalty to Betty and also knew that if any one of them decided to claim an impropriety against any cop that was there, that poor cop was deep in shit.

"Sure guy" was the quick response. With some reluctance at losing the eye candy, he left.

Back on Post 10, Mike climbed the stairway to the restaurant. He had never been in the place and was somewhat surprised. The décor was rather tastefully done though somewhat aged. There were about six booths against each wall of the place and several tables in the center of the room. The kitchen was in the rear. Access to that area was thru saloon type swinging doors.

Romano was met by a small agitated oriental man who gave a quick respectful bow. He was followed by a tiny frail woman. The man spoke in broken English.

"You take story Mr. poreece man." Pointing at a small cut on his forehead, the man continued, "Rook at my head. Some boys do this. They rob me and hit wife too, he stated as he pointed at her. "Come rook at kitchen. They make mess. Everywhere eggs." He swung his arms to indicate broken eggs all over the place. Where other cop here first?"

Mike now knew why the other foot cop wanted out. *This is going to be a pain. He's there with naked women and I'm here with*

someone I can't understand. Damn, there's the sound of heavy bird wings again. Something is going to come out of this. He vowed to do his best.

All three men sat down in one of the booths. Mike unfolded a blank complaint report from his memo book and attempted to get the basic facts down on paper. It took many repeated answers and the assistance of two other employees who spoke better English to get it all down.

After thirty minutes the radio asked, "Central to Apple foot post at the 10-20 please advise." He had gone past the customary time allotment without notifying the dispatcher.

"Apple post 10 to Central, still on the scene at the 10-20, K"

"Post 10, thought you were on the aided case. Advise, K"

"Post 10 to Central. That is being handled by the adjacent post, post 20, K."

"Acknowledged post 10,K". The dispatcher was satisfied.

The report was lengthy. Mike needed to ask for paper to record all the details; the victim and owner of the restaurant, Wei Cu-Lei, had been paying "protection money" to a group of Chinese youths for several months. Lei had gotten behind on his payments so the gang "paid a visit". After they trashed the place they took any money Lei had and left, vowing to return. Following procedure, Mike asked if Lei would look at pictures. Maybe he could identify the men and they could get arrested. Lei broke into a long conversation with the other Chinese that were there, speaking in their native tongue .

"No sir, we not want to go to court," was the reply. "They hurt my famry in China. They very bad boys from Wachung, China. I talk, they hurt my famry in China."

Mike asked if they were not going to court, why make a police report. The reply was, "For insulance. We get money for mess."

Romano assured Lei that he would file a proper report and pay attention to his place in the future, explaining that he was the cop assigned to the block. After going back on patrol, he made a vow to himself. He would find out more about these Wachungs. He would file his report and attach as much information to it as possible. He would follow it up with an Intelligence Report. Mike didn't know why he was so excited by that incident but he could not wait to tell Gino about it. Instinct told him there would be something more out of this. The rest of his tour was rather uneventful. Mike knew it would be several days before he heard anything pertaining to his report.

***

During one of their tours, the partners responded to a dispute in one of the many electronic/camera tourist trap shops. The clerk was arguing with a man who held the leashes of two Dobermans. The dogs were sitting between the counterman and their owner. As the team entered the shop, the arguing toned down.

Mike and Gino were told that the guy with the dogs had bought a boom box several days before and wanted to return it. The customer stated that the radio had been dropped by him as he walked his dogs and was not as sturdy as he was lead to believe. He wanted another one to replace it.

The store clerk explained to "dog man" that he could not return it as he had admittedly caused the damage himself. If the counterman got too insistent, the customer would increase the length of the dogs' leash and whisper something causing them to become agitated and bark. All in all, it was very intimidating.

Gino gave his patented smile to the "complainant" and asked "dog man" to, "Please walk outside with us sir. We can talk better without that guy yelling. Oh, and please make sure your dogs remain calm too." Gino lead the way outside.

"Sir, please remain in here. We will let you know the outcome," Mike told the counterman.

Once outside Gino began, "Sir, how can you expect the owner to give you a new radio when you admitted to him that you dropped it?"

"I never said that. Are you guys getting paid off or something?"

"What the hell?????," stammered Mike.

"Easy partner," Gino said with a smile. He focused his attention back on the dog man. "If we were on the take you would be arrested right now for attempted armed robbery. What do you have to say to that?"

The dog man was an idiot. "You know that these dogs are killers. One word from me and they attack anyone in front of me, even crooked cops."

Mike and Gino had gotten to know each other real well. They both responded in unison with, "If the dogs move we shoot them first, then you," as they drew their revolvers. "What do you think of that?"

Cops and loud voices always drew a crowd. Some people were already out front when the two cops went into the store. Several people had seen the dog man go into the store and were milling around outside hoping to see some excitement. Now they were watching another show unfold. They might even see gunplay.

"You guys shoot my dogs and I'll sue you. I'll have your jobs."

"Tell us how are you going to sue when you're down on the sidewalk looking up at the sky thru a dead man's eyes?" Gino asked. Mike had started to slowly move to the right of the dog man just in case. It made the dog man look in two different directions.

The man was beginning to understand. He was not getting a new radio and the cops were looking for a reason to lock him up and possibly kill his dogs.

He could not help himself, "How can you guys lock me up for attempted robbery?"

Mike answered, "Because you were trying to get a radio you were not entitled to and using your dogs as a weapon by threatening the counter guy with them."

"I never did. He only thought I was."

"Listen, you're full of crap, we all know what went on. You also threatened us. Now leave and take your dogs with you. If we ever get a complaint about them, the puppies are gone, euthanized, and you are going to jail."

Reluctantly, the dog guy yanked his animals leashes and walked away muttering under his breath. Mike and

Gino never went back inside. Gino called central and reported that the dispute was resolved.

Just another day on The Apple.

Chapter Four

During inclement weather, footmen were expected to have raingear with them so they could remain on post. Mike and Gino would wear their gear to post if it was raining as they left the station house. Once on post, the first place they visited if the rain had stopped was King of Pizza near Broadway.

Tony the owner would allow the cops to leave their gear upstairs in his place. In the event they got caught in bad weather without their gear, they could hang out inside, upstairs until the weather broke. They could also take their meals there or "coop" for hours.

Mike and Gino usually spent an hour or two there every couple of days. Sometimes they took their meals in that lofty perch. Meal hours were assigned separately, but they always took them together. They would make the appropriate entry in their respective memo books as if their meals were taken as assigned.

The entrance to the King's upstairs was unique. Unless you knew where to look, there was no apparent doorway leading upstairs. The "walk in refrigerator", unable to be seen from the front of the shop, because it was protected by a protruding corner within the selling area, was the entrance. It was a perfect "coop." More often than not, some foot patrol officer was reclining in a cushioned chair looking out over the street scene thru the one way mirrored windows.

The loft space was ideal for the cops. You could hide there and observe activity on the block, catch a nap or a meal and if necessary, they could use Tony's old office desk to do paperwork. It even had an old black and white TV. It was perfect.

One day, Mike and Gino were lounging upstairs and the radio crackled," Apple post ten, 10-3, acknowledge, K". The team was being asked to call their command.

"Damn, Gino. Do you think it's the CO?"

Mike had explained his feelings about their commanding officer to Gino a few months before. At the time, Gino told Mike,

"Be careful brother, maybe Bryan's on to you. I've heard he can be dangerous. Tread with caution."

The order to call in while they were sitting in "the coop" made Romano nervous. His mind raced, *Are we caught? Bryan will write me up for sure. My career will be in shambles. Gino and Betty were right. He will get me for killing his brother in-law.*

Mike offered to make the phone call. He acknowledged the radio transmission and both cops walked up the street to the sub-station on the intersection of Broadway and 7th Avenue. Using the directly linked telephone on the reception desk, Mike called the desk officer at MTS.

Lieutenant Armini answered. "Romano, I have some interesting news for you."

"Sir?"

"Mike, do you remember the robbery 61 (complaint report) you took some weeks ago, from the Chinese restaurant?"

"Sir?" Mike's nerves were beginning to settle.

Armini continued, "Well, remember the Chinese restaurant incident. When you filed the 61, you also made an intelligence report about the gang that robbed the restaurant. I'm happy to tell you that I was just notified about the results of the intelligence information. You will be temporarily assigned to the Fifth Precinct in China Town, for about a week or so, to work with a detective. You'll be in plainclothes. See me when your tour is over."

Mike could not believe his ears. "Yes, sure, soon as we get in today. Sure, thank you Lou."

Gino was looking at his friend. He saw the elation in Mike face. "What's going on? You look happy. Tell me."

"Gino, tomorrow I'm going to the Fifth to work in plainclothes on the Wachungs, the kids from the restaurant robbery, remember. It's only for a week, but holy crap. Working with a Chinese detective, in Chinatown. Wow." Mike was spitting out the words now. "Are you gonna miss me?"

Gino's answer made Mike glow with pride. "Yeah, a little."

"Thanks."

"But remember, I was here before you and I'll get by with you gone. Maybe they will give me a better partner."

Mike thought he heard a hint of jealousy in his partner's response.

Gino quickly added, "Hey hurry back. It won't be the same without you. Good luck."

***

As the team proceeded back to their post, they observed what they believed to be a drug sale. The seller was standing under a movie marquee, against a poster of a naked woman. There was a blue ribbon strategically pasted across the fluff of her womanhood. The man's head hid her ample breasts.

Gino assessed the scene and quickly said, "You get the buyer and hold him, I'll get the seller," he added, "Hold the buyer, I'll bring the perp down to you. Don't worry, I'll be fine. The guy is almost half my size and I could always shoot him."

Experience told Gino that these type of dealers usually did not resist. The whole block knew Mike and Gino. They had earned the nickname of Leukemia for all their collars. One of their regular collars explained the name. "You two white guys are like leukemia, the white death, you know too many white blood cells and all that. You're death to our business. You see everything that we do and don't miss a trick. We can't escape you. We got respect for you man."

"Got it Gino. Let's not rush or we'll lose the seller."

The two men separated. Mike crossed the street and walked quickly to get in front of the buyer, crossing back over he waited, pretending to look at something in a store window.

As the buyer approached, Mike turned around and took the man by the arm. "Excuse me sir, please stop and wait a minute with me."

The man responded, "What? What did I do?" Why should I have to wait with you? What for? I have to get back to work."

Romano had been on The Apple long enough. People were always happy to see a police officer near them in that sleazy environment.

They were not pleased when there was something to hide. From the man's reaction, Mike knew immediately that the man

had bought contraband. This guy was not happy; therefore he definitely had something he did not want a cop to know about.

"Sir, if you don't stay put, I'll have to put you under arrest. Please give me whatever it was that you bought from that man on the sidewalk next to the naked lady poster."

The response was a nervous question, "What are you going to do, arrest me anyway?"

"Not necessarily. If you're cooperative and only bought marijuana, I could write you a summons. But only if you have proper identification."

"Here, I bought two nickel (five dollars) bags of pot. Yes, I have ID." The man responded as he hurriedly reached into his pocket.

Mike had turned slightly away from the man to keep his gun away from the potential combatant. He grabbed the man's wrist while his hand was still in his pocket and said, "Easy sport. Better come out of there with nothing more than two nickel bags or you're going to get hurt." It allowed him time to react should it be necessary. He never let go of the guy's wrist.

Slowly the man's hand came into view and produced two small manila envelopes, to wit, two nickels of what Mike believed was marijuana.

"Please step into this doorway and behave. Let me have your identification please." Once in receipt of the man's drivers' license, Mike wrote him a summons for possession of marijuana. The summons was returnable in Manhattan Criminal Court in three weeks. He sent the guy on his way just as Gino walked toward him with the dealer in tow as Mike wrote his initials and the summons number on the envelopes for later identification.

"Hey Mike. We have us a marijuana salesman here. Did you get the buyer?"

"Yeah Gino. I got two nickels and wrote a summons. How much does your guy have on him?"

"Well partner, he has ten nickels and $150. I don't know where his stash is though. I didn't have time to look for it. Jones is back there looking now. He'll bring it to us if he finds it."

Mike called the dispatcher for transportation to the station house

· Back at MTS, in the arrest processing room, Mike and Gino began the paperwork. Mike vouchered the two bags of alleged marijuana (alleged until tested at the police lab). He recounted the bags from Gino's arrest and vouchered them too, asking Gino to sign the paperwork and envelope seal as the recovering officer. Meanwhile, Gino wrote up his arrest report and fingerprinted his man.

"Thanks for the help Mike. I have this. Sector Henry is going to drop us off downtown. You get ready for your big case in China Town tomorrow."

After changing into civilian clothes, Mike almost ran out of the station house. He jumped into his car, spun the tires as he pulled out away from the curb on 10th Avenue and almost flew home. He zipped thru traffic like his butt was on fire.

Once inside his apartment, he ran past Betty, picked up each of his children and gave them a big hug chanting, "Daddy's gonna get the bad guys." several times.

He then ran to Betty who asked," Michael," as she called him when she sensed something serious, "Just what is going on?"

"You're acting like a kid at Christmas."

"Betty, remember I told you about a robbery at a Chinese restaurant on my post? That there was some gang extorting money from the owner. Well, I made an intelligence report out and turned it in. It has merit. Today, I was notified that I'm going to work in China Town with the detectives on the case."

"Mike, that's wonderful. You've been promoted? she sked.

"No. It's just a temporary assignment, kind of a reward, to work with a particular detective who handles the gangs. His name is William Lee. I'm only assigned for a week. I have three days left in this set (work week) and hopefully, I'll get to stay the entire next set. I don't know for sure. I have to be there at 0800 hours tomorrow. You know 8:00 a.m."

"Slow down Mike. You're talking too fast."

"Sorry Betty. So far is there anything you want repeated?"

"No, I think I understood it so far. Is there any more? " Betty knew enough to ask. There was always more when her husband babbled on.

"Yeah. Lieutenant Armini told me to dress like a detective. Where's my tweed sport jacket? Don't know if I have to wear a suit. I'll wear the tweed tomorrow. Give me a hug will you? I've gotta calm down."

Betty gave her husband a quick bone crushing hug and said, "Go pour yourself a tranquilizer," referring to his favorite scotch, Dewar's White Label. "Supper is almost ready", she shouted.

"Yeah," Mike responded, as he almost sprinted to the kitchen. Caught up in the celebratory moment, Betty added, "Just wait until you see your dessert"

"Oh, yeah. What time do the kids go to bed?" Mike asked as he sipped some golden colored elixir.

Chapter Five

Mike arrived at the Fifth Precinct on Elizabeth Street, known throughout the Department as "The Chinatown Precinct" at 0745 hours He was nervous. His mind raced as fast as his pulse.

Do I look OK? This jacket is not tacky and run down is it? What's Lee like? Will he treat me as an equal or act superior?

The station house appeared to be as ancient as the old 32nd Precinct. The building was squeezed between two tenements. Once inside Mike walked slowly. He tried to get a feel for the place. He looked down at the floor. It was dark, constructed entirely of wide old oak planks. Looking closely, Mike could see that there were worn portions of the flooring that looked as if legions of warriors have tread on them, giving the appearance of beaten paths. He now was standing in front of a reception desk, manned by an obviously oriental, young uniformed officer. Looking up the cop asked, "Can I help you sir?"

Showing his shield, Mike responded, "Romano, Midtown South". *This is like something in the movies.* "I'm here to work with a Detective Lee. Where can I find him?"

The young officer pointed to a stairway and answered, "Upstairs, third door on the left."

Mike controlled his ascent, as he climbed the stairway, trying not to show how excited he was to reach the landing. The corridors on the second floor had stains on the institutional green walls. It looked as if someone had randomly spilled and splattered coffee onto them, everywhere. Romano counted six doorways along the corridor. The doors themselves were constructed of old brown oak, their varnished finish pitted and peeling. In the upper half of each door was a pebbled translucent window. One could see shadows of people inside, but could not see into the rooms. Next to each doorway an old chipped sign hung, identifying the room beyond. *Bakelite, the fore runner of plastic,* Mike thought, as he reached out to open the door tagged, Detectives.

Once inside the room, Romano saw a lone man. He looked oriental enough. Quickly, Mike looked him over before speaking to him. The man wore a snub nosed .38 revolver under his left shoulder making him right handed. Holding up his pants was a belt and suspenders. He wore a blue button down shirt and no tie. He was looking over some paperwork on his desk as Mike approached.

Mike extended his hand, "Mike Romano, Midtown South, you must be Bill Lee. Very pleased to meet you."

"Hi, Mike. I've been expecting you. Please call me William or Lee. Chinese upbringing you know."

"Sorry, Lee. I'll remember." *He looks pleasant enough. No attitude in his voice,* thought Mike.

Lee accepted Mike's hand and got right down to business. "Mike, Intel contacted me last week about your report. Do you have any idea who those guys were on 'The Deuce'"? (Another nickname for 42nd Street, but it meant the whole street not just The Apple).

"No Lee. Outside of the fact that they are all supposed to be from Wachung Provence in China, I have nothing else. I have no names or anything. Everything I had was included in my report. My complainant is terrified of them."

"Come over and take a look at these pictures. All or some of your guys have to be here."

Mike moved closer to Lee's desk. Lee moved some paperwork aside to reveal several sheets of photos. They were all young kids and looked Chinese. To Romano they all looked alike. He found it hard to distinguish one from the other.

Lee continued, "All of the kids or should I say, most of these young people, range in age from 13 thru 23 years old. They are all either members of a local Chinatown gang or associated with one and paying tribute to the parent organization. Here in Chinatown the parent organization is the Ghost Shadows. All of the smaller groups kick something back to them. Your group would also be paying tribute to the Shadows or they wouldn't last long."

Lee moved out of the way and motioned for Mike to sit, allowing him a closer look at the photos. To Mike Romano, an Italian, they all looked so similar, they could all be brothers. He was barely able to tell one from another. His brow wrinkled as he attempted to determine any outstanding features so he could tell one man from another.

In apparent recognition of the look on Mike's face, Lee spoke, "Don't worry Mike in a day or two they will all look different." He gave a short chuckle as he continued, "Now, you won't be as good as me, but you will be able to tell them apart."

"Thanks Lee." *Good guy, a sense of humor, this is going to work out,* thought Mike. "Right now it's hard for me."

Lee began to speak again. "Now, some background to help you understand the system down here".

***

Lee began Mike's education with, "Most of if not all the oriental businesses here in Chinatown pay tribute to someone. We cannot put an end to it. Your Italian mob calls it protection. Down here, as in China, it's more like a way of life. People consider it a normal business expense. Our job, the Police Department's, is to keep it under control. We know that we can't stop it, so we work to keep it a cultural thing without violence and mayhem. Kind of like a cover on a boiling pot of water."

Lee tapped his desk as he continued, "The young people you see here are dangerous. They are always trying to make a name for themselves. As with all young people, they want instant gratification. They want to get as much money as possible without having to wait for it. The Ghost Shadows are a modern version of old cowboy desperados, young turks. They do not have the patience or style of the Triads of old."

Mike knew what Triads were. They're gangs, like the Mafia families, organized gangsters.

Lee continued with a little triad history. "The history of the triad is ancient. Triads were originally established as secret societies set up to overthrow an unpopular ruler. The first known secret society was called the Red Eyebrows. They were set up to overthrow the Han dynasty in China that ruled from 206 BC to AD 220."

"I didn't know that", stated Mike. "Is there more?"

Detective Lee obliged, "The Hung League was the first known Triad Society. They date back to the time of the pilgrims, to the 17th century. There is a legend that says that the society was founded by five monks and their main purpose was to overthrow the Ch'ing dynasty and restore the Ming dynasty back to the throne." *Just like the origins of the Mafia back in Italy,* thought Romano.

Lee continued, "In the 18th and 19th centuries, other secret societies were formed in China. Some of them claimed to be a part of the Hung League. However, there appeared to be little or no organization among the groups and their militancy seems to have been more concerned with robbing and terrorizing citizens than trying to overthrow the government. By the 1911 revolution, the league lost any legitimate purpose. It and all those who had links to it were heavily involved in organized crime."

Mike was fascinated. He said aloud what he had been thinking. "Just like the origins of the Mafia, Lee. The tongs were started to over throw unjust rulers too, but got carried away and became what they are today."

Lee answered, "Very similar Mike." He continued, "Any one of the triads is like one of the mafia families. They usually deal in extortion, credit card fraud and gambling. Sometimes they will have prostitution operations as well, but not too often. The young gangs, such as the one you came across, use the word Triad to intimidate the victim.

I'm sure that you are aware of the fact that some young Italian street punks sometimes claim ties to the Mafia while actually not having any. It's done to put fear into the victim and make them worry about reprisals if they run to the police."

"Yeah, Lee, that's exactly what happens."

"Well, the Chinese community is much the same way. The possible difference is that these young men are treacherous. They seem to have no sense of honor, not even among thieves."

"Gather up those photos and let's go to work." Mike handed them to Lee who put them into a manila folder. "We'll walk Mike, it's easier."

Romano and his new partner left the station house and walked south on Elizabeth. They were headed for a few square blocks known as the heart of Chinatown. The "heart" is composed of Canal Street on the north bordered by Worth Street on the south with Pike and Center Streets, east and west respectively.

***

Mike, being a New Yorker his whole life, had "been in Chinatown" before, but nothing like what he was about to see.

Walking the few blocks with Lee as he absorbed his surroundings opened up a new world. He tried to absorb it all. The sidewalks were littered with small stands next to almost every store entrance. The sidewalks were a cornucopia chock full of different things from children's toys to fish on beds of ice.

There were vegetables and dried herbs. At least Mike thought they were herbs. People were everywhere. Scattered thru this mass of humanity were small pushcarts manned by little persons he could not understand, hawking foods he did not recognize. Mike found it amazing.

Mike, weaving his way thru the crowded sidewalks, noticed that even though the streets were filled with people moving like schools of minnows swimming with and against the currents of a mountain stream, as far as he could observe not a single person bumped into another. He noted that there was little or no exchange of conversation as they moved about. *I wouldn't understand it if I heard it,* he thought, never sharing it with Lee.

"Mike, we're going into the next soup shop that's coming up. Stay close." Lee announced as they approached Bayard Street.

"Ok", was Romano's quick response and he focused his eyes on the young person lounging next to the doorway of Wong's Soups, their destination.

Once inside, Mike quickly tapped Lee on the shoulder, leaned close, and spoke softly, "Lee, what's going on? Who was that guy by the door?"

"If you turn around now, you'll see that he's gone. While we are in the shop, the young hoods won't stay close or come in. He was probably here to make a collection and we spoiled it."

"Wow, they sure don't try to hide, do they?"

"No, Mike, not at all. They know that the proprietor will not finger them, especially now that all parties know of our presence. If we acted against the group within a short time after speaking to the shop owner, the gang would initiate immediate and probably harsh reprisal action. They know his lips are sealed because of that fear."

Lee then spoke in Chinese to an aging man that included the customary quick, short, reciprocal bows.

Lee then turned to Romano, “Mike this is Mr. Woo, the shop proprietor.”

Woo bent slightly at the waist and smiled. Mike, a quick study, responded in kind but, as habit took over, Mike also held out his hand in western fashion expecting a handshake. There was none. Woo gestured the two men over to a table in the corner.

Mike looked at his surroundings.

The store was about twenty feet wide with a small service counter along the wall on the right side of the entrance. Behind the counter were two men and assorted restaurant equipment. Only about 10 patrons were scattered about. Towards the rear of the shop, in a small recessed alcove, was a stairway leading downward. Over the stairway was a sign written in Chinese. Mike made a mental note to ask Lee what it said. Adjacent to the stairway were double swinging doors covered in what appeared to be stainless steel. Romano assumed the kitchen was behind them. The air was pregnant with a variety of odors.

Once seated, Woo shouted in what Mike perceived as sing song, although he knew better. As if by magic, a tea pot, along with three cups and three bowls of soup were placed before them. The odor coming from the soup was strong, but not distasteful.

Again Woo gestured with his hand, indicating that they should eat. As Romano dipped a flat bottomed spoon into the bowl before him, Lee sipped his tea and began an earnest conversation with the old man. Mike could understand nothing. However, he could see Lee push the manila folder towards the man and the old guy shake his head negatively and withdraw his hand from anywhere near it. Obviously Woo wanted no part of looking at the photos.

The rapid fire exchange continued long enough for Mike to finish his soup. He enjoyed it and wished circumstances were different. *I’d like to get the recipe and try to make this at home,* he thought. *Can’t do it today. That’s for sure.*

Lee was speaking softly indicating the conversation appeared to be winding down. Mike felt totally left out. He understood nothing. He was intrigued, yet felt slighted.

Lee turned to him and said, "Sorry Mike, but sometimes this is the way it is. I'm still trying. We won't be but another minute or two and then I'll bring you up to speed."

Romano forced a smile and replied, "Sure Lee. I'm fine with it. You'll fill me in later."

Mike had no sooner finished his sentence when Woo softly spoke to the Chinese detective. There were slight nods as Lee stood up. He spoke loudly to Mike, almost a shout, feigning disappointment, "We can't get any help here. Let's go." Lee handed the folder of photos to Romano and in apparent frustration stormed out of the soup kitchen. Mike followed.

Once outside, Lee spoke softly to his partner, "Look across the street, two doorways to the left. Do it casually."

Trying to appear as casual as possible, Mike saw what Lee had brought to his attention. Standing in a doorway was the man they passed as they entered Woo's place. He was watching the two cops attentively, as if they were bugs under glass. Next to him was a second man.

Mike was startled as Lee gave him a slight tap on his arm and in a loud voice rapidly said, "Later, let's go" in an effort to move them away from the shop as quickly as possible he added, We have to get there quickly. Our boss is waiting for us."

Mike understood and was unable to think of anything to say except, "Yeah, that was good soup." He felt stupid as he heard his own words. *What a dumb thing to say. Those punks know who we are.*

Lee led Mike along Bayard Street towards Columbus Park, just behind 100 Center Street, New York City's Criminal Courts building.

Stopping near the corner of Mulberry Street in front of a small pizza shop, Lee spoke his first words since leaving

Woo's shop. "Mike, let's stop here and get a slice. We can sit in the park and I'll fill you in."

"Sure Lee. An Italian kid never turns down a slice. Now what the hell happened back there?"

Lee got two slices, handed one to Mike and led them to a bench facing the rear of the Criminal Court building. He took a bite of his slice, chewed twice and began, "Mike, old man Woo was terrified because the man at the door knew he was talking to us."

"Then he was a bad guy?" asked Mike.

"He's the collection man. Apparently he had just arrived to make his collection. The guy must have spotted us coming down the block and waited to see where we were going." Lee took another bite and continued, "As you could see, Woo wanted no part of the photos. He felt that he was being watched. I tried to tell him that he wasn't but could not convince him. At the end of the conversation, he told me that we could meet him inside the big Chinese bank on the corner of Canal and Center Streets any day at 9:30 a.m. He asked me to call him a day before. I think he was placating me so we wouldn't come back. Who knows maybe someday I will call him."

"So, Lee, did you recognize the guy at the door? You never said anything."

"No Mike, but when we left, the second man across the street, he's in my photo array." Lee was opening the folder as he spoke. He glanced over the first sheet. Spotting the second man, he pointed and said," This guy here. He's affiliated with some gang that calls themselves the Ghosts. They probably use the name to scare people into believing they belong to the Ghost Shadows. Either way, they're not nice boys."

"Are we going to go back and collar either of them? After all, they are extorting Woo."

"No Mike. Woo would never be a complainant. I tried that in the store. He told me that he came to accept it as a way of life. He pushed me off by saying, 'It's not too much. Like a tax we pay the government.' "

Mike was disappointed. "Then we have nothing. Do we?" he anxiously asked.

"Not too much here. But, we know the second man is one of the crew working Woo's shop. At least we can identify him and maybe catch him in the act if we're lucky. The Chinese are not good on going to court as you know, but if the guy is armed when we grab him, we don't need a complainant. We always have a weapons charge, hopefully a gun. As to the man in the doorway, maybe we can check more photos later and learn who he is too."

The rest of the afternoon was spent talking to several proprietors. The team covered restaurants almost exclusively, drank tea and ate soup. The two cops' kidneys were floating. Every person interviewed was basically respectful to Lee, but also uncooperative. Only one man in a Vietnamese restaurant even looked at the folder. He claimed not to be paying protection and said he never saw any of the men in the photos. Lee did not believe him.

That evening, Mike told Betty all about his first day as a "Chinatown Detective."

She found it interesting yet added, "Mike, this Lee guy told you the triads are like the mafia, right?"

"Yes. Why do you ask?"

"Well he also said that they are more ruthless that the mob. Right?"

"Yes. Please make your point."

"Well please be careful. I know you're having a good time and all, but I would rather see you back on The Apple with Gino. At least you're used to the place and know what's going on. And the people speak English so you can understand them."

"Don't worry Honey, Lee's a real smart guy. I'll be fine. Now give me a big hug and a kiss."

***

The following day's investigation took a different turn. Lee had made arrangements to have a third man with them. He also was an oriental. Lee had borrowed him from the city wide street crime unit. The cop had never worked in Chinatown. Best of all he was fluent in the Mandarin and Cantonese dialects. His name was John Eng. They were doing an 1800 x 0200 tour in hopes of catching a collector in the act.

Lee also had requisitioned two cameras from the property clerk's office, complete with carry cases to allow two of them to "dangle" the cameras around their necks like tourists.

The plan was to send Eng into a place to get a feel of what was going on. Eng would then signal William and Mike to walk in and attempt to act like tourists. Mike liked the idea. Roll playing was something new to him.

The trio had tried two restaurants with negative results. Eng came out of each one and reported that he observed no suspicious activity. He added that as best as he could determine, none of the men in Lee's photo array were present inside.

The team continued on to Pell Street. Pell was a short block, almost an alley, between Saint James Place and Mott Street. Eng entered a small restaurant, "Fong Hot Soup" thru an entrance that was below street level. Mike and Lee were uncomfortable because they would be out of sight of their team member. To avoid possibly being made, Eng was carrying no portable radio. If he observed something, they would never know unless Eng resurfaced and notified them in person. The worse scenario would be if he ran into trouble. Eng didn't seem to be nervous as he disappeared into the restaurant. Lee and Mike were uneasy. To make matters worse, it was now twilight and soon, darkness would come.

Mike had heard the rumors about all the basements in Chinatown being connected. He had heard that people grew mushrooms and bean sprouts in some of those basements, but never saw them. William Lee had told him that the stories were for the most part true. He added that not every basement was connected to every basement on the block, but sometimes two or three basements did run together. Mike's sixth sense had begun tingling or was it paranoia? The sound of large wings began beating in his head.

He spoke quickly, "Lee, we have to go in. I don't feel right about this." Mike began descending the steps as he spoke.

Lee muttered, "Ok kid, let's go look," and followed his partner.

As Romano passed underneath the red neon sign above the door, he almost tripped. His clothing and skin turned red for that instant. Mike thought, *My God, is this a sign of what's inside?* He quickly chastised himself. He was being stupid. Nothing was amiss. Yet!

The two cops quickly spotted Eng, obviously distracted as he was slowly attempting to make his way back towards the entrance. Eng was intently watching something. He was moving as if he was trying not to attract the attention of a tall man in the far corner of the room. The man was arguing with someone.

Lee, sensing something, almost ran up behind Eng announcing softly in Chinese, "Eng, it's me Lee. What do you have?" Eng stopped moving and in excited whisper asked,

"Where's Mike? I just saw that guy in the corner put a pistol against the side of the man he's arguing with. We got a live one here."

Without waiting for an answer Lee drew his own weapon and shouted something Romano would later learn was "Police. Everybody, down," in both Mandarin and Cantonese.

The tall guy slipped thru a door that he was standing next to. The other man, the possible victim, ran to the opposite corner of the restaurant and threw his hands over his head. Several patrons were startled enough to spill whatever they had in front of them as they dove onto the white tiled floor.

Mike Romano, the would be archangel instantly recalled prior gun fights he was in. They played in his mind's eye like flashes of an action movie. There was the one on 145th Street and 8th Avenue in the 32nd Precinct, rounds bouncing off the concrete as he rolled on the sidewalk with a shooter, the foot race and shots in the same command while running thru the Madison Houses after a long car chase.

Mike once again vividly recalled the night he shot Wilkey, the perverted child rapist, on the rooftop during the blackout. He remembered the pain of being shot. He remembered how scared he was and how adrenalin rushed thru his veins helping him ignore his wound and survive the encounter. His mind raced, *Oh shit. It's going down again.* Eng was the first cop to reach the doorway. He flattened himself against the wall one hand gripping the doorknob and holding the door closed, waiting for his team to get in a tactical position. He was also scanning the restaurant to make sure there were no additional armed adversaries in the room.

Lee followed Eng to the doorway. He took a position on the hinged side of the door. Mike joined his partners and stood behind Eng for a few seconds while the team formulated a plan.

Mike said, "Look guys, I have this stupid camera around my neck. I'll get low in the doorway while Eng opens it and I'll snap the flash at the same time. I'll be a small target so the guy can't get a good shot off if he decides to fight. Hopefully he won't be able to see at all because of the flash and we'll hopefully see him."

Lee spoke first, in a barely audible whisper, "Sort of a good idea, but stay behind the wall next to John and get as low as possible. When John swings the door open, just put the camera out, not you and snap the flash. If the guy is waiting we'll get a chance at him while he's hopefully blinded. If he fires, we may locate him by the muzzle blast."

John held up three fingers as he nodded that he understood. He then closed his fist and began silently counting holding up one finger at a time.

To Mike, it seemed like 30 minutes, before that third finger sprang up, the door swung open and Mike's own finger, as if it had a mind of its own, set off the camera's flash. The burst of light lit up a short narrow corridor, beyond which, the team could clearly see rows of platform like structures with long tray type tops. Something was growing in them. There was no one in sight. The light supplied by the flash left as quickly as it came and the room beyond the corridor was bathed in darkness. The trio then entered the corridor and quickly closed the door behind them thus preventing themselves from being silhouetted against the light from the restaurant. Mike had a pen light with him. He clicked it on and scanned what he could. Visible in the small round beam the team could see trays of large mushrooms growing. The floor appeared damp and slippery. Romano held the light in his left hand, extended away from his body and very low. He thought to himself, *if he's in there, maybe he'll think we're crawling in.*

Slowly the team advanced, feeling the walls ahead so they would know when they reached the end of the corridor. The narrow beam of the penlight did nothing about illuminating the corridor. Once into the room itself, Lee and Eng, each turned on their own small pocket flashlights. The air in the room was permeated with an odor that reminded Mike of an old cave he once explored as a Boy Scout. Employing good tactics, the advancing police officers held their respective lights at arm's length far from their bodies. If the gunman shot, he would aim at the light source believing a person was directly behind it and possibly save them from serious injury or worse. Quickly, three small lights scanned the room.

After two sweeps of the room with no adverse activity, John Eng found a light switch. He used his flashlight to alert his partners to the find. They nodded with their own lights to go ahead and flip on the wall switch. They would take their chances. The room was bathed in light. There was nobody there except the cops. The officers stood up and gave the area a good look.

Mike found it amazing. The place was about twenty five feet square, with neat rows of growing tables filled with mushrooms. The tops of those fungi were as big as saucers, about six inches across. The floor was damp and almost slimy. Walking was precarious. No one spoke.

On the far wall, directly across from the doorway the men had just entered, was another closed door. Lee signaled to his team that he wanted John to shut the lights again. He indicated that once the lights were out again, they would attempt to go thru the new doorway. He motioned to stay low. Lee then signaled Eng to shut the lights.

Once again the champions of justice were in complete darkness. Lee was already positioned next to the doorway when the lights went out. He duplicated Romano's prior entry tactics. Once everyone was positioned, the team advanced again. This time it was different. **Flash, bang,** a shot rang out in their direction. It struck the far wall of the room behind them. Each cop instantly returned two shots each at whoever might be in that other room.

Eng and Mike heard Lee hit the floor. Simultaneously they spoke, softly and excitedly, "You Okay, anyone hit?"

Each man answered. Lee was first, Okay."

"Good", was Mike's response.

Eng came back with, "Me too".

The whole incident took less than two seconds. Then complete silence. Mike wanted to shout to break the tension he felt. His sphincter muscle was so tight you couldn't bang a ten penny nail into it. Each team member instinctively moved forward thru the doorway. In the darkness, they bumped into each other. They were once again in a short corridor.

Oh shit! thought Mike. He knew they were too close to each other. They made an easy target if the guy fired again. The first time they were lucky. He cautiously reached into the darkness. Finding his partners, first one then the other, he gently pushed them in an effort to spread out as best they could in such a confined space. There was no conversation.

As the cops advanced, they heard voices in the darkness. Eng and Lee were able to understand. There were at least two men speaking in the Cantonese dialect. That meant that there was a minimum of two bad guys and they were willing to shoot it out with the cops.

The only thing Mike knew was that he believed he heard two different men. He hoped that there was not more. *We only saw one guy duck into the doorway. Where did the other one come from? We're in deep shit now!* He thought. He wanted to speak to his partners but knew it would give the other men a sound directed target. He took slow shallow breaths to control his anxiety as they reached the end of the corridor and entered a larger space, still hugging the walls.

Eng took the chance of shouting into the darkness in both Mandarin and Cantonese. Later, Mike found out he had announced, "Police, give up. If you fight you are going to die." Romano heard Eng's feet shuffle as he quickly moved sideways as the last word fell from his lips.

Within a millisecond shots were flying. From within the black void in front of the officers, approximately ten feet apart were explosions of sound accompanied by muzzle flashes. It was deafening. In the quick flash of gunfire Mike could see more growing trays. It was not possible to see any shooters. *They gotta be behind the trays and low. I'll shoot low.* Mike's mind was racing.

From Mike's left three quick shots were returned by one of his partners. At that moment, he didn't know which one it was. Revved up by adrenaline and basic survival instinct, Mike also fired three times into the darkness. His shots were low and sent in the direction of the muzzle flash he just saw in front of him. The sound of his own weapon snapped a page from his training to the front of his thinking process. Mike remembered his training. *Stop. Count your shots. Don't empty your weapon. It could cost you your life.*

From his right and slightly ahead of him, two more shots were quickly fired in the direction of the shooters. Mike thought his head would explode with the noise. He ears were ringing. He felt something wet and cold splash on him. *Must be water from the damn trays, that thumping sound, angel wings or my heart?*

The plethora of sound ended as abruptly as it started. The dark abyss was bathed in dead silence. It seemed like minutes had passed since the last eruption of sound. Actually it was only seconds. From somewhere within the black hole in front of the battled centurions came a moan.

Lee shouted in Chinese and English, "Police, give up or we will kill you."

Not the usual, Police don't move kind of thing. What the hell, they are trying to kill us. Turnabout is fair play. Especially here, Mike thought. He spoke out loud, "Damn right guys. We are going to put you down." He didn't even care if they understood or not. It made him feel better to purge some of the tension within him.

Lee spit the words out, "Mike, John, status?"

As his adrenaline rush subsided, Mike answered "Wet and OK."

John Eng followed with, "Ditto." He tried to add humor obviously trying to break the tension and not give away his position.

Lee continued, "Now we have to see who the hell is in here. Use your lights and be damn careful. Don't get hurt now."

Cautiously, each officer snapped his light on and off in attempt to see if they would draw fire. Thankfully they didn't. However, they did hear labored breathing.

Several seconds passed, Mike spoke next, "I'm going to sweep the room with my light. Watch for movement." Again he heard the beating of wings. *Just my heartbeat, he thought.* Mike tried to sound like he had command of the entire situation but he was shaking inside. Fully extending his left arm, he held his light high. Using his right hand to point his revolver as it followed the light into the darkness, he swept the room. He could see wood splinters everywhere. Something that looked like pale worms littered the floor. The place looked like someone doused it with a garden hose. There was water everywhere. With no aggressive response, the other two cops switched on their lights.

The first man the team saw in the light beams was lying on his side. His head was facing them, eyes open. Beside him was what looked like a semi-automatic pistol. Mike could hear someone moving in the direction of the man. He moved his light off the guy, yet the man was bathed in light. Either Lee or Eng had begun advancing on the prone perp. Mike continued to sweep the room and saw a second man sitting against the back wall. Dangling from his finger was a gun.

Mike shouted, "Drop it or you're dead."

As he spoke, a second light was directed on the man. It was Eng shouting in Chinese. The man let the weapon slide off his finger. Eng spoke again and the man used his foot to push the gun away. Mike moved quickly and was on the guy in the blink of an eye, putting one foot on the firearm and his own revolver against the man's face.

Lee had already advanced on the first man and announced, “He’s dead. We got him. Our guy’s gone. How about the guy you men have?”

Eng answered, we think he’s hurt. Don’t know where yet. But he’s been neutralized.” By the time the verbal exchange was over, Mike and John had their man in handcuffs. There was no other movement. Mike mouthed a silent, *Thank God. Only two bad guys.*

Lee found the room’s wall switch and snapped it upward bathing the black abyss with light. He looked around and found the place was in shambles with two perpetrators down, one of them DOA. “Someone call this in.”

Mike attempted to give the wounded man his Miranda warnings. In frustration, he shook his head. “Eng, give this guy his Miranda, will you please before I finish what we started.”

“Sure, Mike.” John proceeded and paused at times, apparently waiting for an answer. The perp did not reply to all the questions. Eng continued on as if he did respond.

“I’m done Mike. He’s refusing to give his name.

Lee shouted back to them, “My dead guy had a 9mm Browning semi-auto. I think he’s the guy from the restaurant. What does your guy have?”

Romano answered, Looks like a Sig Sauer. Also 9mm, but he was carrying hollow points. The son of a bitch. Maybe we should kill him anyway.” The handcuffed man twitched and spun his head around to look at Mike. Romano almost lost it as he shouted, “You bastard. You understand English. Don’t you?”

It was discovered that the dead man had been shot in the forehead, just over the left eye and apparently died instantly. There were other wounds too, a chest wound and one on his right hand. The second man was hit twice. He stopped one round in his right thigh, and another in the right shoulder. Mike was not a doctor but he thought the man was hit at the rotator cuff. *Good for you. That arm will never function right again. You deserve it. You should be dead.* Mike wanted to tell everyone but regained some composure and never articulated his thought. Instead, he called the job in to dispatch.

"Fifth Squad to Central, K. We have multiple shootings. Two perps down, one probably DOA. Three plainclothes unhurt. We're in Fong Hot Soup on Pell Street. Acknowledge, K"

Within minutes, the EMT's arrived just as a uniform sergeant walked in. Every detective on duty at the fifth squad came out also. Minutes later, the Fifth's squad commander and a duty captain arrived. Shortly several teams of uniformed men showed up too. In all at least fifteen men responded.

Once the Squad Commander knew that his men were fine, he began bemoaning the "tons of paperwork" to be done. It would all start right there with the initial statements of the officers involved. Crime scene arrived just as the surviving perp was loaded onto a gurney and brought out to the waiting ambulance. Two uniformed officers were assigned to ride with him.

The responding duty captain looked at the dirty, trio of wet cops he came to interview and saw them pointing at each other and laughing.

The captain thought that it was somewhat bizarre behavior and asked, "What do you guys find so funny here? You all could have been killed and you did kill a man."

Lee and Mike answered in such unison, it almost sounded rehearsed. "Sorry Captain, but look at us." Mike added, "We're wet, slimy and have bean sprouts all over us." He almost laughed again when he added, "At first I thought they were worms."

"You men go back to the Fifth, clean up as best you can, get union reps there if you think you need them and I'll be in for statements in ten to fifteen minutes." Then, with a crooked smile he added, "Get the hell out of here. Looks like a good shooting to me."

Back at the command, because he was assigned there and had a locker, only Lee had a change of clothes. He changed his shirt. John and Mike took turns brushing bean sprouts off each other's backs. They cleaned up as best they good. By the time the duty captain arrived, union delegates from the DEA (Detective's Endowment Association) and the PBA (Patrolmen's Benevolent Association) were present. The Captain introduced himself to each man. The interview for the Unusual Occurrence Report went smooth. The sequence of events was reported along with the Captain's determination that "It was a righteous shooting. The circumstances of this incident indicate that the officers involved acted properly and within Department guidelines."

The trio's weapons were taken for ballistic comparisons. They would be returned later. It was usual Department procedure to offer trauma treatment to cops involved in a shooting incident. All three of the stalwart officers refused medical aid. They did, however, opt to take the next day off.

They planned to meet in Det. Lee's office again on Thursday at 0900 hours.

***

Mike cautiously drove home. He had survived another gun fight and his adrenalin was still pumping. He didn't want to get in an accident, so he forced himself to drive like an old woman. It seemed like the eleven mile ride took forever.

It was 3:00 a.m. when he quietly entered his apartment. He went to the fridge, removed his bottle of nerve tonic, the ever helpful Dewars White Label and poured three fingers into a glass. Mike thought he had been extra quiet and would not awaken anyone in the house. He was wrong. Betty, through a sixth sense, walked into the kitchen. Mike had been lost in thought and was startled as she approached. He did however; notice that she was wearing pale blue, almost transparent baby doll pajamas. Betty knew her husband well.

Before noticing his dirty and still damp clothes she spoke, “What happened now? Is everything OK? Answer me right now Michael Romano” The decibel level was low, but Mike knew by the tone that he should not bullshit her.

“Well,” Bet, as he often called her when he was trying to be extra friendly, “We had a little exchange in the basement of a restaurant. We’re all fine, but a bad guy is dead and another is hurt. We were interviewed and it’s a good shooting.”

Her eyes widened. Before she could speak again, he cheerfully added, “But I have tomorrow off. Don’t have to go back in until Thursday. Pretty cool, huh?” *Poor attempt Romano,* he thought.

“A little exchange was it? One dead and one wounded. What did you do exchange harsh words or bullets. Damn you Michael. When do you go back to 42nd Street, to the perverts, derelicts and drug dealers? It’s safer there. When Michael, when?” Her body shook as she spoke. He could see her ample breasts shake thru her flimsy pajama top.

The scotch had begun doing its thing. He was now oblivious to her verbal lashing and now focused on her feminine charms. “Betty, it will soon end in a couple of days. It will end soon. The assignment was only for a week, one set of tours.” He finished his drink, rose quickly out of the chair and made a quick lunge at his wife, grabbing her by the wrist. He began pulling her toward their bedroom. She offered little resistance. Mike was spent in ten minutes. He slept until noon.

***

Thursday morning at 0830 hours, Mike was back at the Fifth, in Lee’s office. It was the last day of his set (Romano’s work week). Lee was alone drinking coffee and going through several typed reports. Off to one side were the photos they had carried thru Chinatown.

"Hey, Mike. Good morning. It's just you and me. John Eng has an old court case. After today you will go back to your own command. The bosses want you to take those photos with you and show them around. The dead guy from the restaurant has been identified and added to the mix. Hopefully you'll get an ID from your complainant. The DOA was only 19 years old."

Mike thought, *Damn, Lee's all business today and asked*, "William, guess we did good. What about the other guy?"

"Woo Feng, he's been arraigned and is in the Tombs (the city's ancient jail attached to Criminal Court Building). He's being kept in isolation and Intel is working on him. Now we can maybe get some information about the gangs down here. Good work by the way. It was bullets from your weapon struck him without killing him."

"Lee, what about the DOA? Who shot him?"

"John Eng and I did. The report said he was hit three times. The lucky head shot was mine." He added as an afterthought, "Intel confirmed that the DOA is the guy from inside the restaurant that night. The guy's name is Weng Fat. He's from Wachung China, seventeen years old. He's been busted before. Maybe Intel interviewed the owner, the guy Eng saw with Fat in the restaurant."

The two men spent some time going over all the paperwork associated with the shooting incident. They joked a little and later Lee took Mike to a little hole in the wall place for the best Chinese meal he ever ate.

Chapter Six

When Mike returned to MTS on the following set of tours, the place buzzed as he walked in to the muster room. The story of the Chinatown shootout had filtered uptown. There was some time before roll call and Mike used it to his advantage. After smiling at those present, he went upstairs to see the precinct detectives. After some quick talking, Mike convinced the detective squad in MTS to duplicate the photos Lee had given him by using their 1 to 1 Polaroid camera. The camera is designed with a fixed focal point and a bridge attached to the front assuring that the lens is always the correct distance from the original object. Its purpose is to photograph fingerprints or duplicate photos. It was not normal for a patrol cop to get such treatment, but the Chinatown incident gave him some extra weight.

After receiving his Polaroids, Mike thanked the men of the squad numerous times and went down to attend roll call.

Before roll call began, Lieutenant Armini and Sergeant Holbrook called for silence in the room and publically complemented Romano about the Chinatown incident. There were some whoops and applauds. Even the Commanding Officer, Dennis Bryan, Mike's least favorite person in the Department, felt the need to comment on a job well done. Mike enjoyed the minor celebrity status. However, the celebrity only lasted to the end of roll call and then it was business as usual.

Once Gino and Mike arrived on post, they immediately went to the coop above the King of Pizza. Gino wanted to hear all the details and look at the photos Mike was carrying.

It took about half an hour for Romano to tell of his short assignment in Chinatown. Gino was only interested in the restaurant incident and asked Mike to tell him every detail. Mike enjoyed relating everything to his partner.

"Hey Mike, even the CO came out and publicly complemented you. That was great. Does he know you hate him?

Maybe he's trying to get on your good side. It might be a good thing. You could get close to him."

Romano's reply to that remark was, "Yeah, he knows me. Let's see where that goes."

After spending about an hour in their perch, they left Tony's office and went back on patrol. The team responded to the usual disputes in the "camera stores" for the first hour on the Apple, working their way back towards 8th Avenue. Mike was anxious to show the Chinatown photos back at the Cu-Lei Garden restaurant where the Wachung gang had been collecting tribute.

The owner, Cu-Lei, became nervously animated when he saw two uniformed officers enter his place. He first looked at Gino and a few seconds later recognized Mike.

"Why you here officer? There probrem? You catch boys. I not go to court. I tell you that before."

Mike spoke as calmly as he could, not to excite Cu-Lei, "Sir, Mr. Lei, no, we didn't catch the boys, but I have pictures to look at. Please come, sit and speak with us."

As he spoke, Mike and Gino were moving to a booth in the far side of the restaurant. There were no customers present at the time. Two people came to the kitchen doorway, looked wide eyed (as wide eyed as an oriental can get) and whispered to each other. Lei, always the quintessential china man giving instant respect to authority, gave a slight bow from the waist and sat down with them.

Mike began, "Sir we have some information that some boys we are after in Chinatown are Wachungs. Here are some photographs of some of those men. Please look at them and tell us if you know any of them." Romano slid the packet of photos forward. Wei Cu-Lei was not happy to again be involved in the possible prosecution of these men.

"I no need to look at pictures. Men no longer come here to get money. They are gone now." Lei's hand moved away from the photos as if they would burn him.

Mike picked up the photos and separated them placed them one by one on the table before Lei, two rows, six across. He placed a mug shot of Weng Fat in the number two spot, a trick he learned from Detective Lee.

"If you were sure you had the right guy, always put him in the number two spot. Ninety percent of the time you got a positive ID from your complainant." He was not sure why it worked, but it did. In the fifth place position he put the photo of the second restaurant shooter.

Cu-Lei looked closely, or at least acted like he was studying the photos. Mike and Gino studied Cu-Lei. The old man finally touched the second photo if only for a microsecond. Both cops caught it. Gino kicked Mike under the table. Mike instantly opened his memo book and withdrew another photo. It was the photo of Fat taken at the fiasco in Chinatown by Crime Scene. Mike dropped it in front of Cu-Lei with a slightly flamboyant flick of the wrist.

The old man snapped back in his seat. "Ohhh, he shot in head. He is now dead. Yes"? he loudly asked Mike.

There was some conversation at the kitchen door.

"Yes, Mr. Cu-Lei, he is dead. Is he one of the men who took money from you?"

Cu-Lei turned to face the kitchen and spoke loudly in Chinese to the people at the doorway. Now there were three. Cu-Lei's wife had joined the other two. The back and forth conversation was punctuated with what Mike thought was sounds of joy as all the doorway people were smiling broadly.

Cu-Lei turned back to the team and said, "Yes, he one of men. He will not come anymore to take my money." As he spoke, Cu-Lei hit the crime scene image of Weng Fat. "You porice do good. You take some food now. Yes?"

Gino looked at Mike for a sign. Mike shook his head ever so slightly. Gino answered for both of them, "Thank you Cu-Lei, that's very nice of you, but we must go now. We have something to do."

Mike added, "Maybe we will come back later to see you and have some food. Again, thank you all."

As the men got up from the table every worker in the place, five in all, came forward and bowed to each of them. Mike and Gino were slightly embarrassed. They left quickly.

Once outside, Gino turned to his partner, "Good work Mike. What now?"

"Well, my friend, you know the little Chinese take-out on 43rd Street and Seventh, around the corner from that big gift shop."

Deluca answered, "Sure Mike. Been there a long time remember?"

"Well partner, let's take a walk over there. Maybe we can get lucky. We'll do the photo thing."

The team walked quickly toward Seventh Avenue. As they approached the last theater on that side of the block, one of their "regulars", a fellow named Rivera, a pot dealer, saw them moving quickly. Worried, he backed into a nudie billboard almost knocking it over. He tried to act friendly, hoping he was not their target. As friendly as he could he asked, "Hey Leukemia, where you going in such a hurry? Is somebody getting locked up? Need help?"

The two officers never broke stride. Gino answered, "We have things to do, but we'll come back later for you. Okay?"

Rivera quickly lied and answered, "It's Ok man, I'm not doing anything today. You can check me. I'm clean." The officers never broke stride.

They were almost on the corner now. Mike and his partner continued directly to the small take-out food shop. The owner, Woo Fung, recognized Gino.

"Ah, Mr. Gino, you come for something to eat maybe? Who is your friend?"

Deluca responded, "Good to see you Woo, we are here for your help. We want to show you some pictures of bad guys. Can we go in the back please?"

"Sure. For you, OK. Come." He led the two cops into a small back room.

"Mike, show him the first set of photos." They only had one set. Gino was hoping his partner understood and would again leave out the Crime Scene photo of the dead perp.

"Sure Gino, gotcha", was the quick answer. Mike placed the stack of photos on the small table that obviously acted as a desk of sorts. He motioned for Woo to pick them up. Woo looked at each one, separating them into two piles. He then picked up one stack and looked at each one again. He placed two on the side. Both mug shot were the men from last week's incident.

"Yeah, these men come in here sometimes. Sometimes, only one of them. Sometimes this man" indicating Fat, "comes in with a different man. Some of the people who visit are not here in pictures. Why do you want them?"

Mike answered, "Because they take money from restaurants like yours for protection. Do you pay them?"

"Mr. Gino, you understand? It is the Chinese way. We want no trouble. They come here and ask for some money. We give it. They do not take too much."

At that point Mike took out the photo of the dead man and dropped it in front of Woo. "This one will not come back. Maybe nobody will come back."

Woo's eyes widened, almost round, for a Chinese guy. "He is with his ancestors now. Did porice do this?"

"Mike answered softly, for effect, "Yes, Woo, I did it. He and the other man in the photo you picked out tried to shoot me and two other cops." Mike was stretching the truth, but the effect was noted.

Woo gave a slight bow and said, "Mr. Gino, you have a good partner. Woo knows where you walk every day. If I have trouble, I send someone for you two police." He also offered them food to go. They declined, thanked Woo for his help and left.

The two officers headed straight to King of Pizza's upstairs room. As they entered the shop, they first asked Tony for two foot long sausage parmesan sandwiches on crusty Italian bread. Tony handed them two soft drinks and told them one of his assistants would bring the food up when ready.

Not wanting to be disturbed, Mike notified the dispatch that "Apple Post 10 was on meal." Once they settled in, Gino asked Mike what he intended to do about the identifications they received?

"Well Gino, an intelligence report got this started, so guess we file two more. Only this time I can refer to photo numbers. I'm also going to call Lee at the Fifth and let him know what happened so he can pull the report and work with Intel."

After their meal, their day tour continued unremarkably. They never went back to hassle Rivera either. The team returned to the station house an hour early because they had to file the Intel Reports. Mike notified the radio dispatcher that they had returned to MTS for clerical duties. When writing up his report, Mike included the fact that his partner helped with the interviews and the fact that Woo Fung knew Deluca as an attentive foot cop which made the interview easier. *Might as well share the brownie points with my partner,* he thought. Gino commented to Mike that he appreciated the gesture and thanked him.

The following day, almost one hour before the end of a fairly easy tour, while standing in front of one of the "art Theaters" Mike and Gino thought they heard gun shots across the street. They weren't quite sure where the sounds were coming from because they were muted as if inside a building. They were looking and listening, trying to determine the direction and source of the noise, when from across the street, slightly to their left, people streamed out of one of the "porn video stores", shouting and screaming. The sex shop "doorman", having seen the two cops, was running towards them. Normally the man spoke English quite well, but due to circumstances, he was shouting in his native language, Spanish. He almost fell as he was running to Mike and Gino. They were unable to understand anything he was saying.

"Speak English", each of them repeatedly ordered. After several attempts to get the excited man to comply, they abandoned trying to determine what the excited man was talking about and concentrated on the shouts of the patrons racing from the premises. However, Mike and Gino were able to clearly hear the word gun; they raced across the street, leaving their complainant to catch up later.

Police sirens could be heard in the distance as they ran toward the scene. Once at the store entrance, each man cautiously took a position on opposite sides of the doorway weapons drawn and ready.

Now, as seasoned veterans, Mike and Gino knew not to remain standing upright thus making a large target and tactfully kneeled down and peered inside.

The team observed several video machines emitting sparks, many were turned over and in general the place was a shambles. Standing in the center of the room was a single man who looked slightly familiar to them. He was holding what appeared to be a snub nosed .38 caliber revolver, similar to a typical cops' off duty weapon. The man was pointing the weapon at a particular machine and attempting to pump more rounds into it. The firearm only clicked on empty chambers. The gun was empty.

Deluca spoke quickly to his partner, "I think I know the guy." He then shouted, "Police don't move. Drop the gun", as he aimed his own weapon at the man inside.

Mike added, "Take it easy guy. Don't make us shoot you. Throw the gun away." Realizing what Gino had just said, he quickly added to his partner, "What the hell are you talking about Gino?"

Inside the angry gunman was ranting," These sons of bitches. That's me and my wife in there. I'll burn the place down after I kill them."

Gino shouted to Mike, "Damn it, I think he's a cop. He's one of ours. Go easy Mike. I'm sure of it."

The sirens they heard were fading away. They were going somewhere else and not responding to The Apple. Mike was first to notice and called their situation in to the dispatcher, "Apple post 10 to Central, emergency, K"

"Central reads you loud and clear Apple. What's your condition? Post 10, K"

"We have shots fired in a store. The perp may be one of ours, an off duty cop, a member of the service or something. He's in plainclothes. Two uniform officers at the doorway. He's armed but appears to be out of ammo. Send backup units, K"

"Anyone hurt post 10?"

"Unknown Central. Not inside yet. The perp appears fine and we're OK. Tell responding units to look for the crowd. We're midblock on The Apple, K"

"Use caution post 10. Help is on the way, K"

Only seconds had passed since the blue centurions ran up to the shop. The wheels of Gino's memory began meshing as the irate gun toting man turned toward the sound of the radio transmission.

Gino now spoke softly to the man, "Hey guy, you work Midtown don't you. I'm Gino Deluca, this guy next to me is Mike Romano. Calm down and put your weapon on the floor. There's carloads of people coming and you don't want them to see you standing there with a gun. Do you?"

From inside the shop, the man let out a deep sigh of frustration. The look on his face was one of helplessness. He began sobbing as he spoke, "My name is Henry and these bastards have my honeymoon on these machines. My wife's going to die when she finds out."

Gino continued, "Look man, it sucks. What's your last name Henry? Let us come in before the bosses get here and we'll help you. Don't do this alone."

Deluca was doing his best to talk the man down. He just wanted to get the man's weapon before the circus arrived. He and Mike knew the weapon was empty, but when other men arrived, they might shoot the guy. He didn't want the man hurt.

Deluca continued, "Did you shoot anyone?"

In between his sobs, Henry answered, "Henry Slater. I don't think so. But I just wanted to kill the machines so people can't see us. Guess I fucked up. I'm done now. Probably lose the job too. We just got married three weeks ago. Please, please, help me." He finally dropped the gun.

Gino and Mike approached quickly yet cautiously. Mike dropped down to pick up the gun and Gino gave the guy a bear hug, locking the man's arms to his side to prevent any movement. Once Mike had the gun and announced it was empty, Gino loosened his grip on poor Henry but still kept his arms around him. Henry dropped to his knees, head down and a broken man. Gino dropped to the floor with Henry to maintain physical control of the man. Gino remained there a few seconds. As he felt Henry's muscles relax, Deluca released him and stood up, remaining at the ready. The worst was over.

Two people came out of a back room and a guy popped up from behind a counter at the rear of the shop. They stood like statues, wide eyed and awestruck, remaining silent.

Lieutenant Armini and Sergeant Holbrook came screeching up to the curb. In an unusual move, they had been riding patrol together. Weapons drawn, they bounded into the shop. Seeing Deluca and Romano standing over the shooter, their weapons secured made them slow down.

Lieutenant Armini spoke first, "What do you have here guys? Is anyone hurt?"

From somewhere in the back of the room came, "No. We're all good. Thank God you cops came in. Don't know what this crazy man was gonna do."

Gino added quickly, "Boss, he's one of ours."

Sgt. Holbrook nodded and spoke, "Please. Everyone stay where you all are. We'll get to you in a few minutes."

Lieutenant Armini motioned to his two cops to be very attentive to what he was about to do and closely watch the man kneeling on the floor. They both nodded. Armini stood next to Henry and placed a hand on his shoulder while gently putting his other hand beneath his arm and guiding him to a standing position.

Neither supervisor recognized the man. It was impossible to know all the men in "The South". Armini took Gino's word when he addressed the man.

"What's your name officer? he asked softly. "Henry Slater", was the whispered response.

As a safety measure, Armini spoke to Holbrook, "Sergeant, please come here. I want you to do something." He was hoping to get into Henry's head that police brass was present and not to get violent.

It worked. Henry was almost sagging now. "Henry," Armini said softly, "It's procedure, I'm going to have to handcuff you.

Please put your hands in front of you." He was giving him courteous treatment. Rear cuffing was normal procedure. "Gino please cuff him."

Gino looped a pair of handcuffs under Henry's pants belt and gently applied them to his wrists. With the cuffs under Henry's belt, he was unable to lift his arms and injure anyone should he snap and become violent.

There were no words exchanged as the handcuffs were applied. Sergeant Holbrook radioed the dispatcher, informing him that the scene was secure, there were no injuries and that no bus (police vernacular for the ambulance) was needed. He then added that they had one under arrest. Holbrook requested for Emergency Service to secure the scene. In addition, he asked the dispatcher to have precinct detectives respond. The Sergeant was barely audible to those present in the room. Anyone could see that Holbrook was shaken. One of their own had lost it. It could have been any of them.

"Romano, you get into some stuff and now you have Deluca with you to add to the mix. What a team you guys are. Remain until the scene is secured and assist the squad if they need you. Then come in and see me. Got it?" Armini ordered as he guided Henry outside.

"Yes sir, Yes sir" they both answered in turn." They were happy to see poor Henry leave. It made them both very uncomfortable to see a cop in handcuffs. The men were witnessing one of those reoccurring nightmares, common to law enforcement officers everywhere.

After herding all remaining people out of the shop, including ranking officers into the small entrance vestibule, Mike and Gino posted themselves at the doorway and waited for the other units to arrive. As first to arrive on the scene, they were responsible to maintain its integrity. The civilians were strategically placed so they could not wander away. The y would soon be interviewed by the investigation teams.

Detectives from the station house responded first. One of them began interviewing the witnesses in a cursory manner, first getting their pedigree. Two other detectives entered into the shop to look around, then joined the detective with the witnesses, taking special interest in the shop clerk. One of the detectives interviewed Mike and Gino. Still trying to wrap their brains around the incident, they gave the detectives their account of what happened from the time they heard shots to handcuffing Henry.

Emergency Services never arrived. Instead the Crime Scene Unit did. The sergeant in charge asked who was first on the scene.

One of the detectives waved his arm at Mike and Gino. They were asked, "What are we looking for guys beside spent rounds?"

As they walked into the premises, Romano responded first with, "The poor cop who did this was talking about movies of him and his wife."

Gino added, "Something about his honeymoon. Poor Henry, the guy who was responsible for this, told us that he got married three weeks ago. Somewhere in here, on one of the video machines, is a movie or movies of him and his wife taken on his honeymoon without his knowledge."

The sergeant asked, "Do you know which one? There's almost a dozen in here."

Mike responded as he pointed, "Gino isn't that the machine he was pointing his gun at when he ran out of ammo?"

"Thanks guys. We'll start there."

The two foot cops then asked, "Who's the boss? Can we go now? Our Lieutenant wants to see us."

A big burly detective answered, "Yeah, guys, you can go. If we need you, we'll find you at the command. You boys did real good. Nobody was hurt."

Back at the command, Lieutenant Armini and Sergeant Holbrook were waiting for them. The Lieutenant ushered them to a small office. Present in the room was DI Bryan and two men. Sergeant Holbrook remained in the doorway and listened in.

"Gentlemen, I'm Captain Lowery and this is Detective Johnson. We're from the Internal Affairs Division. We would like to hear your account of the events as they occurred in 257 West 42nd Street, also known as 'The Adult Video Store'."

Gino and Mike looked around for two seats.

The captain continued, "Deluca you go with Det. Johnson. Romano you remain here."

Johnson stepped forward and motioned Gino to the door. *Wow*, thought Mike, *this is going to be something. They're going to get separate statements.*

Bryan then spoke, "Captain, please inform me if they say anything that needs immediate attention. I'll get the rest in your reports." He smiled and left the area followed by Lieutenant Armini and Sergeant Holbrook.

Lowery began, "Romano, Mike, you have a good record. I see that you were recently involved in a fatal shooting downtown. Want to tell me about it?" He was attempting to put Mike at ease.

"No sir. I'd rather not talk about it. I'd like to put it behind me. I was scared out of my mind and did what was necessary. By the way, I did not kill the dead perp, someone else did. There were no shots fired by us today. Why ask about the Chinatown incident?"

Mike was getting upset with the IAD captain. He just wanted to get the interview over with and to go home as soon as possible.

"I'm just trying to get a feel for you officer, Mike. You exercised great restraint today. Did you know the shooter was a cop before you entered into the shop?"

"No, we, I didn't. My partner, Deluca thought he might have seen the guy before today. He thought that he might be one of us."

The captain pushed, "And that's why you didn't fire at an armed man. Is that correct Romano?"

"Listen, we didn't shoot because the poor bastard was shooting at video machines. When we were at the door, he was trying to shoot one particular machine. He was also out of rounds. We heard the gun clicking. That's why we didn't fire. Are you trying to say we did something wrong? You guys are always trying to get somebody. Do I need a union delegate? "

"Easy Romano, I'm a captain. Don't get surly with me. This is not about you. We are trying to decide exactly what happened. Right now we are undecided what charges will be filed against the cop. Our job is to determine all the facts and decide how far the cop went in disregarding Department regulations. To me, shooting your

weapon in a shop is doing something wrong. He put people in jeopardy, didn't he? Did he say anything to you?"

"Yeah. Maybe shooting up the machines is wrong, but he wanted to stop some pictures from being seen. He ranted about his honeymoon. He kept ranting something about his wife in a video with him. Apparently they were the stars of one of the movies. You should try to help him. You should find out who made the movie and lock them up. He didn't try to shoot anybody. He just wanted to destroy the videos."

Lowery listened intently to Mike's comments. He answered, "We are pulling the films now. Officer Slater, Henry Slater, told us about the films. No reason to shoot the place up though. He could have called it in. Right now he's under suspension without pay. You can go now. Thank you."

Mike was sitting across from Lowery. He was eager to get out of the room and almost levitated out of the chair, almost jogging out of the room. *Pushy bastard that Lowery. IDA always wanting to get someone. Why don't they go after that crooked Dennis Bryan? He should be under investigation. He's a real bad cop. Not Henry. That poor guy needs counseling.*

Mike went to find Lieutenant Armini. He found him in the muster room with Sergeant Holbrook.

Deluca, having finished his interview walked in behind Mike and asked, "Lieutenant Armini, do you have any information? Is it true that he saw himself and his wife in a porn movie, flipped out and shot up the place?"

Sergeant Holbrook spoke first, "Men this is to be kept as quiet as possible. Officer Slater will be going away for some time. He will be getting counseling and treatment for some time. To our knowledge, with the intervention of the Chaplin's Office, there will be no criminal charges filed. I don't know if he will ever return to work."

"Well, that's something, I guess" Gino echoed Mike's statement.

Holbrook continued, "As we speak, some people are going to his home to inform his wife and explain what happened. They will make every attempt to ease her worry about her husband. The Chaplain's Office will send a counselor with them. They will also bring her to her husband."

Armini took over, "As to Slater's statements. He told us that he had been on his honeymoon about three to four weeks ago. They went to one of those honeymoon places in the Poconos. Which one is not important. The Department is handling that." Mike and Gino had not uttered a word since the two bosses began. Armini continued, "It seems that their resort had two way mirrors in the Slater suite. Color videos were made of Henry and his wife for the two weeks they were there."

The two cops gave mumbled foul expletives.

Armini continued, "You guys fill in the blanks. Slater stopped into the porn shop after work to look at some videos and he saw himself and his wife in the machine. He flipped out. The rest you know."

Mike asked, "But why did he stop at the video place? Did he know he was on film?"

Gino chimed in, "Maybe someone told him. Is that it?

Armini answered, "Look men, you handled the situation like the professionals that you are. Let us do our job now. Mike, you know me, if I can help Slater, I will. Now go home."

Romano and Deluca vowed to learn how to tell if a mirror was two way. Nobody would film them. Of that they were certain. They changed into street clothes, said goodbye and left for their respective homes.

When Mike arrived home, his wife Betty, knowing there would be an interesting answer, asked him why he was late. She had long stopped worrying about her husband. She knew that if something happened to him, she would be visited by a superior officer accompanied by a chaplain. Several years ago, Mike had asked her to give him two hours after his tour before she began worrying. He explained that sometimes there was paperwork or arrest reports to do creating some overtime. If he made a collar and was going to be several hours late, he would telephone her. They had it worked out. Sometimes she would be testy because the kids made her crazy that day, or a meal would get cold, but their system usually went well.

The day's events had unnerved Mike and the only way to cope and purge his emotions, was to retell the incidents that affected him to his wife. Mike gave her a report of the day's events. Betty was horrified to know that hotels and resorts might have filmed them in the past. Betty insisted they review each and every time they spent a night in a hotel or motel, including their honeymoon.

Mike assured her that the Slater incident was a fluke and that all other hotel rooms were fine. He tried to convince her that Henry's filming was the only one that ever happened. Instinctively, he knew there had to be other such incidents, somewhere.

"Mike, can you imagine how embarrassing it's going to be for that poor cop and his wife? People who know them are going to see the film. That poor woman is going to just about die."

Mike silently vowed that he would learn how to determine if he was ever in front of a two-way mirror. He planned to leave early tomorrow and go to the local library before work.

The following day, Mike left home about two hours early.

When Betty asked why, he explained that he was going to the public library to look up two way mirrors. "Just in case Bet, that will never happen to us. Never, I promise."

Betty responded with a soft goodbye kiss and an even softer, heartfelt, "Thank you Mikey, thank you."

At the library, Romano went directly to the section that held technical information. He found what he was looking for. "Place the tip of your fingernail against the reflective surface and if there is a GAP between your fingernail and the image of the nail, then it is a GENUINE mirror. However, if your fingernail DIRECTLY TOUCHES the image of your nail, then BEWARE, for it is a 2-way mirror!" He and Betty would never fall victim like the Slaters. He shared what he had learned with Gino as soon as he got to work.

***

Mike and Gino returned to just another day of routine patrol on their post. It seemed dull after the previous day's Henry Slater incident. To spice things up, they decided to go to the loft office at the King of Pizza and spend some time trying to observe the drug salesmen on The Apple. They sometimes made observations from a chess parlor that sat above one of the store fronts slightly west of the Amsterdam Theater on the south side of their post. Today, it was the pizza loft.

To aid them in observing illegal activity from their lofty lookouts, the team purchased themselves two small collapsible "spy telescopes" from one of the camera/gift shops on their post. The scopes weren't high tech with only 10 power, but they helped do the job. Each one, being slightly larger than a fountain pen when closed could be carried easily. They paid full price even though the owner, Sonny, was a "cop buff" and friendly to all the footmen in the command. Sonny had to order them at a cost of $15 each. He tried to make the little scopes a gift. The team insisted on reimbursing Sonny his cost.

Their investment paid for itself a hundred times over in overtime accrued by arrest processing and court arraignment time.

Gino had introduced Mike to Sonny when they had first partnered up. Sonny owned one of the electronic gift shops on The Apple. He was located mid-block on the north side of 42nd Street. Similar to most of the other shops of the same type, Sonny sold radios, cameras, statuettes, most types of photo equipment, tape recorders and portable televisions.

What made Sonny different from the other owners of the "tourist trap shops" was that he had a commendation from the New York City Police Department hanging proudly on his wall. Sonny had earned his plaque by serving on the Mayoral Advisory Committee. He claimed to be on a first name basis with the mayor in office at the time. Mike would later learn that Sonny knew the mayor well during his tenure at Midtown South.

Mike and Gino had been a team for about four months, when Lieutenant Armini called both of them into an empty second floor office before roll call one morning. It was their first tour in a set of five.

He began, "Gentlemen, there is a new unit about to be formed in this command and one in Midtown North. Your work has been exemplary. Gino, Sergeant Castro, the anti-crime supervisor was enthusiastic in recommending you. Romano, your work and the commendation you are about to receive from the District Attorney's Office, brings your name up."

In turn both men said, "Thank you but for what?" Mike added, "What commendation from the DA's office?"

Armini continued, "Mike, the work you did on the Wachung gang and the identifications you and Gino secured, assisted in building a case resulting in several prosecutions. Seems, your efforts broke up an extortion ring in several other commands, besides the one here and the Fifth. You are to be receiving a commendation for it."

Mike could only grin and slap his partner on the back. Deluca had known Sergeant Castro when he used to supervise the late shift. Gino had been in the command for many years and had been supervised by the sergeant. Sergeant Castro would supervise the new detail. Romano was recommended by Lieutenant Armini to Deputy Inspector Bryan. The inspector hesitated at first, thought a few minutes, and then approved both men to be first chosen for the new detail. Lieutenant Armini continued to explain why a new detail was being formed and what they would do.

"About a week ago, the Mayor and several big wigs were exiting a Broadway show, "Cats", or something and right outside the theater exit, on the sidewalk, was a Three Card Monty dealer. The dealer thought it was cute to ask the Mayor to try his luck at the game. As you guys know, the dealer controls the game. There is no luck. The mayor was furious. He turned to one of his aides and told them to contact the two commands that covered the area and 'Get these people and the drug dealers away from the shows and out of town visitors.' "

Mike and Gino expressed their amazement at the nerve of those street criminals.

The lieutenant continued, "Anyway, the Inspector got a call from Downtown and was ordered to form a plainclothes unit to handle it. As you may or may not know, Anti-crime is not allowed to touch drugs or gambling. It's

Department policy. That's for Narcotics and Public Morals. With the mayor pushing to cut down waiting time after a report is made, a new unit is being formed. The new unit will be called Precinct Conditions Unit and the anti-crime supervisor will oversee you men. Midtown North will also start a unit. Of course, I'll still be your boss. You start tomorrow. We are gathering additional men, but you two are my first choices."

Armini did not wait for a response and ordered, "Be here at 0900 hours. The unit will work 10x6 unless conditions warrant otherwise. Any questions?"

Mike thought about his dislike of Bryan and his quest to somehow, "nail him". *Perhaps, working in plainclothes will give me an opportunity to catch him at something.*

Gino just smiled like a Cheshire cat and said, "Wow, Mike, plainclothes on the Apple and the entire command. We died and went to heaven Partner."

Romano asked, "How is this going to work boss? Do we make collars and call for transportation?"

The answer came quickly, "That has been taken into account, the entire team will find out in the morning. Now go spend your last day in uniform on post."

Outside, Gino shouted, "Look out world, here comes Leukemia." The men proceeded to post.

Once on post Deluca and Romano proceeded to tell all the street people that they were being transferred. One of their regular arrestees, the pot salesman, Paul Rivera, actually told them that they would be missed.

Mike replied, "Don't worry Rivera; the next guys will look after you. Gino and I will tell them all about you later today when we get off duty."

Rivera replied, "Yeah sure, Leukemia, but the next guys don't have your style. You guys don't always bust me and toss me just for fun. The next guys probably will." Rivera seemed genuinely sorry to see them go. He didn't know they would be there in plainclothes. They almost burst into laughter as they left him and continued their patrol. They hid upstairs at the pizza shop almost the entire tour. They were taking no chances. Nothing was going to prevent them from the following day's meeting.

That night, Mike took Betty and the kids out to their favorite restaurant in celebration of his new assignment. Betty thought that Mike was promoted to Detective Rank. He explained to her that cops could work out of uniform in any rank. He would still remain in the rank of Police Officer, but the assignment would give him a step up for promotion.

Chapter Seven

Mike and Gino were in the anti-crime office earlier than necessary the next day. The 8x4 anti-crime team members were already out in the street. Only Sergeant Castro and Lieutenant Armini were present to greet them. Shortly after their arrival, six more officers arrived in street clothes. The entire assembly would be the newly formed Conditions Unit. Mike recognized one or two faces including a friend from his teenage days, Jimmy Carter. Gino knew all the men in the room. They were, in addition to Carter, Alan Rosenburg, Wendell Sloan, Danny Glen, Barry Howe and Mike Hickey.

Lieutenant Armini spoke first. "Spread out and get comfortable men. You all know why this unit was formed. Arrangements have been made for your team to use the old Paddy Wagon that we sometimes use to transport prisoners downtown. This command has a new wagon. You guys are assigned the old green one, it's yours now. The wagon is also your detention facility. Stockpile your collars in it. When you have a maximum of a dozen collars, or two hours before your tour ends, you are to come in, process your arrests and use your van to transport your own prisoners to court. Take turns on who's going to court. The entire team is responsible for the maintenance and upkeep of the wagon. Understood?"

Without waiting for a response, he continued," Make sure the wagon goes to the service shop as scheduled. It's your asses if something preventable happens to it. Fill in the vehicle log daily, no exceptions. Sergeant Castro will explain to you how this unit will operate. Be advised that all assignments given to this unit come through the Inspector and he gets them from Downtown, either the Mayor's Office directly or One PP."

Sergeant Castro took the floor. “Those of you, who know me, are aware that I’m the anti-crime supervisor. Anti-crime is not allowed to make narcotics or gambling arrests. The regulation is city wide. The mayor has requested that this command and Mid-Town North hand pick men to combat street gambling and drug sales. You will not have any undercover officers to work with you like they do in narcotics. You will employ surprise and stealth in drug and gambling arrests. Everything you do will be by observation. If someone buys pot, you will arrest the buyer if possible, record what he or she bought, and then arrest the seller. If a criminal court summons is appropriate for the buyer, you will issue one in lieu of arrest and detention. The seller however will always be formally arrested and processed. Got that?”

Castro continued, “As to gambling, when you observe gambling on the street, especially around the theaters, you will determine the promoter and the lookouts. You will attempt to arrest all persons involved in the game be it three card Monty or dice. We want you to get the lookouts or “slides” as they are called in addition to the dealers and sticks. The sticks were known in the old days as shills.”

Castro explained the meaning of the terms he just used. “The lookouts are called slides because when cops are spotted, they shout, ‘slide ‘em up’. That means, take off, cops are here. The stick or shill is the man winning all the money. That’s how they get the money away from the game in case the police make an arrest. These people expect that only the game operator will be arrested. They will, however, sometimes, leave some money on their board to cause confusion as the onlookers reach for the money and they attempt to get away.” He could see the look of excitement on the faces of the entire team.

He continued, “There will be a lot of overtime in this unit. We want arrests every day you work. If all goes as expected, the unit will eventually be expanded to seven days a week. You men are the first. You will work Monday to Friday for now. There may be changes in the future. You men may be asked to address other problems within the command like selling drinks to drunks or underage drinking in bars. Any questions?"

Alan Rosenburg asked, "Tell us about the wagon Sarge. How is it a detention vehicle? Wasn't it once used for hooker roundups the ladies of the night?"

There were some sexual comments from the men. "Yes, Al it was. The old green wagon was first used for round-ups. When not in use it was used to transport people down to court. Now it's yours."

He continued, "Here's how you men will utilize it. First, everyone signs out a portable radio. Each man must have his own radio. Every day, one of you will be the designated vehicle operator. He will park away from the area you are working and remain in the vehicle. Once collars are made, the arresting officers will call for the wagon. The perps will be locked in the rear and the arrest team will continue. If at all possible we want at least two officers to make arrests daily. If you fine gentlemen get more arrests, so be it. You men work out among yourselves who is the first driver and who will take the first collars. If I'm not here, the desk officer will sign all related vouchers and arrest forms. Got it?"

Everyone nodded their heads. There was some banter exchanged among the men for a few seconds. The new team members were excited.

Sergeant Castro broke in, "Men, pay attention. The keys to the wagon will be kept in this office. If the door is locked, the desk officer will give you a key to unlock this room. The key will be returned to the desk. When this office is empty, the door will be locked at all times. Arrests will only be processed in the arrest processing room. No collars will ever be brought into this office. No exceptions. Now go out back and check out the wagon. You men will be expected to bring some collars in today. Decide who is doing what and go do it. Remember, every man will carry a portable radio at all times. The radio helps insure your safety. You will use channel three for point to point conversation with your team. I will monitor the channel also. If you must reach Central use channel two as you normally do. Sign out your radios and get going. Dismissed"

As all eight officers left the room, Lieutenant Armini stopped Mike and Gino. "You men are two of my best. Make me proud."

Mike and Gino almost danced down the back steps into the parking area at the rear of the building.

The other team members were already outside. Team Leukemia looked the vehicle over. It was the old NYPD green paint that struck Mike. Emblazoned on the side of the huge box portion of the van was the word "POLICE". On top of the cab was an old red "bubble light" rotating beacon and an old chrome bullet type mechanical siren. The front of the vehicle had push bars attached to the bumper. On the cover of the engine compartment, also written in white was "NYPD Police." The double rear doors had the old type Police Department logos, silver grey in color. Overall the machine had the look of a hardened veteran with small dents and dings in various places.

Once inside the van, Mike examined the "bench type seats" on each side of the passenger compartment. The tops were hinged, and could swing up to reveal storage. Each seat was approximately four feet long and 28 inches high. Plenty of storage for confiscated contraband materials.

Inside the rear compartment, thru a bolted single door, was the prisoner compartment. It was lined with wooden type bench seats fastened to the side walls and two overhead metal bars running the length of the compartment. The tops of those benches did not open. Alan Rosenburg verbally noted that during prostitute roundups, if the seats were full, the girls were handcuffed to the ceiling rails. *We'll have no use for them,* thought Romano. All in all, there was ample room for the entire team, their equipment, and many arrestees.

Deluca announced that it was now about 1030 hours and they should begin their first day as a new unit. Everyone went back inside the station house to sign out radios and gather whatever equipment they guessed they might need. Mike and Gino each brought with them two pairs of handcuffs and assorted manila envelopes to temporally store contraband that they carried in canvas shoulder bags.

Danny Glen numbered several thin strips of paper. "The one who draws the highest number drives first. Agreed?" he asked.

There was some rumblings, but all agreed; lots were drawn. Alan pulled the driver's seat.

By 1100 hours the team was aboard the truck. Alan Rosenburg was not happy about being the first driver. He would have liked to make the first collar. On the ride to the area of 42nd and Broadway it was decided that Mike and Gino, being the first two men picked for the unit, would take collars downtown. If they made enough arrests, the second team would be Barry Howe and Mike Hickey. If they didn't go downtown today, they were first up tomorrow. The game plan was to set a routine if possible. No one man could handle more than three prisoners safely. If there were six collars, two men would go and so forth.

The first stop for the wagon was on 45th Street, west of Broadway. The seven street men would attempt to make Three Card (Monty) collars on the sidewalk around the Times Tower. Experience showed that there was usually at least one game set up there.

The cops spread out, trying to look inconspicuous. Mike and Gino spotted a Monty game behind the Times Tower just across the street from the discount theater ticket sales booth, where a large crowd was gathered. They backed off a safe distance and spoke to the team via the radio, point to point on channel three.

Gino spoke softly, "We have a game behind the Tower. Do you guys see it?"

Each member of the unit replied in turn, "Got it. We see them." Only Danny Glen added an additional comment, "There's two guys sitting on mailboxes near the building, looking over the crowd. Lookouts. We gotta get close. Gino, you and Mike get close to the game; we'll spread out and try to get the lookouts. When you move, we grab who we can. Ready?"

Mike and Gino approached the game from different directions. They managed to get right up to the game board. The dealer had the board set up on a cardboard carton. The board itself was a box cover with a few sheets of newspaper flattened out on the bottom. The newspaper allowed the dealer to quickly roll it up with any money "on the table" and hopefully get away if he spotted cops. Not all dealers left money behind to cause confusion. Some of them were just too greedy.

The dealer spoke constantly as he shuffled the three cards. "Hey, here it is my man, the red queen" He would show it. Next he continued, "Look here black king and black king. Now all you have to do is find the red queen. Ten will get you twenty, twenty will get you forty." The cards were constantly being manipulated as he spoke.

An obviously well-heeled tourist put a ten dollar bill on the board. The cards moved. He attempted to pick up what he thought was the red queen. The dealer gently slapped his hand away. "No my man, you cannot touch the cards. If you do you lose. Now how sure are you?"

The tourist replied, "Very sure. It's the one on the left."

"My man, put another ten down to back up your feeling and I'll pay you forty if you're right."

Another ten went down. The dealer turned over the indicated card. The tourist was correct. With great fanfare he paid the gambler. "Now that was easy. Try again. Play one hundred, win two hundred."

In the crowd was the shill. He stepped up and dropped a hundred dollar bill on the board. Naturally he won and was paid two hundred dollars.

He shouted to the tourist," Go for it guy, it's easy. Don't let this man take all my hard earned money. You get some too."

The tourist asked, "If I bet more do you still pay double?"

"Sure my man, but not too much, I gotta make a living too. Most people bet ten and lose but you're good, you two guys are gonna kill me today."

"I'll bet one fifty. You'll pay three hundred? "

"Absolutely, here we go. Just drop your money down." The dealer began moving the cards as the money hit the board.

"The middle card," was the choice of the hapless tourist.

The dealer turned the center card over. It was a black king. "Sorry brother. Try again?" By the time he finished speaking, he had pocketed the money.

The crowd was unaware that the dealer controlled the order of the cards as he threw them. He would hold one card in his left hand and two cards, in a stacked fashion, one over the other in his right hand. By manipulating his fingers that held the two cards he could drop either of those cards at will. The fast movement and constant banter confused the victims. There was actually no gambling, which is chance based on odds, because the dealer controlled the cards at all times. Legally, the charges at arrest were recorded as 225.05 Promoting Gambling, 2nd Deg. and 225.30 Possession of Gambling Paraphernalia, the cards.

Romano reached across the game board and grabbed the dealer's clothing while shouting, "Police." At the same time

Deluca had the stick or shill in a bear hug from behind. From the mail box men, first came the words, "Slide 'em up," followed by very loud cursing as they were snatched off their perches. The team had their first four arrests. At first there was mayhem with people scurrying in every direction. When they realized that a plainclothes team was working, they all remained behind to watch. The public, curious as always about the workings of the police didn't want to miss anything. The wagon arrived quickly and the four men were stuffed into the rear. The crowd actually applauded.

***

The team was proud. It had taken less than ten minutes from arrival on the set, to their first arrests in their new assignment.

Once in the van, the perpetrators were searched. In addition to the $150 recovered from the playing surface, the dealer was holding $300 in twenties. The stick or shill man had almost $800 on his person. The lookouts apparently had only personal money. They each had less than twenty dollars on them. The cards and all money recovered from the games was placed in the manila envelopes and marked appropriately. All the property would be vouchered at the precinct and receipts given to the respective defendants. The appropriate copies of the vouchers would be given to the writing Assistant District Attorney to substantiate the arrests.

The team then left the Times Tower area and moved to 8th Avenue and 45th Street with their charges and their van. They parked on 45th between 8th and 9th Avenues. Leaving Alan in the driver's seat with the prisoners, all unit members partnered up and spread out. Mike and Gino proceeded to The Apple, post 10.

It was a nice day. As they approached the corner of 42nd and 8th, they ran into Lorraine, the call girl Mike would always remember as the garment center hooker. She stopped them.

"Hey Gino, you and Mike have the day off?" she asked.

Gino replied, "No, a new assignment. We work plainclothes now. What's happening?"

The call girl replied, "Finished work for the day. I'm just walking back to get my car and go home. Congratulations on your promotion. Do you guys need anything?"

Mike thought, *there goes that offer again. Wonder if Gino ever did her. Gotta ask him some day.*

Deluca replied, "No thanks, but you'll see us out here from now on. Keep an eye out and let us know if anything happens that we might be interested in. We're out here for drugs and gambling. Just stop us like we're paying customers or friends and let us know. See you later and thanks."

Mike's unasked question was answered when she replied, "Sure thing Gino. I'll make believe Mike is a paying customer. And you know there's never a charge for you. You're a friend. Later." She then turned, shook her stunning derrière and sauntered down the block.

As the plainclothes centurions passed the subway entrance, on the corner of 42nd and 8th, on 42nd, a small dark skinned male stepped in front of them and said, "Grass, herb, valiums, anything you gentlemen might want. Got anything and everything to help you enjoy your day." Without waiting for an answer, he continued, "Nickel bag my friends?" and held out three nickel bags in the palm of his hand.

Gino, with his little goatee and mustache looked like a more likely candidate to the dealer. Gino reached into his pocket and withdrew several bills while asking, "Can I get two nickels and some valiums for my friend? He's a little tense today?"

Mike took the hint and looked around as if very nervous while he shuffled close to the man. He would be in position to grab the seller when the time was right.

"Sure man. Just let me call my associate, he has the V's." He turned to call to a tall thin man lounging just below street level on the first landing of the stairway. "Hey brother, need some V's up here."

With the dealer's attention diverted, Mike, too anxious to make the arrest, did not wait for the second man to get close. He lunged at number one, grabbing his right arm and twisting it behind him while holding the guy's ear and shouting, "Police, you're under arrest". He snapped on the handcuffs almost without thinking.

Gino was on the move in the same instant. He jumped down to the landing, two steps at a time in an attempt to apprehend the second man. The guy was too quick and ran down into the station and across the platform toward the stairway on the other side of 8th Avenue.

As Deluca ran, he withdrew his portable radio and shouted his position to his teammates hoping for assistance. "South Conditions Unit; Gino in foot pursuit of suspect, tall male Hispanic running on 42 and 8 subway station in west direction towards Show World entrance."

"Gino heard the quick responses from the team, "10-4 Gino, we're on it."

Wendell Sloan added, "I see him now". Next came,

"Ummph, shit," heard over the radio. Wendell continued, "We got him. Dropped him, he's down. I'm here with Barry."

When Deluca joined his teammates, they already had him cuffed and lying face down on the station floor. Gino thanked them for the assist and "tossed" (searched) the detained man. In his pockets he had only loose little blue pills believed to be valiums.

"Thanks guys, he must have thrown any large quantity he was carrying as he ran. Anyone see anything on the ground?"

The replies were negative.

Gino then called his partner, "Mike I got the other one. I'm on my way. See you in a few minutes. You OK?"

"Good as gold Gino. Take your time. I'm in the stairway. There's no problem here." Mike added, "Listen, walk your man out on the east side of the street, come up to the street next to the little sex show on 8th next to the bar. That way we can walk them to 45th and 8th for the wagon without alerting the whole street. The other guys have to collar up too. OK?"

Deluca replied, "Good move partner. See you there in the doorway."

As Gino came up out of the station to the street, the radio crackled, "Conditions wagon ready and waiting," it was Alan. He had heard everything.

By the time the two dealers were loaded into the wagon; the rest of the team had three men in custody and announced that they were walking their charges from mid-block on 44th to Broadway. Mike and Gino jumped into the wagon for the ride. They would mark their evidence envelopes as they rode.
It was going to be a good first day.

By 1500 hours. (3:00 p.m.) the new Conditions Unit had thirteen men in the back of their truck. They decided it was time to return to the station house and process the arrests. They had at least two hours of paperwork ahead of them.

When they arrived at the rear of the precinct, Alan parked the wagon close to the rear entrance of the station house. The team had handcuffed each man, one to another, to make removal from the wagon safer. Unloading thirteen men could be a problem if one or two of them acted up or attempted to run. Cuffed together, if a man tried to cause a ruckus, he would be dragging everyone else.

When the desk officer, Lieutenant Fondalar, saw the parade before him, he commented, "Nothing like a new broom to sweep clean. You boys have been busy." He picked up the desk phone and notified Lieutenant Armini that his boys were back and he should come down and take a look.

"Ok, gentlemen take them into the processing room and get started. Someone come out here to see me when you know how many vouchers and whatever else you might need."

Once in the arrest processing room, the team assessed all the evidence that they had gathered. They separated the gambling evidence, the cards from the money confiscated during each arrest. The money taken from the playing boards or observed in play at a game was kept separately. The drug collars were dealt with entirely separately. Their money and drugs would be kept away from the gambling evidence. Drug dealers were considered lowlifes by the team. Even the gamblers looked down on them. The prisoners began asking questions.

"Hey are you guys new? Is this gonna be a steady thing? Where are you DT's (street talk for detectives) from?"

The men who actually ran the games were concerned with their money. They wanted to know if it all was going into evidence, be returned to them or pocketed by the cops.

Mike and Gino pulled Alan, Jimmy and Danny to the side.

Gino spoke first, "Listen guys. These men know that they are in for a long night. Why don't we voucher what we took from the games and then use some of their personal money to feed us all. We can also return each man's pocket money back to him. The game money is enough for court. There's nothing in the regulations that say we can't feed our prisoners. After all, we have to eat too and it's going to take hours to do all these collars. As to the drug dealers, it all gets vouchered. They get nothing returned."

There was some quick discussion among the cops and all agreed to follow Gino's lead.

The arduous task of processing the collars began. While the team partnered off to do the paperwork, all men were fingerprinted and sandwich orders were taken. Wendell and Barry volunteered to go out and secure the food and soft drinks.

The prisoners were aghast. "Hey, you DT's are cool. Nobody ever fed us before. Are you really gonna give us our money back?"

Mike answered, "Yes we are, some of it, but be cool because if you break our balls, we keep it all and no food. Got it?"

All went smoothly once things got under way. By 1830 hours, all processing was completed and the arrests were ready to be transported down to Central Booking at 1PP (One Police Plaza). The entire unit was already on overtime.

Mike and Gino had five men between them. It was agreed that Gino would take three collars and Mike two. They would also drive downtown in their own vehicles so they could sign out at 1PP and go directly home. It was going be a long night.

The other men were broken up in much the same manner. Alan and Jimmy had two each; Mike Hickey and Wendell had the remaining four men. Barry and Danny would transport the prisoners, return to command and sign out. They would not get much overtime that night. With the system the men of the unit worked out, everyone would accrue approximately the same amount of overtime each month.

The first working day of the Midtown South Conditions Unit was a roaring success. The mayor's office would hear about it.

***

The Conditions Unit was operating two months when Mike was called into Dennis Bryans' office. As he entered, his heart raced and the beating of birdlike wings pounded in his head. He thought, *here we go. Now something's gonna happen to change everything. What the hell could the crooked bastard want?*

"Yeah, Inspector you sent for me?"

The reply was friendly. "Sit down Romano. I need you to do something for me. Your work ethic says you're the right man for the job. OK?"

Mike decided to play it cool. "Sure boss. What do you need?"

"Well officer Romano, Mike, I've watched your activity since you have been here. You are one active guy. Good collars. No sick time and all that."

Mike thought, *I'll bet you've watching me. I've been watching you too you fat shit.* He answered, "Well I like my work. Thank you for the opportunity to be in the Conditions Unit."

The Great Pumpkin continued, "Well Mike, you might not know it, but I live on Staten Island. On Fridays, I usually walk some part of the command to see how things are going, end of the week and all that. The traffic around here is terrible, especially on Friday afternoons."

Seeing that he had Mike's full attention, Bryan continued, "I would like to get a head start on going home from the street. It would be easier for me to jump into my car and not have to return to the command. So I'm asking you to come into my office every Friday, open the center drawer of my desk, take my spare car key and take my vehicle to 8th Avenue somewhere between 43rd and 45th streets, park it in a metered space, place my Department parking permit on the dash and lock the vehicle. Of course, you don't have to feed the meter."

Getting no response, the Pumpkin continued, "When you get off duty or return to the command for any reason, put the key back in my desk where you found it. This is between you and me only. If your team asks, tell them it's a personal favor to me and say nothing more. Only you will be in the car and only you will ever handle the key. Can you do that?"

Mike's thoughts were racing. *Why should I do this for you? You suck. You're a criminal. You probably want to set me up for a fall. Kiss my ass.* Mike brushed aside his negative thoughts. *Opportunity is knocking Romano, or is it angel wings I'm hearing?*

"Sure inspector. You want this every Friday? What if you're not working?"

"If you don't know, just check the roll call sheet. Do not ask anyone. Just look at the roll call sheet yourself. Just make sure to park the car no later than 1400 hours and don't forget to drop the plate on the dash. There's no way I want a summons. Try to always put my car in a metered spot, no bus stops or other restricted zones. Got it? This is strictly between us."

"OK. I'll take care of it. What if I take a day off or vacation?"

The answer surprised Mike, "No days off on Fridays. If you put in for vacation or a day off, come and tell me before hand and we'll change the parking day if necessary. Can I count on you?"

Romano's' curiosity and the beat of those angel wings had him hooked. "Sure boss. When do we start?" He would never learn why Bryan picked him for the job.

"This Friday. Now go to work," Dennis waved his right hand towards the office door. Mike was being dismissed.

Mike told no one about the conversation with Dennis, not even Gino. He remained low key for the entire tour. He could not wait until he got home that night to tell his wife about the latest development in his ongoing saga with Dennis Bryan.

Betty was less than enthusiastic as Mike finished his recount of the job Bryan had given him. She was very concerned that Bryan would try to harm her husband's career.

Coyly she spoke, "Mikey", as she called him when she was trying to hide concern or be cute, "Be careful. He probably knows that you want to catch him dirty. He might be setting you up for something."

Mike replied, "Don't worry Betty. I intend to be very cautious, including making memo entries when I pick up the car and drop it off. I'll even record if there is something on the seat or floor and the general condition of the car. Of course I'm not going to touch anything inside except the steering wheel. Now give me a hug and wish me luck."

The work week went rather slowly for Romano. On Wednesday, he and Gino went downtown with ten arrests. By Thursday, he could not contain himself any longer and told Gino about his conversation with Bryan. He knew that Gino would want to know why he was moving the CO's personal auto on Friday. What was the real reason? What was Dennis doing?

Deluca, always cautioning his partner said, "Mike, be careful of this guy. Maybe he knows you want to hurt him and will hurt you first. But we can follow his route, sit inside someplace and watch him if you want to. Just say the word."

Mike's anticipation about Bryan's car made time move slowly.

Friday finally arrived. At about 11:00 a.m., at his request, Mike was dropped off at the station house. He told his team that he would meet up with them in half an hour on 8th Avenue and 44th Street.

Cautiously, Mike entered Dennis Bryan's office and opened the center drawer of his desk. He saw a single car key on a round ring that was about the size of a quarter. Attached to it was a note; "Romano, please put the key back later, without the note. The black Buick in the CO's parking space is mine. Thank you."

Mike quickly went to the rear of MTS, located the Buick and looked over the exterior and recorded its condition in his memo book. Slowly, he opened the driver's door. He sat down and started the engine. *Wonder if your paycheck or graft paid for this beauty you fat bastard. Did you ever have your perverted brother-in-law in the car?* Mike's head snapped around as he heard what he thought was a large bird take off behind him. *Mike,* he thought, *you're going nuts.*

Mike gave the interior a visual inspection. Seeing nothing out of the ordinary, he put the car into gear. What he did notice though was the faint odor of booze lingering in the atmosphere. Mike thought as he smiled to himself, *Guess he's still a lush.* Fighting the urge to look for a bottle, he drove out of the parking area.

Mike drove the Pumpkin's Buick up 10th Avenue to 42nd Street. He swung right to 8th Avenue. Going north on 8th, he found an empty parking meter on the east side of 8th just below 44th Street. He parked, put the Department's parking plaque on the dash and locked the vehicle, checking the doors twice.

As Mike turned away from the vehicle, Gino materialized next to Mike, startling his partner. He had been waiting in a doorway. "Mike, did you find anything incriminating inside. Did you toss (search) the car?"

"No Gino. The inside is clean as a whistle. It does have the faint smell of booze though. Bet if I looked, I'll find a bottle somewhere."

Deluca was going to say something but was cut off by Mike who continued, "I'm not looking inside the glove box or in the trunk. He probably has it rigged somehow so he can check and see if I opened anything. I'm not giving him any chance to stick me."

Mike then went into the canvas shoulder pouch he always carried and extracted his memo book. He recorded his earlier observations about the vehicles interior, then added the time, date and final position of the Pumpkin's car. He also noted that he observed no contraband in the passenger compartment.

The two friends joined their team for the rest of their tour. Romano and Deluca only assisted their teammates that day. They were not catching any arrests. Both men wanted the weekend off with their respective families.

Chapter Eight

Michael Romano had been doing "the personal favor" of parking Dennis Bryan's private vehicle along 8th Avenue for three months. The stalwart, angel with a gun, had meticulously made memo entries every time he entered and left Bryan's auto. He and Gino had observed Bryan walking to his auto; entering it and driving off on several occasions, but could not say that they observed any suspicious activity, until one day in September when Bryan walked into the parking lot on the south east corner of 42nd Street.

The "Leukemia" team was sitting at the upstairs windows in Cu Lei's restaurant watching some of the local dope dealers when Gino spotted Dennis Bryan walking toward the parking lot. Mike was watching someone thru his pocket telescope and didn't notice Bryan.

Gino slapped him on the shoulder and almost shouted, "Mike, there goes Bryan, into the parking lot. He looks like he's headed for the attendant's booth. Check him out."

Mike changed his position slightly, realigned his scope and replied, "Got him".

Both officers focused on Bryan. Chatter between them was excited and constant.

"Mike, what do you think he's doing there?"

"Don't know Gino, we never saw him there before".

"Look, there's the old bum, Cadillac, looking right at him. We gotta go talk with him later".

"Yeah, maybe he can give us some info."

The banter ended when both cops observed something in Dennis' hand. It looked like a parking ticket stub. It was too far for them to see the small piece of paper well enough to be sure. The little pocket scopes had their limitations. Whatever it was, Bryan handed it to the attendant.

Mike spoke, “I don’t see his car. Do you? What the hell is going on? Is he getting another car?”

The attendant took the stub, went into the booth, bent down, out of sight for a few seconds and then went outside and walked up to Bryan. He handed Dennis a letter sized envelope. Bryan took the envelope and put it inside his sport jacket, probably into the jacket’s breast pocket. There was a quick exchange of words and a nod of the head between the men. Dennis then turned and walked out of the lot. He passed directly in front of Cadillac who sat leaning against the chain link fence.

Mike articulated his excitement with “Holy shit. We got him.” He heard his own heart thumping or was it beating wings?

Gino countered with, “Easy Mike. We have nothing but a guy putting an envelope in his jacket.” He then added almost joyously,

“But it sure looks like a payoff. Let’s go see Cadillac. ”

The drug dealers were forgotten. The team almost ran from the restaurant. Rushing across the street, they raced to question Cadillac. Mike and Gino knew what every police officer knows, that local street people were a cornucopia of information. Cadillac, when sober was one of the best, almost as good as Lorraine. Gino, having been in the command for years, knew the old man well.

He opened the conversation. “Hey, Cadillac, how’s things going for you? Need anything? Is there anything we can do for you?”

The old man was only half drunk. He answered quickly,

“Say hey Gino. Haven’t seen you in a long time. The street talks about you and Mike. Is that Mike?” Without waiting for an answer, Cadillac held out his right hand to Romano.

Mike looked down at the dirty woolen gloves on the hands of the old man. The fingers were cut out exposing his fingers up to his palms. Mike’s instinct was to not touch the man, but he was there to make a friend. He extended his hand. *I'll wash as soon as we walk away from here. Poor old bastard. What a life.* He thought.

Mike steeled himself and shook hands. "Hi Cadillac, I'm Mike. Pleased to meet you buddy."

Gino spoke again. "Cadillac, do you know the guy that was just here. The big red head? He went up to the booth and talked with the man inside and left. "

"Yeah Gino. That's the boss of the cops at Midtown. He comes here almost every Friday, at least I see him almost every Friday. Maybe he comes every Friday. Sometimes I'm not here, you know." Without taking a breath he asked, You guys got any money? Like five bucks. I can eat and get a drink."

Mike responded by reaching into his own pocket. "Look man, I see the bottle sticking out of your coat pocket. Here's five bucks, spend it all on food will you? And thanks for talking with us."

"No problem. You guys got a standup rep on the Apple. It's my pleasure."

Once away from the parking lot, Mike turned to his partner.

"We got him Gino. The son of a bitch was making a collection. He's his own bag man." (Bag man is an old expression for the man who goes out with a paper bag to collect weekly or monthly graft).

"Sure Mike, that way he doesn't have to share or if he does, nobody knows how much he collects." He added. "Now what the hell do we do with the info? It's dangerous to accuse a precinct commanding officer. We have no proof. We need proof."

"We'll watch him every chance we get. Maybe someday we can get proof." Mike opened his memo book and made an entry, recording the incident. Gino thought he was crazy and told him so.

"Don't worry, Gino; the bosses never read our books anyway. Even when they give us a “scratch” (signature with time and date) to prove they supervised us. They never read anything.”

The months that followed were productive for the Conditions Unit. Each team averaged 30 to 50 arrests per month. Mike and Gino continued to monitor Bryan and noted many visits to the parking lot. Mike hoped that someday he could use the information against Bryan.

Chapter Nine

Over time, the team became friendly with the regular precinct detectives who would come to them for assistance in gathering information when necessary. “Leukemia” was the most prolific team in the unit and made the most arrests.

The local street people came to know about their fairness. It was paradoxical, being known as the white death and being respected for their fairness. Their interaction with the street people resulted in their development of many snitches.

One afternoon while his unit was processing some arrests, Mike went up to the Squad’s office to deliver some information as to where a local burglar was reported to sometimes hang out. As he was speaking to a detective, Mike happened to glance over to the holding cell area. He almost cried out in disbelief.

Inside the holding cell were five men, four whites and one black man. All were fairly well dressed in sport jackets. He recognized Rocco Banducci, the nephew of a reputed big time crime boss, Carlo Banducci. Rocco had been dating his sister-in-law Kelly for several years. Mike had been in Rocco’s presence on many family occasions. The man had charm and told Mike that he was in the toy business. He liked Banducci.

As Mike stared into the cell, he looked right at Rocco. Banducci locked eyes with Mike and shook his head ever so slightly as if to caution Mike. Mike caught the motion and turned away.

“Hey Lieutenant, what do you have these guys for? Running a con game or something?” he asked.

“No Romano, Guns, police shields and a stolen van” came from one of the detectives.

The Lieutenant glared at the detective with a disapproving look, turned to Mike and spoke, "Thanks for dropping off that information Romano. Go back to work. We have things to do." Mike knew he was being pushed out of the office.

"Sure boss, have fun," was Mike's reply. He took one last look at the men in the cell and left the room. As Mike left, the door to the office, the door that was wide opened when he entered, was closed behind him. He returned to his teammates, never mentioning what he saw.

Mechanically, Mike assisted his team mates with the processing of the day's collars. His thoughts went to the reputed background of the man he knew as Rocco Banducci. There were rumors within his in-laws' family that Rocco might have mob connections. His sister-in-law had been dating Rocco steadily for the last four years. He and Betty had enjoyed the man's company on many occasions. They had even invited the couple to visit them in their apartment. While Kelly would visit, Rocco would never come over. *Strange*, thought Mike, *we have been out to dinner in public places, been at my mother-in-laws many times, been together at weddings but he never comes to my apartment. Someday I'll ask him why. Right now I have to find out what happened.* Mike couldn't wait for the tour to be over. He made sure that he only assisted with the processing and did not even drive the van downtown. He signed out promptly at 1800 hours.

The minute he walked into his apartment, he quickly told his wife about what he saw in the squad's office.

Betty was a little surprised. "Are you sure it was Rocco? Did you talk to him?"

"Look Betty, I told you, he motioned me away when I looked him right in the eye. Please call your sister and find out if she knows anything."

"No Mike. She'll only get upset. I'm not going to be the one to tell her that Rocco was arrested and you shouldn't tell her either."

"Ok, Ok we'll wait until tomorrow."

Mike, arriving early at work the following day, went right up to the squad office. The squad boss was not present. He spotted Det. John Rich who was friendly with him. Romano had given him the location of a homicide suspect once and Rich got lots of notoriety out of it. He owed Mike.

"Hey, John, those guys in the cage yesterday, who were they? They almost looked like business men. What the hell could they have done?"

The answer peaked Mike's interest. Naturally he did not mention his association with one of the men.

"At about 0800 hours we got a call from the desk to assist a sector car with a collar. They told us they might have known mobsters in custody. It seems that these guys were sitting in a stolen van parked in front of the 34th Street entrance to Macy's Department Store. Apparently the van had been stolen a few hours before and by luck, the owner happened to spot it. He called 911. When the sector car responded, the guys were inside. They were all placed under arrest for Grand Larceny Auto. Under the seats, we found phony police badges, handcuffs and guns. We have no idea what they were doing there or what they had planned. Once in our office, they asked for attorneys and never said a word except to give us their names. We sent them downtown as soon as possible. The case was taken over by Organized Crime. Why the interest? You guys have something?" Mike tried to remain casual, "No, I thought that I recognized the black guy. So are they known mobsters or what? Who are they?"

"The black guy was the driver. We don't know who he is. He refused to give his name or be printed. We booked him as a John Doe. The tall guy is the nephew of Carlo Banducci and the other three are in the same crime family. Some shit isn't it?"

To cover his inquiries, Romano added, "Hey John, if

you can get me a photo and ID on the driver, we'll add him to our photo book downstairs. Maybe our street people can ID him for your guys."

"Thanks Mike. I'll try."

"Thanks for your time John," Mike answered as he left the office.

Two days passed without any news on Rocco. Late in the evening of the third day, Mike received a call at home. It was from Rocco. "Hey Mike, how are you? Thanks for not coming over to me the other day. It might have gotten complicated."

"Are you OK Rocco?" Can we talk? I gotta know what's going on, maybe I can help."

The response answered Romano's question about the validity of Rocco being a real Banducci, "Sure Mike, meet me at the Privateer Diner in half an hour. You're the only cop I respect in the world. We can talk there. Don't bring your wife."

"Of course not. She can stay with the kids. See you soon."

"Betty, that was Rocco, I'm meeting him. He's ok. Be back soon."

Betty responded, "Be careful Mikey, I know you like him but be careful. Don't mess up your career." She did not try to stop her husband. She knew by the tone in his voice that he was going, no matter what she said.

Walking into the diner, Mike looked around. He didn't see Banducci. He continued into the rear dining room and he spotted Rocco sitting alone. His heart pounding, Mike walked up to his table and down on the opposite side. The two men reached across the table and shook hands.

Banducci, not one to mince words, spoke first, "Ok Mike, what do you want to know? I'll tell you what I can, but first, let me give you some background. OK?"

"Sure Rocco, go ahead", was Mike's response.

"Mike, I respect you. Someday you'll know why. Enough to say that I have been involved with my family for many years. Sure, I have money, nice clothes and all, but it comes with a price. Now what I'm telling you is our secret. I'm trusting you. Keep the trust and I'll always be your friend. Do you understand?"

It all sounded cryptic. The conversation was sounding like a movie script. Mike's head was spinning. *What does he mean, someday I'll find out why he respects me. I thought it was because we're friends and he dates my sister-in-law. What secrets is he going to share?* Mike's mind was in fast forward. *I'm a cop. Am I about to be compromised? Holy shit!* He brushed his fears aside.

"Sure Rocco, go."

"Well, the Banducci's are my family, my blood. I am the nephew of Carlo Banducci. My father, Frank, was deported back to Italy back in the 60's. He was Carlos' brother and has since passed on. An uncle and two of my cousins were found in car trunks. The Feds are always watching me and trying to either put me away or deport me. They can because I was actually born in Italy. From time to time I get taken into court, put under oath and questioned about anything and everything."

Mike was all ears. "What do you mean?"

Rocco continued," For instance, they'll ask, where I was on any given day to catch me in a lie and charge me with perjury. They have even tried to get me by saying that I lied on my drivers' license. They claim that my birthday is fraudulent. But the date I use is on my original Baptismal Certificate from a church back in Italy, in the rural town of Sepino in southern Italy, where I was born. Back then, in the twenties and thirties, midwives were common. I was born at home with the birth recorded by the attending midwife."

Mike began to ask, "Is that ......?"

Rocco held up his hand, "Because I like you, I never come to your house. You must have noticed that. If they are watching me, it might go bad for you, having me in your home. In a public place or your mother-in-law's house it's ok to be with me. You have no control over those situations and you shouldn't be implicated in anything by association."

Mike was fascinated by the conversation. His friend was a bona fide mobster and he was sitting here, in a local diner with him, nice as you please.

Rocco continued, "Now, as to the day in question, when you saw me in the squad's holding cell. I and some friends were sitting in a van on 34th Street. We were going someplace. The black guy was driving us. We were waiting for someone. Apparently the van was stolen. We got caught. I'm waiting for the court process and I'm out on bail. Stay away from it. I don't want you to get painted with the same brush. Anything else?"

"Yeah Rocco. I was told by a detective that you guys had guns, handcuffs and phony police shields. What the hell were you doing with that stuff?"

"Well Mike, all I can say is that the stuff was there. I have a good lawyer. Don't worry about it."

"But what were you doing out there and with that stuff?"

"Sorry Mike, but that's all I'm going to say. Thanks for your interest though. Hope you understand now why I never come to your home."

Mike knew he was being dismissed. "Ok Rocco. Can I get you a drink or something?"

"Thank you Mike, but I gotta run. See you later. Remember, don't get involved. You have a career and a clear record. Don't blow it." Banducci got up, left a twenty dollar bill on the table, smiled at Romano and walked out.

Mike was surprised at how calm he felt. He had just been told that he knows a known mobster, probably a 'made man' and he's not upset with it. *Saint Michael,* he thought, *I sure hope you're around.*

When he got back home, he repeated the entire conversation to Betty and was surprised to hear she knew all about Rocco Banducci. She told him that she kept the information to herself because he was always so righteous. Betty, on the other hand expressed surprise that he didn't get all worked up about their friend.

"You know Betty, I'm more than surprised that I'm not all fired up over his revelations too. But I just have to find out more about the case against him. If he didn't do anything like he says, maybe I can help."

"Michael Romano, you are totally insane. Stay away from it."

"Sure Betty, I promise." It was the first time he ever lied to her. Mike had a need to know all about the case against Rocco. He was annoyed that Banducci would not tell him what they were doing on 34th Street that day. He realized that he would probably never know the real truth why Rocco and the men were in the van outside Macy's that day, but he would find out what he could.

***

Several weeks later, Mike had time on his hands while processing several arrests in the courthouse downtown. He visited the docket room and convinced a clerk to put Rocco Banducci's name into their data banks to see what came up. The response was immediate. Up popped the next scheduled court date and his past record. He had been in and out of jail since he was eighteen. His next court appearance was in exactly half an hour on that very day.

Mike went over to the State Court building, checked the court calendars, and found the appropriate court room. On the wall outside the courtroom he saw the names of all five men listed. He was only interested in one, Rocco Banducci. The charges were extensive; two counts of Criminal Impersonation of a police officer, 5 counts of Criminal Possession of a Weapon, Criminal Possession of Stolen Property and Grand Larceny of an auto.

Mike remembered Rocco's caution to him, stay away from the case. He also remembered that Betty would go crazy if she knew that he was there. The need to know was too compelling.

Cautiously, he opened the courtroom door and walked in, taking a seat in the back row. His mind raced, *what harm could it do to watch the proceedings? I'm a New York City cop and have the right to be here. I can't possibly get in trouble just sitting here.*

Rocco Banducci was standing before the judge. There was conversation between Rocco and his attorney. All Mike could hear was the attorney speaking to the judge, "If your honor would give us a few minutes, I'll confer with my client again."

Rocco turned away from the bench to give his ear to his attorney and spotted Mike. He looked visibly shaken at the sight of Romano. He waved his arm toward the door and loudly told his attorney that he was stepping outside for a smoke. Mike took the clue and left the room. He was in the corridor before Rocco was even away from the attorney's table.

Outside Rocco grabbed Mike by the arm, pulling him away from the doorway and down the hall. Shaking Mike's arm, earnestly he said, "What the hell are you doing here? You can get in trouble. Get out of here."

Mike pulled away and answered, "Rocco, I'm Ok here. I'm a cop in a court house. Stop worrying. There could be a thousand reasons for me being here. If anyone asks, I'll tell them I'm studying your case. Anyway, what's happening with it?"

"You're a horse's ass Mike ", was the first comment from Rocco. "If I answer you, will you leave?"

"Yeah Rocco, I'll go right away."

"They offered me 5 years based on my record and

family background. My attorney is holding out for two years. He thinks he can get me down to two years if I plead guilty to a set of lower charges. If he gets it, I'm probably going to take the plea."

Mike couldn't control himself. "Listen, I lost a similar case with guns under a seat. Of course the bad guy wasn't a "Family member". The guns were thrown out because they were under the seat. The reasoning behind the throw out was that anybody could have put them there without the occupants' knowledge. Where was all your stuff?"

"Under the seats Mike. Nothing was on our person. Nothing at all."

Mike began in a sarcastic lecturing tone, "Then the driver could have put it there or the real owner of the van. Only the driver knew the van was stolen. Not you. Right? Maybe, even the driver didn't know the stuff was there. Plead not guilty and stick to it." Mike was on a roll now. He kept telling himself that he was helping a friend. He wondered, *did I just cross the line? Am I now one of them.* Mike shook it off.

Rocco cut Mike off as he was about to speak again. "Get the hell out of here. You'll know what happened in a few days. Go."

Mike Romano's common sense kicked in. Still thinking about his friend and if he did the right thing in giving advice to a known criminal, Mike turned and left without looking back. His head was pounding again. Or was Saint Michael sending him a message?

Two weeks went by without any word about Rocco's court case. Mike even questioned Betty about it hoping that her sister knew something. Betty claimed that her sister Kelly knew nothing about the outcome of Rocco's last day in court.

It was April 28th, his son Donald's birthday. Betty's mom hosted a party for her grandson at her house. As the little celebration progressed, to Mike's surprise, Rocco Banducci arrived.

He looked happy as he entered the dining room. After greeting everyone and giving the little Romano an expensive toy as a gift,

Rocco leaned over next to Mike's ear and whispered, "Thanks, Mike. The not guilty plea worked. We'll talk later."

Mike could hardly wait until Rocco called him on the side and said, "Mike, will you walk outside with me a minute, I want a smoke."

"Sure Rocco", was the quick response, as Mike moved thru the kitchen toward the back door of the house that lead to a small covered porch and the rear yard.

Once outside, Mike walked directly to a far corner of the yard, followed by Rocco. He didn't wait for Rocco to speak first. "Well what happened? Did anyone plead guilty to anything?"

Still curious about the circumstances about Banducci's arrest he continued, "Would you please tell me why you guys were there that day and what were you going to do?"

Rocco lit a cigarette. "Well, Mike, first let me say something. I truly thank you for your advice. The damn attorney charged each of us $35,000 to handle the case. Your advice got all charges dropped at the evidentiary hearing. The only man they had to plead guilty was the driver. He pled to the stolen van. He's just begun serving two years. His family is being taken care of. Thanks again."

Mike still wasn't satisfied. "But Rocco, what were you guys going to do? What happened with the attorney?"

Rocco's' answer was tinged with annoyance, "Do not ask about the arrest again and the lawyer doesn't work for us anymore. Got it?"

Mike assumed that the "us" Rocco was referring was the Banducci Family and he did not even want to think what Rocco meant about the lawyer.

Banducci saw the hurt look on Mike's face. He knew that Mike risked his career by stopping to see him in the court house and spoke to ease the hurt, "Mike if you ever need a favor from me, do not hesitate to ask. If I can do it or get it done, you have it. It doesn't matter what it is, anything. Thank you again. Let's go back inside."

Later that night, Betty asked Mike why he and Rocco disappeared into the back yard. She did not buy into the cigarette bit. Mike explained that he had given Rocco some advice on something and he just wanted to thank Mike without the family nosing into his business. Betty appeared to accept her husband's explanation. She gave Mike a quick little peck on the cheek and with a knowing smile said, "Sure, Michael, just a little advice."

Chapter Ten

One sunny afternoon, while attempting to lock up several pot dealers in front of Madison Square garden, the team got into a foot race as the perpetrators scattered in all directions. Barry Glen and Wendell Sloan chased one man, Deluca chased another. Mike ran off in pursuit of a man he picked out. There were plainclothes officers and bad guys running around like a scene from an old episode of Keystone Cops. Rounding a corner of the open plaza, Mike thought he saw a man hit Gino. Deluca cried out in pain and dropped to the plaza floor. Abandoning the pursuit of his target, Mike rushed to Gino's aid.

"Gino, what the hell happened, what did he do to you? Are you hurt, cut or anything? Talk to me."

Thru clenched teeth, Deluca responded, "I grabbed him as he ran past me; he never stopped running and my leg twisted. My feet never moved. I heard a snap and let go of the guy because of the instant pain. I think my leg's broken. The guy was just running to get away, he never touched me. Just get me help."

Mike snatched his radio from his shoulder bag, switched to channel 2 and told the dispatcher to send an ambulance, with a rush, that a cop was down with a leg injury.

Once in the hospital emergency room, it was learned that Gino's knee socket had broken. The doctor speculated that his foot must have been anchored by suction between his sneakers and the smooth plaza floor and the twist of his body dislocated his knee cap and somehow fractured the top of his tibia, the "socket" where his knee sits. The doctors explained that he would probably never be able to fully extend his leg again, even after extended therapy. His police career was over. Gino Deluca would be pensioned off. Mike would now be without a steady partner. He would miss the man that he considered one of the best partners he ever worked with.

That evening, Betty tried to console him. “Look Mikey, you and Gino can still be friends. We’ll keep in touch with him and his family. It’s not the end of the world. Just think he will get three quarter pay, tax free for the rest of his life. You always tell me that he enjoys tinkering with electronics, now maybe he’ll open up a little shop. He’ll make more money. There’s a silver lining on every cloud. He’ll be fine. Now come here and let me make you feel better.”

Mike put his head on his wife’s shoulder and sobbed.

“This is one of the reasons I love you Mikey, you have heart.”

Later that night, alone with his wife in their bedroom, Mike forgot about Gino for almost an hour.

***

Three days had passed since Gino’s injury. Mike was again driving the “War Wagon” as he had done since Gino got hurt. He was parked, waiting to be called by his team mates. His portable radio squawked,” Midtown South Conditions Unit ten one your desk, K”

Mike answered quickly. “Midtown Conditions, received and acknowledged, K”

Romano exited, locked the van, found a payphone and called the desk. Sergeant Holbrook answered. “Romano, since you have no partner right now, we’re having a car pick you up and bring you in here to do a favor for us. What’s your location?”

“I’ll be next to the van Boss. It’s on 38th between Broadway and 6th. Give me a few minutes to give the keys to someone.”

The team had no detainees in the rear so Romano went looking for a team member. By the time he walked half a block, Al Rosenberg approached.

"Hey Mike, what's going on. I heard the ten one."

"Sergeant Holbrook is sending a car to pick me up. He said something about needing a favor. Don't know what it is. Take the keys, the van is locked. I'm going back to get picked up. Talk to you later."

When Romano arrived at the station, he was informed by Holbrook, "Lieutenant Armini thought you would welcome the chance to chill out after losing Gino and since you're qualified on all Department vehicles, you're needed to drive the peddler truck to the repair shop in the Green Point section of Queens and bring a patrol car back."

The lieutenant knew his man. Mike was happy to make the run to Queens. "Sure Sarge, it would be my pleasure. Thanks."

The peddler truck was a big Ford with a 20 foot open flatbed behind the cab. The bed had removable wooden staked sides and a hydraulic powered lift gate. The entire truck was painted in the old Police Department green. It was normally used to gather the pushcarts of illegal food venders and peddlers within the command. It was also used to transport barriers for parades and demonstrations. The vehicle was scheduled for servicing.

Mike left the rear of the station house, and drove the truck south on 9Th avenue, turning left on 33rd Street intending to go directly into the Queens Midtown Tunnel. It didn't work out. Mid-block between 7th and 6th Avenues, Mike Romano got involved in something that would be directly related to his quest to gather information on his corrupt commanding officer, The Great Pumpkin.

As he drove east, Mike saw an employee of a parking garage putting cars into the street. He was double parking them along the street. The mid-day traffic gave Mike plenty of time to observe the man. He watched the guy double park three cars. There were double parked cars one hundred feet on either side of the garage entrance. They were impeding the flow of traffic and adding to the congestion. Mike was still unhappy about losing Gino and not in the best mood. He was slowly coming to a boil.

Legally parked at the curb, opposite and slightly down from the garage entrance, was a white van belonging to some plumbing company. The side view mirrors protruded out severely. With all the double parked cars, not legal by any means, it was very difficult for Mike to navigate the street. As Romano approached the garage, an employee added yet another card to the mix. Mike was forced to move the truck even further to his left.

As he drove forward, concentrating on not clipping autos, the side view mirror on his truck caught the plumbing van's mirror mounting arm breaking the glass and ripping the arm partially loose from the truck's door. Mike stopped his vehicle directly across from the garage and exited his own truck very agitated.

Walking up to the garage employee who was still sitting in the car that drew his attention, Mike saw the driver smiling at him thru the open window. He stood in front of the window, identified himself as a police officer and simultaneously shouting at the driver to "Return that car to the garage."

Ignoring the police shield hanging around Romano's neck, the occupant looked straight into Mike's eyes and said, "Go to hell. You don't scare me. Kiss my ass and then drop dead."

Mike ignored the remark, "Move the car back into the garage now."

Once again the man refused and while still smiling, removed his right hand from the steering wheel, thrusting it into the seat cushion out of Mike's field of view as if reaching for something. He may have thought that he could intimidate Mike. He was wrong.

Instantly, Mike drew his revolver, thrust it under the man's chin and ordered him to remove his hand from the seat, "Bring your hand up, put both hands on the dashboard, and they both better be empty or I'll put a hole in you."

The man complied at once.

Mike had been channeling his full attention on the man in front of him and didn't notice another man exiting the garage and shouting to the gathering crowd. When Mike was satisfied that the garage employee had no weapon, he began to relax. It was then he heard the shouting. "Look at the cop. He's going to kill my employee. He's gonna shoot him. Don't let him do that. He's crazy. The cop is crazy."

Mike knew this could escalate into a real mess, but he was committed and had to do something. Directing his next question to the person stirring up the onlookers, he shouted, "Does this idiot work for you? Shut up and behave or I'll lock you up for inciting a riot. Stop shouting or I'll handcuff you to a pole."

Mike was trying not to lose control of himself or the situation without much result. The situation was getting ugly. The crowd was getting larger and the traffic began piling up. Car horns were voicing the driver's impatience. It sounded like New Year's Eve.

Mike fought to regain control of his emotions. He took a deep breath and continued in what he thought was a firm authoritarian tone, "Tell this man to give me his driver's license, if he has one and we can avoid something ugly. That's the only talking you're allowed. Don't continue to excite the crowd."

The response cranked Romano up another notch, "Fuck you. He doesn't have to do anything. I'm calling your boss. I'll make sure you lose your job. You're crazy."

Mike beat him to the punch. He removed his portable radio from his canvas shoulder bag. It was already set to channel 2 because he was going out of borough. He keyed the radio, "Midtown Conditions Unit to Central. I have a large crowd gathering at the scene of an arrest. This unit is requesting backup and a supervisor on 33rd Street mid-block between 6th and 7th Avenues. Use caution, I'm in plainclothes. Please acknowledge, K"

"Acknowledged, plainclothes."

The dispatcher continued, "We have a 10-85, assist police officer in Midtown. Officer requests units on 33rd Street 6th to 7th Avenues. Use caution, officer in plainclothes. Units respond, K"

Several units answered. Mike did not pay attention to the responses.

Turning to the apparent garage owner, Mike assured him that, "My boss is coming and you are going to get arrested too."

Mike ignored the crowd, even though he returned his weapon to its holster, was intently busy watching both of his adversaries while waiting for backup. In his mind, Mike formulated his next actions; *I'm locking up this idiot for inciting to riot and summonsing the shit out of this smartass driver.*

As his thoughts began to take shape, Mike heard rapid **cl-clop, cl-clop** sounds approaching his position. He happily recognized the sound of a steel clad horse shoes galloping on pavement. Charging up from 7th Avenue was a mounted officer in response to the call for assistance. Mike waved his shield above his head to identify himself.

The mounted cop asked, "Are you OK?"

"Thanks, I'm fine. Thank you for responding so fast.

"No problem. We're all brothers in the same family. Right?"

Without waiting for an answer, the first thing the mounted officer did was to skillfully direct his horse to move the crowd back away from Romano. Mike's original antagonist and the garage owner were now shouting at the mounted cop. Their words could not be heard over the sound of the approaching sirens. Three marked police cars were slowly manipulating thru the congested scene and moving closer to Mike's position. Walking, much faster than the approaching police cruisers, was Sergeant Holbrook.

"What the hell is going on here Mike? What hornets' nest did you stir up? Are you OK? Is anyone hurt?"

Without waiting for a response he turned to the people that were trying to pass the mounted officer, "You people back up or I'll order multiple arrests. Better go back to work or whatever else you were doing."

Mike now had the assistance of four uniformed cops and the sergeants' driver working to clear the street and make sure the crowd left the area in an orderly manner. The mounted officer walked his animal back and forth near Mike to insure his safety.

Holbrook turned to Romano, "Ok Mike what have you got?"

Pointing to the man still sitting in the double parked auto, Mike began, "Well Sarge, this guy was pulling cars out of the garage and parking them in the street. I saw him and another guy park at least six cars as I drove up the block. The car he's sitting in caused me to break the mirror on the plumbing truck there and I ordered him to move. After I identified myself, he cursed me out. When I ordered him again, he dropped his right hand onto the seat and I put my weapon under his chin to protect myself. I didn't know what he had there. Maybe he was pulling a gun. It escalated from there."

"Ok, now what did that guy over there do?" he asked pointing at the assumed garage manager.

"He came running out of the garage and yelled for the people on the street to attack me. He accused me of wanting to shoot and kill his employee. He tried to get a riot started as far as I'm concerned. When I asked for his help with his employee, he got abusive. I want to lock him up for inciting to riot."

"Easy, Mike. Let's do this one step at a time. What do you want from the guy in the car?"

"I want his license. And I need summonses. I only have one or two in my bag."

At that, Holbrook went over to the man sitting in the auto and ordered him to produce his license. As the man was giving his license to Holbrook, the garage owner started up again. He was now directing his wrath at Holbrook.

"You cops, you all stick together. You're all crazy and power mad. I know people. I'm gonna bury you all." Turning to the few remaining people on the sidewalk, he continued, "See, you all see that these cops are crazy. Help me."

Holbrook turned to the two closest uniformed men and ordered, "Mike is right. Put that man under arrest and transport him to the station. Romano will be in soon to do the processing." It took seconds for them to handcuff the bigmouth. He screamed like a little girl as they stuffed him into a patrol car. Mike felt vindicated as the car manipulated its way out of the street.

Holbrook then went over to his own vehicle and withdrew several sheets of forms. He handed them to Mike. "Romano, I don't have any summonses, but fill out an accident report and return to the command. Here's the driver's license, get some summonses from someone and write whatever summonses you feel are necessary. I'll leave a car on the block until you leave. Don't get into any more trouble."

The mounted cop reached down and handed Romano his summons book. "Here officer, use as many tags (police slang for summonses) as you have to. I'll stay here too." In an attempt to ease the tension he added. "After all you have my summons book."

Mike wrote the driver several summonses; double parking, blocking traffic, failure to comply with the directions of a police officer, failure to carry auto registration and failure to carry an insurance card. He even wrote one for reckless driving.

After Mike sent the driver back into the garage, he completed an accident report and left a note on the van. It was another forty minutes before Mike left to return to his command.

Chapter Eleven

Mike parked the peddler truck along the curb on 36th Street behind the station house. As he entered the building, he was met by Lieutenant Armini.

Armini grabbed him by the arm, "Don't say a word. Come with me." He guided Mike into the far right corner of the muster room away from the bathrooms to make sure what he had to say would not be overheard.

Mike spoke first, "But Lou, what's going on? I followed orders and came right in."

The answer shocked Mike, "Stay here. Do not speak to anyone and only come out of this corner if I come to get you. Understand?"

Romano could only think of the incident on 33rd Street. *Boy oh boy, I started a shit storm. Something heavy is going on.* "But Lou, what's happening? I didn't hurt anyone. Am I being accused of anything?"

Armini continued, "There's two PBA delegates and a lawyer for the guy you arrested inside with DI Bryan in his office and he's pissed. Stay here. I'll come back for you." Mike was left with his mouth open as Armini hustled out of the muster room towards Bryan's office.

While Mike sat in the corner of the muster room, several men walked up to him and asked if he knew what was going on in the boss' office. He told them that he did not have any idea. Truth of the matter, he didn't. He only knew that it was related to the incident on 33rd Street that he was involved in about an hour ago. Curiosity and anticipation finally took over and he began to walk around, ignoring his lieutenant's orders.

Even though the CO's office door was closed, muffled, earnest words filtered out. Mike thought he heard words that sounded like; "dismissed", "law suit", "job loss" and "retraining". Ever inquisitive and ballsy as ever, he moved close to the door and heard, what he thought were the words, "take care of you". He quickly retreated to the muster room.

It seemed like hours before Lieutenant Armini came out to get Mike. Actually it was only twenty five minutes according to the big clock on the wall.

Armini spoke softly to Romano, "When we go in there, say as little as possible. They want to void the arrest and can't without your permission. I do not want to order you to allow it, but, weigh your options carefully. It could get very messy. DI Bryan is quite upset. So much so that he even took a swallow of whiskey in everyone's presence. Let's go."

Entering the office, Mike observed, Joe Valenti, the senior PBA delegate and John Kelly, one of the other delegates. Sergeant Holbrook was standing next to a distinguished gray haired man in a dark blue pinstriped suit. Deputy Inspector Dennis Bryan stood behind his desk, all puffed up, his face redder than usual. Mike almost smiled as he thought, *ears sticking out, bright red face, big round head, almost no neck, he is the Great Pumpkin damn it. Get a grip Romano and control yourself, it's going to get messy.*

Dennis spoke first, "Officer Romano, Mike, we have an incident here that never should have happened. There was no cause to arrest Mr. Rosen for anything. His attorney is here to assure that his rights are protected and to secure his timely release," Dennis was pointing at the man in the blue suit as he spoke.

Bryan asked, "Do you have anything to say?"

"Sure do Inspector. First, I acted properly. Rosen's employee did not comply with a lawful order of a police officer. He blocked the street causing me to destroy another man's property, the mirror on the plumber's truck. If I didn't hit it someone else would have."

Mike was almost spitting his words out as he

continued, "Next, they, Rosen and whoever, charge people to park in the garage, why put their cars in the street? If there's no more room in the garage, tough shit, don't take in any more cars. That's stealing. Those people are guilty of Larceny."

He was on a roll. The beat of wings was thumping in his ears, "The owner, or manager, the guy you call Rosen, was asking the crowd to interfere with my lawful duty. He told them to get me. That would have caused a riot. It would have been ugly. People would have been hurt. Ask Sergeant Holbrook, he was there and witnessed it. He even told the guy, Rosen, that if he continued, he would authorize his arrest."

Mike was interrupted by the attorney. "As you know officer, I represent the accused. The second man involved in the incident is also my client. You put your revolver under his chin. That's menacing, a crime on your part. We can file a complaint against you and you can be charged criminally. Have you anything to say?"

"Counselor, your client refused a lawful order and put his right hand, which I could not see into the seat cushion of the car he was driving, in what I thought was a menacing manner. I drew my weapon and protected myself. I did not hit him or shoot him, which he probably deserved. I acted properly. A police officer does not, unlike a civilian, have to retreat." Mike was quickly getting annoyed and losing his temper.

Bryan picked up the conversation again. Speaking calmly he began, "Officer Romano," *how proper and polite you can be you bastard,* thought Mike, "We discussed this matter and our conclusion is as follows; finish the paper work on Mr. Rosen and void the arrest. You may keep all the summonses you issued to Mr. Lupe, the garage employee. Mr. Levy, here will represent him in court and will deal with the summonses. You are an active officer and make many arrests. You have an exemplary record. Do not tarnish it with this incident. You certainly do not need one more arrest to increase your numbers."

In a slightly menacing tone, Bryan asked as he slapped his desktop, “How about it Mike?”

Mike thought, *you graft taking piece of shit. They probably paid you off, or soon will. Now you want to involve Mike Romano. It is not going to happen.* Mike recalled the envelope exchange he and Gino observed back on 42nd street some time ago.

Mike responded, “First, let me speak to Officer Valenti, my delegate in private. Then I’ll give you my answer.”

Before Bryan answered, he moved from behind his desk, “Sure, but stay in this room Romano. It will have to do.” Bryan then motioned for all others present to move to the far side of his office.

Joe Valenti was standing behind a set of file cabinets, now out of sight of everyone in the room. All anyone could see of Valenti was above his shoulders. He motioned for Mike to come closer. Mike did, keeping his back to all in the room. Joe spoke, loud enough for all to hear. “Mike I think that you should do this. The boss is right, you don’t need this arrest. You have a great detail and make lots of overtime. Let this go. You can continue working and everything will be fine. Whatever happens with the summonses in court, that’s for the judge to decide. You’re not a traffic cop. That’s my advice.”

The other occupants of the room were unable to see Joe’s hand movements as he spoke. Mike was the only person who saw Valenti move his hands in a manner that one would use to count money as it was put into other person’s hands.

Mike felt his blood pressure rise as he watched Joe’s hands move. He fought within himself not to turn around and spit in Bryans face. It was now confirmed that some kind of deal was made. What he didn’t know was why. Was this a one-time single payoff or did the Pumpkin and Rosen have a working relationship? Mike remembered that the loud fancy paint job on the front of the garage was duplicated many times in both midtown commands. *Were the suspicions he shared with Gino correct? Was there a payoff or steady money involved? Did he really hear the words, "Take care of you", while he listened at the door? How stupid and greedy could Dennis be?* Romano vowed to himself that one day he would find out for sure.

Mike turned to face the main group, "Ok, you can void the arrest but I don't trust anyone. Here's what I want. Mr. Levy here will sign my memo book stating that every word in my book concerning the garage incident is true and there will be no civil, departmental or criminal charges against me now or in the future as a result of this incident. I also want DI Bryan to sign my book after the attorney."

Dennis Bryan almost lost it. His face lit up like a frightening Jack O' Lantern at Halloween, "Just who the hell do you think you are Romano. Just because you are considered a good cop, don't go about making demands. We are doing you a favor. Your career could end right here and now."

Lieutenant Armini stepped into the conversation at this point. "Inspector, let me take Mike outside and talk to him. Maybe we can resolve this quickly." When receiving no immediate answer, he moved Mike outside and back to the muster room.

"Are you nuts Mike? You are my best, smartest cop and you want to throw away your career and any chance for advancement because of one stinking arrest?"

Mike didn't know if Armini knew about any money exchange. He decided not to take any further chances and did not bring it up. He wanted to keep the good relationship he had with his lieutenant.

"Listen Lou, I don't trust lawyers in general, that blue suit in there got here too fast. If they want to void the arrest, I want them to sign off on it or it stands. I'm the arresting officer and I'll choose to keep the arrest. Hell, facts are facts. I'll take my chances."

"Mike, I admire your convictions but I don't think they will go for it. I'll go inside and try to work it out. While you sit here, check your notes and make sure your record is accurate. Good luck."

As the lieutenant walked away, he turned towards Mike and reinforced his authority with, "Do not leave this room without me Romano. That's a direct order." Armini returned to Bryan's office.

Mike had nothing about the incident in his memo book. The last entry he had was the assigned trip to the shop with the truck. He sat there and recorded the entire incident into his book. It took three pages including the reverse sides. At the end of the entry he wrote, "The undersigned attests to the fact that the above recorded incident is true and accurate. The undersigned also agrees that no charges of any kind, be they procedural, civil or criminal will be brought against the recording officer by either the Police Department, the person known as Mr. Rosen, who was first arrested and subsequently released or his representatives, now or in the future." Mike felt that now he was ready to reenter the cluster fuck in Bryan's office.

Ten minutes later Armini came back to get Mike. "I don't know what the hell is going on, but they agreed to your demands. You are one lucky son of a bitch. Let's go."

Back in the office, only Joe Valenti, the attorney and Dennis remained. Upon entering, Lieutenant Armini excused himself with,

"Gentlemen, I have other duties. Officer Valenti will be here to witness the conclusion of this incident. Thank you all." He then left, closing the door behind him as if he knew that the entire incident smelled like rotting flesh.

Joe asked for Mike's memo book and handed it to Bryan. Mike found it interesting that Bryan's hands shook as he read it. Almost dropping it as he put it down on his desk and pushed it in front of Levy. "As per our agreement, if Mr. Levy is gracious enough to sign this, the incident will have a successful conclusion and be closed."

Levy looked down at the book and apparently without reading it, signed at the end of the entry. He left it on the desk. Bryan picked it up and handed it to Mike, "Here Romano, go inside, void the arrest and go back out to work with your team. It's done."

Mike still did not have any supervisor's signature in the book. He wanted to beat the seeds out of the Pumpkin, but maintained his composure. "Yes sir. I'll be back for a signature on the voided arrest papers." Without waiting for an answer, he turned and left the office."

Back in the arrest processing room sat an agitated Rosen. Mike explained in the most business-like manner he could muster that he, Rosen was going to be processed as if his arrest would stand, fingerprints and all, only then the arrest would be voided. The wording would be something like, "Further investigation indicates that the parameters of the crime charged herein was not fulfilled."

Rosen, spoke to Mike for the first time since he was stuffed into the patrol car. "Hey officer, sorry I spoke like that, but you got carried away. Proof is they're letting me go. Do you have to finger print me and all?'

Mike, his blood pressure off the chart, responded with, "Listen, we can do this without much conversation. Let's do that and you can leave quickly. OK.? Break my balls and all bets are off. I'll even add charges."

Rosen understood. The processing went quickly. The arrest was assigned a number and recorded into the arrest log. Once a boss signed off on the actual paper, a copy would be appropriately filed, voided and the actual arrest number would be used again. The copy of the voided arrest would have a line drawn thru it and a "V" added to the originally issued number. It would be placed in proper sequence with all other arrest reports.

After completing the paperwork, Mike had an officer sit with his arrestee and went back to Bryan's office to get the DI to sign off on the arrest sheet.

"Are you nuts Romano. Commanders do not sign arrest reports. Now get out of here before I file charges against you."

Mike could not help himself. Before he realized it, he responded. "We'll talk again." He heard his own words and made a hasty retreat.

Sergeant Smith was attending the front desk. When Mike asked him to review the arrest report and sign off making the "void" official, he too refused. The sergeant did however phone upstairs for the Integrity Control Lieutenant. Lieutenant Blaise came down to the desk.

"Mike, I heard about the incident on 33rd Street, the arrest you made and the need to void the arrest."

Mike wondered if he knew the whole story. Blaise's next comment didn't help answer the question at all. "Next time, don't act so hastily, be sure of the parameters of the charge and act accordingly. You're a good cop. Try not to make this mistake again." He then signed the report. Mike didn't know how far the corruption went and chose to remain silent about the probable payoff.

After reluctantly releasing Rosen, Mike made a copy of the voided arrest for himself, put it safely into his locker and spent the last few hours of his tour with his teammates. Their time together was spent discussing the garage incident. Each man not busy processing an arrest had an opinion. Naturally, Mike did not tell them everything about the circumstances leading to the final result.

Mike promised himself that he would watch Bryan even closer if it was possible. Friday was three days away. He also wondered what would happen when he normally moved Bryan's car. That would be interesting.

***

At home that evening, he never told Betty about the incident. He did not want to worry her. He only told her that it was a slow day and he did not make any arrests.

The following day was Thursday. Mike arrived at the precinct at 0915 hours. The desk officer called out to him as he passed the desk on the way to the Anti-Crime office.

"Romano, DI Bryan is waiting for you in his office. Sign in first then, go see him forthwith. I'll tell him that you're here."

Mike was shaken. The hair on the back of his neck stood out. He sensed something bad was about to happen. He signed in and went to Bryan's office.

The door was closed. He knocked twice. From inside came, "Come in Romano, I've been expecting you."

Mike entered, leaving the door open. "Yes Inspector. You wanted to see me?"

"Please close the door."

As Mike turned and closed the door, Bryan indicated for him to take one of the chairs that faced his desk. Romano shook his head and chose to remain standing.

"Mike, we had a good relationship going. Didn't we?" Bryan did not wait for any answer. "When the Conditions Unit started, you and Deluca were the first men chosen. You kind of lead the team, setting a goal for the other men. It hurts me to do this, but for a while, you're going back into uniform and on foot patrol. Do you understand or want to say anything?"

Mike was weak at the knees and took the chair. Inside he was shaking for two reasons, losing a coveted assignment and wanting to punch the graft taker in the face.

He spoke, hoping that his emotional state did not come thru, "Look Boss, we got along great up to now. You even have me taking care of your car, moving it on Fridays. I thought the garage incident was closed."

Getting no response, Mike quickly tried another tactic. "Betty and I, she's Irish you know, (hoping to play the ethnic card, Bryan was rumored to be a bigot and not like Italians) we're saving for a house. This is going to hurt."

Mike continued, trying to get a definitive answer, "It's only for a month right. When do I go back into uniform?"

"Tomorrow, Friday, is your last day in the unit. When you swing back in, you're in uniform. Sergeant Holbrook is aware of my decision and so is Lieutenant Armini. See Holbrook for an assignment. I'm allowing you to remain in the day squad on 10x6 tours. You're a good cop Mike, but I decided that you need some time to think and learn to calm down. See me in a month. Oh, don't move my car either. Dismissed!"

Mike left the office devastated. He went to meet with his team and tell than what happened. Some of them were surprised and said nothing, others, like his old friend, Jimmy Carter, reminded him that Bryan said it was only for a month. While they were consoling him, Mike heard someone behind him. It was Lieutenant Armini.

"Mike, don't worry about that fat bastard, you are still my best man and I'll try to make sure that you get back into the unit. I'm not even requesting a replacement. When the arrest numbers go down, he'll want you back out there."

"Thanks Lou. I hope you're right. Not only do we have fun doing what we do, but it's gonna cut into my earnings. This is really going to hurt." All Mike could think about was Betty. She was looking forward to buying a house. They were ready to go into contract. Now there will be a big cut in overtime money. It was going to be tight. He asked the Lieutenant to see him outside and walked into the hallway.

"Lou, can you make sure that I stay on the Apple. I can still do my thing and make collars if I stay there. Bryan said that I can stay in the 10x6 squad. Can you do it for me?"

"Sure Mike. I'll arrange it. Don't worry. You still have two days, today and tomorrow. Go get 'em."

Chapter Twelve

The men of the Conditions Unit were a loyal team. It was decided that the rotation system they used would not apply to Romano for the next two days. Mike could have as many arrests as he wanted. Maybe he could even collar up on Friday and spend his swing (regular days off) downtown in court accruing overtime. They all felt bad for him. First they lost Gino, now their unofficial leader.

Once outside, the men headed for the 34th Street area of the command. In addition to the usual reports of Monty games and pot salesman, there had been complaints about men accosting tourists as they shopped in that busy area. The team parked their van on 31st Street east of 7th Avenue and proceeded on foot towards Herald Square, a small landmark park near Macys and Gimbles department stores.

Mike was walking in a daze. He was still upset about losing the coveted assignment and was worrying about how he would break the news to his wife. Two team members were following behind him, trying to give him some personal space. As Mike approached the corner of 34th and Broadway, he was confronted by a tall thin man. Mike never noticed the guy until the man spoke. To the street person, in his dazed state, Romano must have looked like a dumbfounded tourist.

The man asked, "Hey sir, are you shopping for a gift for your girlfriend?"

Without thinking, Mike instinctively answered, "Yes. Why?"

"Because, I have here some items that I think will make an impression on her. Come over to the side and I'll show you some fine gold chains and things. All guaranteed to be 14 karat gold at half the price of any store around here, actually any store in the city." The man was carrying a small attaché case.

The police officer bell went off inside Mike. He was now alert. The guy was one of many people in the command that was selling bogus gold chains and rings for the real thing. It was standard for the hawkers to either claim their wares were the real thing or as in the case of a chain, have a real 14k clasp, marked as such, claiming the whole thing was 14k gold. The crime is called fraudulent accosting. In New York State, section 165.30 NYS Penal Law states, "A person is guilty of Fraudulent Accosting when that person accosts another person in a public place with intent to defraud such person of money or property by means of a trick, swindle or confidence game."

Mike engaged the man in conversation in order to fulfill the requirements of the law.

"Sure pal, but I don't want anything too fancy. I don't have a lot of money to spend. Can you keep me under $100 dollars?"

The man bit. "Yes sir. Allow me you to show a few of the chains and pendants that I have in my case here", as he rested it on top of a mail box.

Once the case was opened, Mike pointed to a pretty twisted gold color chain and asked, "How much do you want? Is it really gold?"

"Yes, indeed it is a beautiful chain. It is 14k gold." Holding the clasp in front of Mike, he continued, "Look, you can see the markings, and you can have it today for seventy five dollars. For another twenty five, I can give you a pendant of your choice. In any store it would run you three times that price. Here hold it and take a closer look."

Once the complete offer was made, Mike grabbed the man in a bear hug and announced that he was under arrest. Barry Howe and Danny Glen ran up to assist him.

Danny asked, "What do you have here Mike, a chain Guy?"

Turning to Barry he added, "Call for the van. I don't feel like walking."

Barry called to the van on the point to point channel and Wendell answered, “10-4. Where are you?”

“We’re on 34th Street and Broadway near Herald Square. We didn’t get very far. Mike has one under. ”

Wendell responded, “Listen there’s a delivery truck close to me and I may have trouble getting out, can you walk the guy? Are you alone? ”

Mike answered using his radio. “Mike here. I’m with Barry and Danny. We can walk to the van,”

As Mike walked his handcuffed man, followed closely by his two team mates, he was stunned to hear, “Listen man. I can’t handle an arrest. I’m on probation. I’ll pay you to let me slide.”

Mike thought, *Here we go. My second bribery arrest. One in the old three two and now another, when I need it most. Thank you Saint Michael.*

He put his hand into his shoulder bag as if to steady it, and keyed the transmit button of his portable as he spoke. He knew that Central, even though they were on channel 3, ran tapes on every transmission. He would have to get the conversation on tape.

“Listen man, I’m not above that but I have partners. How do I explain it to them?”

“You can share the money with them. If it’s not enough, I’ll send my girlfriend home to get more. Just let me call her.”

“Sure, just as soon as we get back. But we gotta keep this quiet. Ok?”

“Yeah man and thanks, I’ll have her bring money for each of you.”

“Ok. Now, no more talking about it. We’ll work it out in the station house. When we get there, I’ll say that I arrested the wrong guy. Nobody will see your paper work or anything. I’ll say that I arrested you for robbery and your phone right guy. Then I can let you go. OK?"

As Mike approached the van, he stood aside to allow Danny and Barry to get in. As they passed him, they looked at him with wonder. Were they hearing right? Wendell quietly asked Barry and Danny, "Did you guys hear that last transmittal?"

Barry answered, "Yeah we did. Not sure what's going on," he said while staring at Romano.

As Barry was putting the arrestee's case into the under seat storage box, Mike opened the door to the rear of the van and put the man inside. He then loudly cried out as if in pain and said, "Listen you guys take the van in, I have to find a bathroom."

He leaned over towards Barry and whispered, "Break down or something, I'm running back to set this up and take your time." Mike then ran out of the van.

It was four blocks back to the command. Mike dodged thru traffic and pedestrians as quickly as he could, arriving breathless.

Lieutenant Fondalar was on the desk. "Mike what the hell is going on? I heard about you getting re-assigned. Are you alright? You look like shit."

Mike responded quickly, drawing deep breaths as he spoke, " Forget that,…I have…..a collar coming in…..he bribed me to let him go……want to set up a recording…….he will send home more money…..get Lieutenant Blaise down here…… Is Bryan in?"

"Easy son. Let me understand this, Mike. You made an arrest and the man bribed you. You say he will send for more money and you want to take it and make the arrest? Is that correct? No, Mike your friend DI Bryan is not in. I don't know where he is. He should be working. I think he took a day (off). He doesn't need my permission you know."

"Yes, Lou. I know it goes better in court.........he was getting his breath now) and with the job if you get it on tape. I held my radio key open so my team could hear and Central could record it, but I want the transaction recorded here too. Is Blaise in?"

"No Mike he isn't. Where is the bad guy?"

The team is bringing him in. I need a room to use and have him call his girlfriend for the money."

"Ok Mike. I'll make a call to Internal Affairs and try to get a recorder here. Use the interview room at the front when he gets here. I'll try to set IDA up in another room."

Twenty minutes went by and the van had still not arrived. The boys were doing a good job buying Mike some time. There was however, a plainclothes Sergeant asking for Mike.

"Officer Romano, I understand you have a bribery arrest and you want to record it on tape. I'm Sergeant Conway from the Manhattan South Internal Affairs Office. The Lieutenant said we can use the front interview room. Let's go. You can fill me in as we set up."

Both men walked into the interview room. Mike was sure that this collar would save him from losing his coveted spot in the unit. He was thinking, *how could that idiot drop me from the unit? I just got him points with the brass by making a bribery arrest in his command.*

"Ok Romano, here is a machine that can record about one hour of tape. We have to put it somewhere the perp won't see it and be alerted. Some place close to him, so it will pick up the entire conversation. It's your command, so any ideas?"

Mike responded quickly because he had been going over the logistics in his mind as he ran, "Sure Sarge. We can put it in a paper bag on top of a file cabinet like it's just someone's lunch or whatever. How is the machine turned on?"

Conway responded, "Manually in this case. We'll turn it on just before putting it in the bag. Where is the perp?"

"My team is bringing him in. We should have enough time to turn it on when we know they're here. They'll come in from the back of the station house and stop at the Desk first.

"Ok Mike. I'll put a header on now and turn it back on when you tell me they're in house."

Conway recorded the date and time and purpose of the tape. He also added the fact that there was a waiting period.

Within minutes, Barry came in looking for Mike. When he found Mike he asked, "Did we stall long enough? Did you get it all set up? Can we bring him in now?"

Mike quickly answered, "Yeah, I'm gonna interview him alone in the front room. There's a tape in there that will record it all. Count to one hundred and then bring him in. I'll meet you at the desk."

***

Internal Affairs Sergeant Conway turned on the recorder and placed it in a brown paper sack and deposited it on top of a file cabinet chosen by Mike. He quickly left the room. Passing Mike he gave a quick encouraging word, "Play him good Mike. Go get him."

As the detainee was passed over to Romano, Mike told his team members, "Just hang loose guys, me and my man here have some information to exchange about some bad guys."

Romano thought that his remark would keep the perp at ease and not make him realize he was being set up. Lieutenant Fondalar turned his head as if not caring what went on in front of him. Mike's team backed off.

Once inside the interview room, Mike relied on his instinct and removed the handcuffs from his arrestee. Mike felt the man would not become violent, especially because he wanted to be let go. Knowing that several cops were just beyond the door, he felt reasonably safe. Mike smiled at the man as he visualized the Sergeant and his fellow officers bumping into each other in an attempt to hear what was going on inside. The poor sap thought Mike liked him and smiled back.

In the center of the room were a table and six chairs. Mike placed his charge close to the file cabinet on the far side of the table, away from the door and directly in front of the very important paper sack.

Mike began the conversation. "Look man, I told my friends that we were talking about information, like you were giving up some bad guys. That way we can continue our conversation about being let go. If we're going to do business, we should know each other's names. Mine is Mike, and you are?"

"John Norton, Officer Mike"

"Ok John Norton, what are you offering?"

The man responded, "You counted the money I had in my pocket when you arrested me. You can keep the money, two hundred sixty dollars if I remember. Is that enough to share with your friends?"

Mike asked, "What if it's not?" Romano never actually expected the man's next statements.

If it's not, I'll call my girlfriend and have her bring more. How much do you want? I can't go to court. Another arrest and I'll do serious time. I'm on probation and for sure I'm gonna get violated.

You guys can keep the jewelry too; wholesale it's worth about five hundred."

Mike could not believe this guy was so stupid or so desperate. *He was actually bringing his girlfriend into the crime. She too could be charged with bribery.*

"Ok. You call her and tell her to bring as much as she can and we'll settle on a fair amount. Is that good for you?"

"Sure officer. Can I use the phone?"

Mike pushed the telephone across the table and his perp called his girlfriend. Mike was not able to hear her side of the conversation.

"Ok. She said it will take her about ten minutes to get here. She's bringing five hundred more dollars. Is that good?"

All Mike thought of was the tape recorder and staying in the unit. *This is definitely going to get me to stay in the detail. The tape will clinch the arrest.*

"Let me get all this. We keep the money you had on you, and the money your girlfriend is bringing, and the stuff in your case. Right?"

"Yeah. You get all that and the case too. Now you're going to release me like you said when we're done. Right? We got a deal?" the poor man asked.

Mike almost felt sorry for him, but he was worried about his own ass. "Sure my friend. It's all set."

They passed the time with small talk. Mike asking about how many chains and pendants did the guy sell? He was surprised to find out the man cleared about fifteen hundred a week. He also learned that his girlfriend was five months pregnant. Mike never asked why he was on probation. He didn't care. It would all come out when his rap sheet was run downtown after he was re-arrested and charged.

At least fifteen minutes had passed when Lieutenant Fondalar knocked and opened the door. "Romano, there's a woman to see you. Can we send her in?"

Mike thought he saw a look of relief on the lieutenant's face. He guessed that the Lieutenant was also anxious to finish up with this arrest. After all it was on his watch and he was indirectly responsible for everything that happened while he was in charge. The lieutenant wanted it to go smoothly.

"Sure Lieutenant, send her in. Thank you."

In walked fairly young, semi cute female. She looked slightly disheveled. She was definitely pregnant. Mike was beginning to feel sorry for the arrested guy again.

The lieutenant closed the door again after cracking a slight smile. Romano motioned for her to sit next to her boyfriend. Both persons now faced Mike. The girl's first words were to her boyfriend.

"Johnny, here, I brought what you asked for," she said as she reached into her jacket pocket.

Mike tensed up and dropped his hand down to touch his revolver. He would be ready in case she pulled out something besides money. He quickly relaxed as she dropped a packet of bills on the table and pushed it towards her boyfriend.

John unwound the rubber band that bound the cash and started counting the money. They were all twenty dollar bills. He counted aloud. *Thank you God*, thought Mike, *for giving me this idiot to arrest. Thank you.*

When John had finished counting, Romano took the money put his hand over it and turned to the girl and said, "Ok would you please go outside and wait for John on the benches next to the front door. John will be along in a few minutes. I have to do some paperwork to explain why he's going home. Thanks."

"By the way, what's your name Miss?" Mike asked, making sure it was recorded on the tape.

The girl was obviously nervous, "Ann, Ann Pollack", was the reply.

The girl turned to John, kissed him on the cheek and left, closing the door behind herself.

It seemed like only a split second before the door opened again and Sergeant Conway walked in. He introduced himself to John.

"Hello, I'm Sergeant Conway of Internal Affairs and you are being charged with bribing a police officer."

John quickly answered, "What do you mean? You can't do that, we have a deal!"

Conway walked over to the paper sack, removed the recorder and rewound the tape. “Listen, when you’re arrested and then try to pay a police officer to let you go, it’s a crime. It’s called Bribery. Do you understand? You wanted to give money to Officer Romano and his partners. That’s three cops, three separate counts. Do you understand me?

John must have been the biggest idiot in the world or really desperate because his next comments almost knocked Mike out of his seat.

“But, look Sergeant. I can’t go back to jail. My girlfriend Ann is pregnant, she needs me home and I’ll get hurt in there. Do you want money too? I’ll send her home to get more. How much do you want?”

Sergeant Conway lost it and leaped out of his chair almost jumping across the table at John. “Listen you idiot, I’m an Internal Affairs sergeant, we have you on tape and you want to pay me off. I don’t believe this.”

Regaining some of his composure, he continued, “You are under arrest for bribing a police officer,” Conway’s composure was short lived, “Shit, an Internal Affairs Sergeant too, you moron and that’s all there is to it. I don’t give a rats’ ass what happens to you in jail.”

Conway turned to Mike, “Romano cuff him and put him in the holding cells. We have to talk about his girlfriend.”

Mike handcuffed the man who was now sobbing. “Officer you can’t jail me. My girlfriend needs me.”

Conway broke in saying, “Shut up you moron or we’ll arrest her too.” He was still enraged and shouting.

Mike hoped that she did not hear the last statement and flee even though he was certain that Fondalar, Barry or Danny would prevent her from leaving.

When Mike left the room to put John into the cells, he saw Barry and Danny sitting with Ann on the bench. She sat between them. When the cops saw him with John, they each grabbed one of her arms. Barry turned to her and said something. She began to sob.

Mike knew that someone now had to decide if she was going to be arrested and charged also. He would leave it up to Sergeant Conway; after all, he was in from Internal Affairs.

In the arrest processing room, John was confused and questioned his situation. "Hey Officer Romano, why didn't the sergeant take money like you did?"

Mike could not believe his ears. "Listen John, you are under arrest for bribing a cop, several cops. It is against the law; just the offer alone is Bribery. I did not take the money, I arrested you. You broke the law, especially my law. Now let's make this go easy. When you get downtown your legal aid attorney will explain it better."

"Yeah but, I can't go back to jail man. Is my lawyer going to get me off?"

As far as Mike could tell, the guy wasn't high on drugs. He must have been real stupid. He almost began feeling sorry for him again. "You just sit tight. I have to go back inside and talk with the sergeant again."

Once back in the interview room with Conway, Mike began to feel better about his current situation. He was thinking that now he could tell Betty about the events as they occurred, beginning with the garage incident. He was sure that his collar would guarantee his chance to remain in the unit. He felt vindicated.

Sergeant Conway was marking the tape with the date, time and his initials. He carefully put it back into its original box, sealed and marked it. He handed the cash to Mike and instructed him to put his own initials on each bill, all seven hundred and seventy dollars. Mike was told to gather the case and the jewelry. He was instructed to voucher each item, including the cash, then bring the completed paperwork and items back to Conway and he would personally sign off on them.

"Any other regular paper work can be signed off by your command, Mike. Now before you go start this, what do you want to do with the girl? Legally she is a co-conspirator in this crime because she brought the money here and knew what it was for. I don't care. It's your call."

Mike's brain was running at light speed. "Sarge, do you think we can get her to sign a statement about what she did, let her go home and let the assistant district attorney decide her fate in the complaint room?" He was reluctant to arrest a pregnant woman.

Sergeant Conway was still obviously amazed by John's reaction to the arrest. "In eight years of dong this Mike, I never experienced what happened here today. Yeah, go see if you can get her to write a statement about bringing the money here. If she does, we'll let her go home."

Mike walked over to Barry and Danny as they sat with Ann. Barry asked, "What's going on now Mike? Do you need the girl? Is she in too?"

Smiling at the girl, Mike answered, "No Barry, she will be allowed to leave if she helps explain what she did. I need to talk to her. Thanks. I'll fill you guys in later. Thanks for your help."

He then spoke directly to the girl, "Hello, Ann, do you remember me from inside the other room." Mike was trying to be as friendly as he could be. He did not want to arrest her too. He already had what he wanted, he had John. It was good enough for him. Now he had to smooth talk her into giving a statement. "Unfortunately your boyfriend is going to stay under arrest. He will be taken to court tonight and formally charged. Maybe they will set a low bail and he'll come home in the morning. You have the option to go down to the court house and wait if you want to."

"Yes, I want to go home, I mean."

"Hold on, that's only if you write down on paper what John said to you on the phone and what you did as a result of that call. Will you do that for me so you can leave in a few minutes?"

Her reply came as expected. She was scared and apparently not very bright. She and John were mentally compatible.

"Yes Officer. Just give me some paper so I can go home and wait for John."

Mike brought her back into the interview room and in the presence of Sergeant Conway; she wrote, dated and signed the required statement. Mike thanked her and escorted her out of the station house, leaving the written statement with Sergeant Conway. Conway signed off on the statement as a witness. Copies of the statement and all vouchers were made for Sergeant Conway. He also took a scratch copy of the arrest report. Conway did not wait around for the conclusion of the arrest processing.

As Conway was leaving the building, he shook Mike's hand. "Well done Romano. If you ever need a hand again, with anything, call the office and ask for me. You're a credit to the job and your command."

Mike telephoned Betty to say he made a bribery arrest and he hoped to see her sometime during the night, possibly in the morning. He had a lot to tell her. She was excited about the arrest. Mike hoped she remained happy after he told her about all the events of his day.

***

Following the bribery arrest, Mike spent the entire night at the courthouse processing the collar. John Norton was finally brought before the judge; bail was set at five thousand dollars. Not having anyone to post the bail, John was held remanded until his next court date.

Mike finally signed out of court at 5:00AM the following morning. It was not worth going home and possibly upsetting Betty, so he returned to his command. Mike went down to the basement, grabbed an alarm clock he kept in his locker for such occasions and went to the lounge, set the clock for 0900 and went to sleep.

At 9AM, Mike cursed the alarm when it rang and forced himself awake and took a quick shower. He had learned to keep at least one clean change of clothes in his locker. Mike quickly put the fresh clothes on and went upstairs to sign in for a day's work.

As per Dennis Bryan, it was to be his last day with his unit before having to go back into uniform and regular foot patrol. After signing in, he went directly to Bryan's office hoping to use the bribery arrest to plead his case regarding getting dropped from his unit. The DI was not there. Mike vowed to see Bryan before he left the building for the day.

Because it was possibly his last day with the unit and still tired from the long night in court, Romano volunteered to be the van operator and sit with any prisoners for the day. He also wanted to use the down time to gather his thoughts. Mike planned to have his act together when speaking to the Great Pumpkin. He knew that his thought process had better be extremely sharp before he spoke to Betty later that evening. He also knew that however things turned out, Betty would be difficult.

By 1600 the team had arrested ten men. They returned to the command to process the group. Mike was pleased to learn that Bryan was in and excused himself from assisting with the processing.

As Mike approached Bryan's office door, he still wasn't sure how he would begin the conversation. The office door was opened. Mike knocked on the door jamb as he stuck his head in.

Bryan solved Mike's dilemma by speaking first, "Romano, come in and sit down," gesturing for Mike to sit in one of the chairs opposite himself. "I heard about your bribery arrest. Excellent police work."

Mike smiled, as hope entered his thoughts, *Wow, it worked. I'm staying in the unit.*

Romano's hopefulness ended as fast as it came with Bryan's next statement, "Nothing like going out with a bang is there?"

Mike was floored. He could not believe his ears. *That son of a bitch is still dropping me from the unit.* His brain went into overdrive as his mouth went into gear.

"But Inspector, we had a good relationship. Gino and I were the first ones picked for the unit. Lieutenant Armini and Sergeant Holbrook tell me I'm their best man. I know that I bring you the most collars in the unit. Hell, the unit was even written up in New York Magazine."

Mike began to feel embarrassed as he heard his own words. He sounded like he was begging and changed tactics.

"How will it look downtown? One of your elite Conditions Unit men makes a better then textbook bribery arrest. He makes an arrest where the bad guy sends his woman home for more money and also tries to bribe the IAD sergeant handling the case. As a reward, you drop that honest cop from his unit."

Mike didn't know if his heart was pounding in his head or he really was hearing the beat of Saint Michaels' wings. Now he was getting cranked up and challenging his boss. The vision of Valenti making payoff motions with his hands now filled his head.

"Well Boss? How are you going to explain that one if asked?"

"Officer Romano", *getting formal now are we?* thought Mike, "You did good work, but it does not change my decision. I had to answer downtown for the garage incident, which caused me lots of grief. My decision stands. You go back into uniform. See me in thirty days. Maybe then you can go back into the unit after you had time to think about the error of your ways."

Mike wanted to say; *sure you had to answer downtown. You probably had to share the money you fat pig,* but he didn't. Instead, he took a deep breath and answered, "If it has to be that way, so be it, but you will see me in one month. Count on it. I'm holding you to your promise." Mike was slightly gentler then he wanted to be in his response, but still challenging.

"Sure, Romano. Go see Sergeant Holbrook; he'll give you a new post. Because you're basically a good cop, I'm letting you stay in the 10x6 detail. Keep your nose clean and you can get back in the unit."

Mike couldn't control himself and threw another verbal punch at the Pumpkin, "Sure Boss. I'll see Holbrook. We'll see each other in one month like you said. If I don't get back into my unit, we're going to get to see each other a lot."

Bryan's reply took some of the bluster away from Mike, but stiffened his resolve. Bryan saw the look on Mike's face. There was a venomous threat in his voice, "Easy Mike, I am your boss and the Commanding Officer here. You, on the other hand, are only one of my police officers, on the bottom of the pecking order, I might add. True you're an excellent worker, but still only a cop. See you in thirty days. Now get the fuck out of my office."

Within minutes Mike found Holbrook. The sergeant was almost apologetic as he told Mike that as of that coming Monday, he, Mike Romano, would be back in uniform. However, it was arranged, that Mike would return to The Apple and continue doing 10 x 6 working tours. Mike was also informed that he would not have a steady partner because there were no free men and he would work with a different man each day if one was available. Mike silently went to the locker room and checked his uniforms. He would be ready. He was nervous because that evening, he would have to tell Betty. He also vowed to leave something behind for Dennis to worry about.

Before leaving the command for the day, Mike went into the arrest processing room. His former team mates were still there. Seeing several large bags of marijuana on the table, he manipulated them, finding one with a loose opening and deliberately picked it up. As planned, a good amount of seeds dropped out.

"Opps. Sorry guys. I'll clean it up, just wanted to feel the weight. Good collar. As he swept the seeds off the table into his palm, he said, "Sorry to leave the team. Dennis said I can come back in a month. Hope to see you then. Now, I gotta go."

Mike then walked over to the trash barrel, as if dumping the seeds; instead he put most of them in his pants pocket. He went to his locker, gathered up some personal belongings and signed off duty.

As he left thru the front doors of the station, he passed Bryan's office. The door was open. The Pumpkin was not there. Mike was pleased. He walked outside and sat down on the brick planter outside Bryan's office window putting several items down on top of the planter wall. Acting as if he was looking for something, he reached into the planter with one hand and in one quick motion dug a three foot long trough in the dirt. Quickly, he spread the marijuana seeds, and covered them. In a barely audible mumble he announced, "Here you go you crooked Pumpkin, let's see how long it takes before you or someone else, like Lieutenant Blaise, notices your little garden."

That evening, when Mike got home, he barely acknowledged his wife and went to the rear of his apartment to see his children. He needed more time to think. Spending time in the children's room helped.

Betty knew the signs. He was hiding something. "Michael Romano, get out here right now. Tell me what's going on," she yelled.

The tone of her voice told him that Betty knew he was hiding something important. *Women and their sixth sense*, he thought. *Can't hide anything from them. Might as well go out there and tell her right away before she gets upset and the shock of battling Bryan will put me in the doghouse.* "Coming Betty. Be right there my love"

She was in the living room when he approached her. "Michael, the children were hungry, so we ate early. There is some heated food on the table for you in the kitchen. But let's have the whole story before you eat it or I'll throw it away."

He took her in his arms and attempted to kiss her passionately on the mouth. She began to respond, but instantaneously caught herself and pushed away. "Don't be cute Michael. What happened?"

Cautiously he responded, Sit down Honey, it's not that bad."

He then proceeded to tell her everything from the incident at the garage to the last minutes of the conversation with Bryan. "Thank you for not interrupting me. Any comments?" He had watched her facial expressions as he delivered the saga. Romano knew there would be some comments and opinions.

Betty began, "Well, for one thing. It appears this is only a small setback financially. If my memory serves me well, you still made many arrests and overtime when you were in uniform with Gino." She paused, waiting for a response.

Mike quickly jumped at the chance to lighten the mood. "Sure Betty. There should be little overtime loss. There's really nothing to worry about, Right?"

"Sure there is Michael;" she was serious again, "You still have Dennis Bryan to contend with. You already know the man is treacherous. Your own PBA delegate indicated to you that there was money exchanged. You even think it occurs often!! Just what makes you think that you can tackle that man? He will hurt you as soon as he can and that little stunt with the marijuana seeds under his office window was not too smart. What if someone saw you?"

"Well, Betty, as I told you, I have my memo book about the garage incident signed off by the guys' attorney. I made a great bribery arrest yesterday and I'm sure, if I have to, I can call the IAD sergeant for help if I get the goods on Bryan or if he tries to hurt me."

"Michael Romano, you are not Saint Michael and Bryan, bad as he is, is not Satan. I know you. Let it go and do your job. You have a family to support. Do not push that man. He obviously has powerful friends. Do you understand me?"

"Betty, I promise," he lied again. "I'll even bring my memo book home for safe keeping, just in case I ever need it."

"You should bring it home. That's smart, but there is no just in case. You will stop your crusade. And you better pray that nobody saw you plant those seeds. Understand?"

Betty knew her husband. She hoped her stern words cautioned him enough to be extra careful. Yet, she knew in her heart of hearts, that if given a chance, Mike would still battle DI Bryan. He couldn't help it. My husband is a *righteous idiot,* she thought. But that was one of the things she loved about him. Always trying to do the right thing and correct injustice.

She looked at him. He looked like a sick puppy. Holding out her arms she said, "Come here lover, your supper can wait. Come inside and get dessert."

Mike grabbed her and immediately began to feel better as he pulled her towards their bedroom.

***

The marijuana plants grew to almost 2 feet tall within two weeks. It was Blaise who realized what they were and had them removed. As the Integrity Control officer, Blaise personally read a precautionary notice at every roll call for a week. Bryan was visibly shaken by the event.

Every time Mike heard the announcement he almost lost his composure.

Chapter Thirteen

Returning back to work after his two day swing, Mike was reassigned to his former Apple post, post 10. The local shop owners and even some of the street people were happy to see him.

One of the first merchants he went to see was Gino's longtime friend Sonny Levine, the owner of the shop where they purchased their mini telescopes. Mike wanted Sonny hear about the garage incident, the bribery arrest and the conversation he had with Bryan. However, he would leave out his belief that Bryan was on the take.

Mike told the story while sitting in Sonny's rear office. He thought that Sonny, with his prior service on a Mayoral Advisory Committee might have an opinion as to why the arrest was voided and asked, "Sonny, you know lots of people downtown, can you think of any reason the arrest was voided?"

Sonny's only comment was, "Mike, the man is a Deputy Inspector for God's sake. Don't take him on alone. The voided arrest stinks. He should have let you bring the man to court and allow the Assistant District Attorney in the complaint room decide if he wanted to refuse prosecution and throw it out but he didn't. I don't know if I can find out what happened. But if I hear anything, I'll let you know."

"Thanks Sonny. I really appreciate it. And thanks for letting me vent."

"Anyway, it's good to have you back here on a daily basis."

***

Two weeks, and four arrests later, Mike had the chance he was waiting for. There was a family gathering at his mother-in-law's house and Rocco Banducci was there. When the opportunity presented itself, Mike spoke quickly and quietly, "Rocco, I have to speak to you alone. I need some information."

"Sure Mike. Can you meet me at the Privateer Diner tomorrow night?"

"Absolutely. How does seven o'clock sound? Is that good? I'll come directly from work."

Having detected the sense of urgency in Mike's voice, Rocco responded quickly, "Done. Michael, are you alright?"

"Yeah, I'm OK. Just need something clarified. Maybe you can help. Thanks" There was no other mention of their future meeting, just the usual family chatter.

The following day, Mike made sure he did not get involved in anything. He spent most of his tour up in the loft office at Pizza King. About once every hour he hit the street to show his face on post in case a supervisor checked for him. Romano never spent more than ten minutes outside. He was determined to sign out exactly on time. The evening meeting was too important.

As the end of his tour approached, Mike telephoned Betty to say he would be a few hours late. The phone call was their usual procedure when he knew that he would not return home by 7:00P.M.. He also told her not to save him any supper; he would eat before coming home. Mike claimed that he assisted in an arrest and had to help process multiple persons.

Mike was anxious to get to the diner where he last met with Rocco. He shot from 35th Street in Manhattan to Astoria Boulevard in Jackson Heights, Queens like a Grand Prix driver, making the trip in record time. It would normally take at least forty five minutes to an hour at that time of day. He made it in thirty five minutes.

Mike quickly entered the diner and walked directly to the rear dining room. Banducci was already there sitting at a table with a cup of coffee in front of him. As Mike approached, Rocco smiled and said, “Mike, you look like a wound up clock spring. What the hell’s going on? You sounded all upset yesterday. Sit down and tell me what’s got you in that state. Maybe you should order a drink to calm you down.”

Mike waved the waitress over. “Scotch, Dewars if you have it, on the rocks.” Rocco was correct in his assessment of Mike’s demeanor, he was getting more hyper. He continued without taking a breath, “Rocco, did you eat yet? Do you want a drink? I’m hungry. Please order something. It’s on me. This is gonna take some time.” Mike could not calm down.

They both ordered food. Rocco declined any alcohol. As Mike sipped his drink, he began, “Remember when you told me that if ever I needed something, to just ask you. Well, I need information on my commanding officer, if there is anything available.”

Seeing a puzzled look on his friend’s face, Mike didn’t waste any words; he went directly to the bottom line. “I think he’s on the take. I need to know if it’s true.”

Rocco’s face broke into a gentle smile as he spoke, “OK, Mike. I’ll try to help. But start at the beginning.”

“Well, it started on 35th Street in front of a parking garage…..” Mike related the entire garage incident. He then went into the many conversations that occurred in Bryan’s office. As Mike finished his second drink, he concluded his dialogue with that day’s conversation with Bryan.

Rocco had been listening intently, with hardly a comment except to slow Mike down. “Mike, sounds like you stepped on somebody’s toes. I’ll check on it. Now finish up and stop worrying. You’re family. Someday I’ll explain more.”

Mike assumed Rocco made that comment because he was dating his sister-in-law, Kelly. He assured himself that could be the only reason Rocco would say that filed being called "family" to the far recesses of his memory.

Three weeks went by before he even heard from Rocco again. Once again they met in the rear dining room of the Privateer Diner.

The conversation they had was enlightening. "Well, Mike. Your information was correct. There was money exchanged regarding the arrest of Mr. Rosen." Rocco smiled as he said the man's name.

"Rosen is not his real name. What name did he give you?"

Mike responded quickly, "Larry Rosen. I don't remember the address he gave me. Why?"

Rocco only replied, "That's not his real name. The guy is Italian and owns thirty five garages in the midtown area. The arrest was voided for eight thousand dollars. Rosen called that Levy guy, the lawyer, as soon as he got to the station house. The attorney, however, took on the case without notifying the proper people. He also took a fee from your Mr. Rosen. He no longer works for us."

"What do you mean? No longer works for you."

"The lawyer worked for a group of garage owners. There is a procedure for these sorts of things. He didn't follow it. That's all you have to know."

Mike was surprised at the question directed to him as Rocco continued. "Now Mike, what do you want done with Bryan. Do you want him to lose his command, get transferred or get gone?"

Mike's third drink arrived. He took a sip, using the time to digest what he had just heard. Mike's thoughts were full of questions. *This mobster guy is asking me if I want something done to a police official. What the hell is going on? Who the hell is he and who am I to get this treatment?*

Mike countered with, "What do you mean, what do I want done with Bryan? I don't fully understand. Why do I get that kind of choice, why me? I'm nothing but a cop. You may like me, as you so often said, but I'm sure your friends don't. Hell, they never even met me."

"Mike, you did me a favor and gave me advice when I got arrested. Your advice kept me out of prison. The DA wanted to send me away. Remember? The favor is being returned. That's all you have to know. My offer was made."

Mike could not believe his ears. He was a cop and knew enough not to get in bed with guys like Rocco. He also was smart enough not to disrespect the offer and wherever it came from, Rocco himself or higher up in the Banducci Family. He hoped his answer would be correct, "Thank you, Rocco, for the offer and the information. I think now that I know exactly what happened and just what Bryan is all about, I'd like to try to handle this myself. But, thank you."

Rocco chuckled, "Always the good cop Mikey," Rocco's affection for his friend came out in the tone of his voice, "I knew you would say something like that. Romano the cop never crosses the line. But the offer is still good. If ever you need it. That's why I respect you kid. You're always you."

The conversation had made Mike uncomfortable. He made excuses a few minutes later and went home. At least he now had reliable information that Bryan was a bad cop and possibly involved in much more. The thing he had with his dead brother-in-law was probably only one of his crooked activities. Yet, he could not report what he just learned to anyone. They might ask how he received his information and Mike could tell no one.

Mike never mentioned the meeting and confirmation of Bryan's corrupt behavior to anyone, not even Betty, but filed it in his head for possible later use.

Chapter Fourteen

Thirty one days had passed since Mike was returned to uniform. He decided it was time to see what Bryan had to say. Directly after roll call, Mike went to the DI's office. The door was closed. Mike knocked three times.

"Enter," was the only response.

Opening the door, Mike observed Bryan sitting behind his desk shuffling papers. The big man looked up. When he saw Mike, he quickly commented, "Well Officer Romano, I see you are right on time."

Mike saw a slight sardonic smile on the man's face. He thought, *you fat, great Pumpkin shit. Now I know what happened. I hope you choke on the money. If I can't get you, I now have someone who will. Let's rock-n-roll.* "Yes Inspector. Your words to me were to come back in thirty days and I might get my detail back. What's the chances?"

"Well Romano. There's still some noise about the garage incident, so you stay in uniform for another month and then come see me again. That's your answer. OK?"

"Well, Boss, needless to say I'm disappointed." Holding his Italian temper in check, Mike continued, "But, I'll play it your way. See you in exactly thirty days."

Bryan realized that Mike was twisting his shorts with his last comment. Reluctantly, Dennis had to give Romano credit. Not too many people would come back at him like that. The cop had balls. Bryan's own ego dictated that he answer Mike's last remark and waited until Mike reached the office door, "This isn't a game Romano, its police work and a command decision. Remember, I'm still your commanding officer."

Just as Romano was about to leave the building, Lieutenant Blaise called to him, “Mike, come upstairs with me please. I have something for you.”

Mike was not thrilled that the ICO called him to his office in front of anyone who might have been in the vicinity. Dealing with the in-house IAD representative made other cops nervous. Mike swallowed hard and answered, “Sure thing Boss. Right away.”

Once in the lieutenant’s office, Blaise turned to Mike, smiling at him, as he announced, “You received a commendation from Sergeant Conway and a certificate to prove it” and handed the award to Mike.

It was his second one. Back in the three two he had made a bribery collar, and he had to do his own write-up requesting Department recognition. The award certificate was sent to him thru department mail. That was an impersonal and standard procedure. This time, he never submitted any paperwork due to the Bryan problem. It was not foremost in his mind. Sergeant Conway must have been impressed enough to send it in on his own.

Mike relaxed, “Thank you sir. I didn’t know about the request for recognition. Who sent it in?”

“No one from this command. Sergeant Conway wrote it up for you. It was a good job you did on that collar Michael. What was the outcome in court?”

“I don’t know. The guy must have pled guilty because I was never notified to go down on the collar after the initial arrest.”

“Well, you should be proud. The Integrity Review Board will call you down to speak to you. I’m sure you know that one of the duties of the Board is to review bribery arrests and reward the officers for their exceptional performance and dedication to honesty. I saw in your personnel file that this was your second bribery collar. Your first one was in your old command. Is that how you arrived at The South?”

"No Loo. I requested the transfer. When I made the first bribery collar, I elected to remain in the 32 precinct. I was having fun and had a good partner."

"Well, they'll call you in again. They will probably offer you another transfer if you want it. You live in Queens don't you? You could transfer closer to home."

"That would be great but we hope to buy a house in Staten Island soon, so I'll stay here. By the way, does the CO know about the commendation?"

"Sure. He gets notified when I do. Why?"

Mike thought, *That shit. He never mentioned it and he's still keeping me in the bag (police slang for uniform).* He answered, "Just curious. I just saw him in the lobby and he didn't mention it. By the way, I'm still on foot post. Do you have any input?"

"Not at all Mike. It's his command and he assigns men where and when he wants to. It's his call. I'm only a guest here."

"OK, thanks for the certificate. I'll put it in my locker then go out to my post. See you."

Several weeks passed without any Romano vs. Bryan incidents. It was now getting close to the holiday season. Mike was always looking for another way to possibly get back into his beloved unit and decided to ask Sonny if he could help him start a merchants' association on the Apple. Mike thought it might help him return to his plainclothes unit. If nothing else, it might embarrass Bryan.

After a short conversation about the possibility to hold a merchants meeting in Sonny's store, Mike got his answer. "Mike, some store owners, the legitimate ones, have discussed it for some time. We have never done anything about it though. Why do you want to see one formed? It could mean lots of work on your part."

"Well, I think it would help my cause. The more I do to put good stuff in my personnel file, the more chances I have to get back into plain clothes. Anyway, it might be fun and maybe it will unnerve that shithead Dennis in the process."

"Boy, you really can't leave well enough alone. But ok. I'll talk to some people I know downtown and see if they think it would be good to push it. Personally, I think it's a great idea. With the holiday season coming, people are usually in a good mood and it probably will be easier to get the merchants to join."

Two days later Sonny told Mike that he would help him take on the project. Sonny would do most of the work. All Mike had to do was visit each merchant as he made his rounds and get them to sign up if they were interested. Sonny would supply the forms and do the follow up on the applications with the help of some political interns from downtown.

Within a week, Mike had seventy five percent of the Apple's business owners signed up. The missing twenty five percent included all the sex shops and one or two others. Mike and Sonny were not surprised.

At the end of the week, after he gathered most of the applications for the new association and gave them to Sonny, Mike decided it was time to visit Bryan's office again.

"Inspector, don't you think that I should be returned to the Conditions Unit? It's been some time now. You made your point."

"What point do you think that is Romano?" Without waiting for an answer, Bryan continued, "The point is, I'm the commander of this station and what I say goes. You're lucky that I'm understanding and take your work record into account every time you smart mouth me. I can transfer you at the stroke of a pen. You do a good job on the Apple for me or you will remain in uniform indefinitely. Now get the hell out of here."

Mike did not argue and just silently walked away with the beating of angel's wings in head.

***

The Holiday season was approaching. Just before Thanksgiving, the Romanos closed on a small house in Staten Island. The merchant's association had their first meeting without incident. Everything was going smoothly.

It was exactly two weeks before Christmas when Mike responded to a dispute in one of the trashy electronic/tourist gift shops on his post. The incident resurrected the dormant war between himself and Dennis Bryan.

The would be archangel was met just outside the shop entrance by the clerk who initiated the call for police assistance. The man informed Mike that the shop owner did not want to exchange a portable television that an irate apparent past customer was arguing about. The customer stated that he had purchased the set two days

before and finally opened the carton earlier that very day to find the power cord was cut. There was no plug on the end. The man had no receipt with him, claiming it was at home. The clerk, thinking that the exchange was bordering on the verge of becoming physical, called 911.

The business' owner, an Armenian immigrant named Aram Samour, was happy to see Mike walk in. Romano had never had much interaction with the man. Samour had a reputation in the command of not liking police officers. Rumor had it that he once had a cop transferred for soliciting a bribe. Mike was cautious.

"Aha, Officer Romano. It's a pleasure to see you. Please explain to this man that we do not sell damaged goods here. We do not cut wires on televisions set here. Please explain to him."

The customer began, "Look at this cord officer. I get home and open the box and the cord is cut. Why won't he exchange the set or give me my money back. He knows I bought it in here only two days ago. Ask him"

Turning back to Samour, Mike asked, "Sir, do you know if this man bought this set two days ago?"

"I do not know him. If he came in here to buy it, I was not here and my employee does not recognize him," he answered while pointing to one of the two counter men.

Mike continued with, "Are there any other employees here today that we can speak with?"

"No officer. I sent another man on an errand. He is not back yet."

The irate man countered with, "Officer he's lying. He knows me. He is a thief and a crook. I want him arrested."

"Take it easy Sir. Nobody is going to be arrested. Do you have a receipt for this? It would have the store name on it and a date?"

"No. I was so angry when I opened the box that I left it home." The man continued, "He knows this is his TV. Look at the shelf. There are many, many more of them."

Mike looked where the man indicated and saw a shelf loaded with the same type of cartons. The brand name and carton markings were similar. Many of the boxes had the same model number as the customers' set.

"Yes sir. I see them. But without a receipt I can't expect this man to refund money to you or even force him to exchange your set for another one. He is breaking no laws. I'm a police officer not a judge."

The man began to turn his wrath on Mike. "What do you do, get paid to protect him? Does he pay you to help cheat customers?"

The man had just assailed Mike's character. *Now you did it.*

Romano responded sternly, "Listen, if you accuse me of taking money again, I'll arrest you for disorderly conduct and voucher your TV. It will take you weeks to get it back. Why don't you go home, get the receipt, come back like a gentleman or take this man to court. Go to Small Claims Court and make a complaint. It's free. Are we clear? This conversation is over."

The "customer" mumbled something unintelligible, put his set back in the carton, picked it up and walked toward the door. As he exited, he turned and shouted, "You are thieves, you and your policeman."

Mike chose to ignore the remark and spoke to Samour, "If he comes back today call 911 again." Mike then removed a blank complaint report from his memo book, unfolded it and recorded the incident. The report was marked, "Closed-referred to court." He would file it later when he signed out for the day.

As Mike rested on a glass counter, folding his report, Samour took his hand and put a small black plastic box in it. "Here, this is to say thank you. It is almost Christmas. You will like the watch."

Mike reacted as if he was stung by a hornet. He quickly put the box down and said, "Thank you, but I am only doing my job. It is not necessary. If I take it, the man will be right."

Mike then opened his jacket to put the completed form into the inside pocket and Samour boldly reached over, held the jacket opened and stuffed the box in saying, "It is a gift. Do not worry. I am saying thank you."

Romano's brain went into overdrive at that point. *He's trying to set me up. The stories are true. That will never happen. I'll walk outside with the watch still in my jacket, call Lieutenant Armini and come back and arrest this jerk. Dennis will have to put me back in the unit with two bribery collars in his command.* Mike smiled at Samour, "Thank you. He closed his jacket. "Thank you, but keep this between us. Thanks again."

As he walked out of the store, Romano again recalled his first bribery arrest. He was on patrol in the 32 and was about to issue a summons to a man for driving through a red light. The man offered to give him ten dollars if he would forget the summons. Mike had keyed his portable radio and made the man repeat the offer so it would be recorded on the dispatch tape. He then arrested the man and got a guilty plea in court. During the resulting interview with the Integrity Board, he elected to shelve his reward then too.

***

Mike stood in the alcove entrance of the store, never actually leaving the property and called the job in. "South foot post ten, on the dispute, condition corrected, referred to court. Central please ask the South Day Squad Lieutenant to respond to this location, K"

Lieutenant Armini heard Mike's call and answered, "Day Lieutenant here, unable to respond immediately. What do you have post ten? , K."

Mike wanted to make sure his voice was on the dispatch tape. He answered, "Post ten here. Central, please inform the lieutenant that I have an integrity problem at this location and need his assistance. K."

Mike heard his lieutenant's response. "Central, please advise post ten to leave that location, notify dispatch of his new location and remain there until I can respond. I will notify Central when able to respond to his new location, K"

Mike acknowledged that he would change his location and await instructions. He went directly to Sonny's store.

Arriving at Sonny's, Mike went directly to the rear office, followed by Sonny and immediately notified the dispatcher, "South post ten to Central, K"

"Go ahead South ten, K"

"South ten, I'm at 255 West 42nd Street awaiting the South Day Lieutenant, K".

Lieutenant Armini heard the transmission and answered before the dispatcher, "Acknowledged, South Day Lieutenant heard the foot post and will respond. Put us both

10-62, out of service at that location, K."

While he was waiting for his boss, Mike opened the watch box. Inside was a Casio wristwatch. It looked medium priced. He examined the watch closely, turning it over. To his surprise, it had a serial number.

He turned to Sonny and asked, "Sonny, do you know if it's normal for a Casio watch to have a serial number? I've never seen one."

"No Mike. I usually carry the more inexpensive ones. I don't remember any with a number. Let me check my stock."

Returning from the front of the shop, Sonny informed Mike that he did not have any Casio watch with a serial number on the back. He added that he had about six models on his shelves. He had no explanation as to why the watch in Mike's hand had a serial number.

Mike got nervous. The hairs on the back of his neck began bristling. He began to believe that Samour set him up. He was impatient waiting for Armini. It seemed that he waited forever. Actually, his lieutenant arrived within five minutes.

Armini entered the rear office. "Mike, I'm here. The counterman said that you and Sonny were back here. Now what happened?"

"Well Lou, I adjudicated a dispute in a store down the block. I made a 61(complaint report) to file later and when I was getting ready to leave, the owner, Samour, tries to give me a watch. I told him no but he shoves it into my open jacket. My mind goes off and I figure I can get another bribery collar. So I went outside and called for you."

"Let me see the watch. Is it expensive?"

"Here, Lou. It has a serial number on the back. Sonny doesn't have any Casio wristwatches with a serial number. I got a feeling the guy set me up."

"Ok Mike. Because you and Bryan are always going at it, I'm going to call IAD and get some input as to how they want to handle this."

Turning to Sonny, he asked, "Can I use your phone please?"

"Sure Lieutenant. Please help yourself." Sonny left the room.

Armini was on the phone for several minutes. "Mike, they're going to speak with their legal department first before giving me an answer. Relax awhile. Central has us both out of service at this location. Please use the time to record everything about the incident in your memo book. I'll sign off on it as the responding supervisor."

Ten minutes went by when the dispatcher squawked, "South Day Lieutenant ten-one your CO, Acknowledge, K"

Armini was not pleased. He acknowledged the radio message and telephoned the command. Once he had Bryan on the phone, Armini became agitated. What Mike heard made him shake inside.

"What do you mean, lock up the cop? Who told you something so crazy? Romano is above reproach. He made a fantastic collar while still in plainclothes. That perp even tried to bribe the IAD sergeant. Romano's one of my best, if not my best man."

Mike began pacing the floor as he listened. He thought he was going to be sick. *Talk about a career going down the tube. These idiots want to lock me up. No way. I'll sue the pants off the entire Department. Bryan is going to pay for this.* His mind was racing.

Armini ended his call with, "Yes sir. I'll call them right away and be guided by what I'm told."

"Mike, I don't have a handle on what's going on, but according to Bryan, some genius in IAD said you should be locked up for accepting the watch."

"But, Lou. I never accepted the watch. I called as soon as I got to the door. I never left the property with the watch until Central told me to change my location. I put the thing on tape as an integrity problem. Was I supposed to say I want to lock someone up for bribing me? Would that have made those morons happy?"

"Mike, go easy. I'm only telling you what Bryan said. I have to call IAD back. Let me do what I can."

Armini made the call. Mike heard him arguing with someone. He turned to Mike and asked, "What was the name of the Sergeant that handled your bribery arrest?"

Mike spit out his response so strongly, the words were almost visible, "Conway, Sergeant Conway. He's one of their own. Damn, he got bribed too. He promised to help any time I called. Get him."

Armini gave the sergeant's name and circumstance of Mike's last bribery incident to the person on the other end of the phone. His conversation ended with, "Yes sir. I'll call back in fifteen minutes."

Turning to Mike, Armini spoke softly. "Mike, I'm on your side. You heard me arguing with the IAD shitheads. Lawyers. I don't like any of them. Bryan seems to have it in for Italians. I'm the only supervisor in this command that does not have a patrol car assigned to him. Bryan gives me the crap that I'm a better supervisor if I walk. I'm closer to the action. He's full of crap. The guy's a bigot but I can't fight him, I'm on the captains list."

"Yeah. I noticed it's very rare that you drive up to a scene or a post visit. Most of the time you're on foot. I never knew it wasn't your choice. Sounds silly but I feel better. Do you think I'm gonna get locked up?

"Not if I can help it. Just wait it out. I'll promise you that I'm not authorizing the arrest if it comes to that. Bryan is going to have to do it. I don't think he will. You remember the garage incident; he never signed your book. Correct?"

"Thanks," was all Mike could mutter as he slumped into a chair in the corner.

The lieutenant called IAD back at the appointed time. After an even more animated conversation, he turned to Mike with the results. "Ok Mike, this is what is going to happen. You and I are going to go back to that store and return the Casio."

Mike didn't believe his ears. "But that's crazy. The guy gave me a bribe. At the least he gave me an unlawful gratuity. That's the correct charge. Right?"

"Calm down Mike. We are going to do exactly what IAD says. Now be quiet, not a word, because I want to get all this down on paper. They want a written report of this entire incident. During my first call they claim that you left the store with the watch, had second thoughts and called it in. After the first call, IA apparently spoke to Conway who put in a good word. They backed off on collaring you."

Armini then walked out to the front of the store and asked for a writing pad. Sonny produced a lined yellow legal pad within seconds, handed it to the lieutenant, who returned to the office, sat down and scratched out three pages. He looked at Mike often to reassure his man that he would be fine when he completed the process as instructed.

When he had finished, Armini thanked Sonny for the use of his office and notified the dispatcher that he and post ten were changing locations. "South Day Lieutenant to Central. Post 10 and I are proceeding back to 255 W.42nd Street on the previous condition, K"

The dispatcher quickly acknowledged the transmission as both cops returned to Samour's store.

As Mike and Armini entered his store, Samour actually looked happy. He came forward with an extended hand and said,

"Hello, Office Romano. You liked the little gift and came for another one for the Lieutenant. Yes?"

Armini's hand twitched. For a second, Mike thought his lieutenant was going to draw his gun. Instead, the lieutenant took a deep breath and said, "Listen sir, you are either the dumbest man alive or the most devious. Either way you're lucky today."

"Why are you so upset Lieutenant? Officer Romano did a nice job for me. Saved me a problem and I say thank you to him. It is your holiday of Christmas, he is your man and I say thank you to you too. It is our way."

Armini was getting red in the face as he spoke, "Look Mr. Samour, is that your name? It is NOT OUR WAY."

Bringing his voice down a few decibels, Armini continued, "Police in this country do not accept gifts. If you try that again you will be arrested. Do you understand?" Throwing the box containing the watch he gave Mike on the counter as he spoke. Samour was about to respond when Armini threw his hand up to stop him from saying another word. He touched Mike on the shoulder and walked out with Mike trailing behind him.

Once outside, Armini turned to Mike, "Finish your tour and don't worry. This thing is over. Next time someone tries to give you something, lock him up right away, ignore it or take it and keep quiet."

Mike opened his mouth to respond but Armini beat him to it. "I know taking something is not your style, so pick one of the first two options. Just stay out of trouble for a while. Go find a spot where you can hide somewhere on post and stay there for the remainder of the tour."

"Yes sir, Lou. I know just the place," was Mike's response. He was thinking about Tony's loft office at King of Pizza. It was on post and he could always look out the windows. If an assignment came over the radio or a supervisor was looking for him, Mike knew he could be on the street in less than a minute.

As the lieutenant walked away, he turned and said, "Mike near the end of your tour, put yourself out of service an hour early and find me at the command. I'll show you the finished write up."

Mike headed straight for Tony's loft. He remained there until one hour before end of tour, put himself out of service on clerical matters and went directly back to the station house to find Armini.

Chapter Fifteen

Mike had just walked thru the front doors of the command when Deputy Inspector Bryan saw him. "Romano, go find your lieutenant and both of you come into my office."

"Ok Inspector. He asked me to come in also. As soon as I find him we'll both be right there." Mike thought, *what dirty, sneaky thing is on his mind now. Bet it's not good.* He found the lieutenant in the muster room. Together they went to Bryan's office.

Bryan was in a foul mood. "One of you, close the door." Looking directly at Mike, he began, "Romano, I brought your lieutenant in here so he could verify what I'm about to say. Just in case you feel it's personal."

Armini had a sick look on his face. It was personal and he knew it. Someday he would get away from this man before he blew his top. He needed another year in the command to satisfy his career path requirements. Midtown South looked good in his personnel folder. He hoped Mike would not explode at whatever Dennis was about to say. He knew it was not going to be good.

Dennis continued, "Officer Romano, I do not know what has gotten into you. From being one of the best cops in the command, you have become a big headache. What you did today, taking a wristwatch as a gratuity and then calling it in on the open airwaves created a good deal of shit for me."

Mike interrupted, "But Boss, I didn't take a gratuity. The guy forced it on me and I called it in on the radio to cover my ass. I still think it should be a collar."

"Romano, do not interrupt me again or I will transfer you to the North Bronx. That will be some ride from Staten Island. Do you understand me?"

Mike's only response was, "Sir". He wanted to remain in the command and continue finding a way to sink this graft taking pig of a man.

Bryan continued, "The incident you created caused me to get calls from Internal Affairs, Chief Galick himself. I also received a call from the Borough Commander, Deputy Chief Leventhall. After I spoke to them, we all agreed that you should be arrested for receiving Unlawful Gratuities. You did not arrest Samour, was that his name? Arrest him on the spot. Instead you left the store. They believe you accepted the gratuity then had a change of heart and tried to cover your tracks."

Mike was ready to shout, *you're probably lying. You just want me. They should arrest your fat ass. You know I wouldn't take a dime. I'm not like you. You're a criminal and probably a pedophile like your brother-in-law.*

Bryan continued, "Look, I had one hell of a time convincing them that you were a good cop and made a bad decision by walking out of the store. I assured them that you had an accurate, full account of the incident in your memo book and except for the fact that you walked outside to call for a supervisor, you had no intentions of doing anything wrong."

Mike's mind raced, *Damn right I do. You know I have an accurate account of the incident in my book. You were asked to sign the last one. Is it possible that you are afraid of poor little old me?*

"Now, here is the reason that I asked for Lieutenant Armini to be present. After all he is your supervisor. If he has any objections to what I'm about to say, he can voice them when I finish." Mike saw a slight crooked smile on the big man's pumpkin red face.

"You are going to have a post change effective tomorrow. You will remain in the Day Squad and you may keep your 10x6 tours. You will however, have posts 16, 17 and 18, on the "Deuce" as we call it, but you know that. That's both sides of 42nd Street between Broadway and 6th Avenue. You will also cover post 18. That's 42nd to 43rd on the west side of 6th Avenue. I expect you to be there all day, and remain there every day you are scheduled to work. Leave the post without proper procedure and you will answer to charges and specs. Got that? Do you have any comments, Lieutenant?"

"No Inspector, Personally, I'm pleased that you are leaving Mike in my squad and keeping him in the command. Thank You"

"Romano, do you have any comments?"

"Well Inspector, I'm a little disappointed in the response I got from IAD. Guess I should say thank you for allowing me to stay in the Day Squad. At least I have posts on the "Deuce". How come I have three posts? I understand that they may be considered one due to proximity, but it's a big area for one man. Usually there are at least two men there. Am I correct?"

The big man's face glowed brighter as he answered, "Because, Romano, I think that you can handle it."

Mike wasn't sure what to make of his next remark, "After all, you seem to be a one man police force, at least a squad. You can do it Romano. I'll personally be watching you."

Mike knew it was a veiled threat and his back came up. Once again he tried to twist the Pumpkin's brain, "Does that mean that I'm up for getting back in the Conditions Unit?"

Bryan was almost gleeful as he answered, "No, Romano. That's it for that assignment as far as you're concerned. You can remain in this command and in uniform if you stay out of controversy. Now if there's nothing else, you are dismissed." He turned to Armini and asked, "Lieutenant?"

Mike couldn't help himself. He had to ask, "Inspector, since you took my part in the watch incident, would you like to sign off as it's recorded in my memo book?"

Bryan started to bristle and was about to say something when Armini cut in, "We have nothing else to add here

Inspector. Officer Romano and I are fine with this." Turning to Mike he said, "Mike, come with me, I want to see you outside a minute."

Armini almost pushed Mike to the stairway that led to the basement locker room. Once in the stairway, Armini commented on the conversation in Bryan's office. "Mike, I still say the man doesn't like Italians. He makes me walk the command. You obviously caused some kind of grief for him with the garage incident. I don't have any idea as to what's going on there. Today you tried to do the right thing with a gratuity and he pulls the rug out from under you. Mike, what is going on between you two? Is there something I should know?"

"Lou. I can only say that I know he is not a very nice man. Yes, it is personal with me. He thinks that I'm just a smart ass. I'm not. He screwed with the wrong guy. Someday he's going to learn that he never should have started with me. I'm not going to say any more about it. Please respect that."

"Mike, I liked you from the first day I met you back in the Three Two. You do your work and except for these two incidents, I never have to worry if you're going to do something that will embarrass the job, yourself or me. Keep your eyes open on the new post. The man wants to hurt you yet, for some reason, he's holding back. He's not going all out. He can give you an administrative transfer and put that blot on your record. He's not doing that either."

The conversation between them was candid, so Mike gave a little. "Well Lou, remember when I made the collar at the garage. Remember when I asked the big shit to sign off in my memo book. Well, he didn't, because I think he was personally pissed off. I broke something up. Please don't ask me what it was, just know that my source is good. He's been gunning for me since."

"Mike, what are you saying? Are you talking about something illegal? He's a big boss in the Department. It's unlikely that he would get involved in something shady. Those now. It's too risky, especially for a man in charge of a show piece command like this one."

Not wanting to confirm anything about corruption, Mike answered, "Lou, maybe I want to believe because of how I got screwed. It's just a feeling I have that he's less than lily white."

"Well Michael," Armini was serious now, "just keep your feelings to yourself. Don't tell a soul. You should not have even told me. That kind of talk could get you hurt, or worse. If you have anything solid why don't you call your friend Sergeant Connors?"

"Can't say for sure Lou, but I trust you. Besides it's only a feeling, something I want to believe. He is probably not banging me out completely because I helped organize that merchants association. The Association is happy with their beat cop. You know they can sink a Commander's career if the guy attacks who they consider their man. Maybe he's afraid of them. Don't know, and I don't care."

As he spoke to his lieutenant, Mike heard the beat of large wings, maybe an angel's, in his head. He knew he was right. Dennis Bryan was probably afraid of the Association. The Pumpkin could not possibly know just how much Mike knew about him. He would stay with that assumption.

At home that night, Mike kept the day's events to himself. He did not want to worry his wife. After all, he was still on 42nd Street. Nothing really changed. He told Betty that he had a terrific day. He played with his kids, ate dinner and later made love to his wife.

***

The next day, as he walked to his new post, Mike took some time to stop at Sonny's store. He wanted to tell his friend about the results of the previous day's events. After all, he and his lieutenant had used the man's office and telephone. Mike felt that he owed Sonny and he was entitled to know the final result of those anxious minutes. Besides, he had to tell him that he would not be on post ten anymore. Bryan made that abundantly clear. Mike also wanted Sonny's continued assistance in organizing the merchants on his new posts.

Mike explained most of the past day's events regarding the near arrest of Samour, leaving out the private conversation with his lieutenant. When finished, he asked, "Sonny, do you have more applications for the merchants association? Once I get to know the people on my new post, I would like to get them to join too. It might help me get back on the Apple or back to Conditions."

Inwardly, he thought, *Conditions, never. But more merchants in the association will get more people to know me and hopefully like me. That way Bryan can't transfer me without getting a powerful bunch of civilians pissed off at him. There's not a commander in the job that wants the general public on his ass.*

Sonny assured him that he had plenty of applications and would assist him any way he could.

Mike thanked Sonny for listening and expressed his appreciation for his future assistance. Reluctantly, Mike left the premises and continued on to his new post.

After crossing Broadway and stepping onto the sidewalk that began his new foot post, Mike began to closely observe his new surroundings. He had been on the block many times while in plainclothes in his beloved Conditions Unit. The difference was that during prior visits, he concentrated on the potential arrest at hand, usually Three Card Monty teams. He was always alert to possible danger, but never absorbed the flavor of the block. Now he observed his newly assigned post was not as sleazy as the Apple. As he toured the area for the first time, Mike took mental inventory of the businesses and persons that he would be responsible for.

On the north side of his new post he saw was a very large electronics/camera store on the corner of 42nd and Broadway. Further down the block were two shoe stores, a large chain restaurant that specialized in fried chicken and the like, two sandwich shops, one of them a national chain, a cheap steak restaurant, two more electronic/camera gifts shops, a travel agent, a fortune teller, another national chain sandwich shop and on the corner, of 6th Avenue, a luncheonette type restaurant. Around that corner on the short block to 43rd Street was a Chinese take-out, another gift shop, a health buff vegetarian restaurant and messenger service.

The southern side of his new post was slightly more businesslike. On the corner of 6th Avenue were the offices of the New York Telephone Company. The building gave an air of respectability to the block, at least on that side. Continuing down the block back towards Broadway was a temp agency, an office supply store that also sold office furniture, yet another large sex show, still another gift shop, a small "discrete" adult book store and still another smoke shop.

After his mental inventory of his new assignment, Mike decided to begin the first tour of his new post by visiting each shop keeper on 42nd Street and introduce himself. He did not go into the sex related businesses or the fortune teller. At his assigned meal hour, Mike disregarded Bryan's order and left his post. He did not notify the radio dispatcher and headed for the loft back on his old post above the King of Pizza. To cover his ass, Mike carefully noted in his memo book that he left post for meal. Such an entry was a Department requirement. *Dennis Bryan can go to hell. He'll never admit to confining me to post.*

On the second half of his tour, Mike visited the vegetarian restaurant. The owner, Herman, was a big man about 6'-6" in height and looked very powerful. Herman's size and slightly effeminate way, instinctively, made Mike slightly uneasy.

Herman, on the other hand, was especially happy to meet Romano. When he learned that Mike was permanently assigned to the post, he was even more pleased.

"You know officer, Mike, if I can call you that, we never have a cop around here. Most of my customers are from the phone company and the big office building mid-block across 6th Avenue, 55 West, just across from Bryant Park. They sometimes get hassled by pot dealers and such. It's bad for business. I'm very happy to see you here. I respect the Police Department and also have a friend who is very high up in rank. We often visit Fire Island at the same time. For some reason the cops around here seem to always avoid me. You didn't and I thank you for that. Stop in anytime for lunch or coffee. It's on me."

Mike decided to push his homophobic feelings aside and give the big guy a chance. He thanked Herman for his offer and continued on his way. Mike was unaware that Herman would become a true friend and he would spend much productive time inside his restaurant. Mike continued making his store visits. Although he spent only a few minutes in each establishment, introducing himself took up his entire tour.

***

Just as predicted by Lieutenant Blaise, Mike had his interview with the Integrity Review Board. It was two weeks after Christmas when the Board summoned him. They offered to transfer Mike to any command of his choice. Trying to capitalize on the offer, he requested reassignment to his old position in the Conditions Unit. The board members explained to him that assignments within a command were the exclusive rights of the commander in charge. It was Board policy not to interfere with a command decision. Mike was disappointed, yet tried to remain blasé about it.

He explained that he was unable to choose a new command and asked if he could have some time to think before requesting a transfer. Sergeant Conway was one of the members sitting in. After a short conversation among the board members, his request was granted. They would allow him one year to request a transfer or lose the privilege.

Mike thanked the Board and left relatively happy. He still wanted to try to hurt Dennis Bryan, if it was possible. He had a full year to try, and he would do so if given an opportunity.

***

To his surprise, Mike grew to enjoy his new foot post. After his first week of writing an occasional parking summons and adjudicating some gift shop disputes, he decided to pick up the applications for the merchants association from Sonny the following day.

New applications in hand, Mike entered the big corner gift shop on Broadway and asked for the owner by name. The store was the biggest of its kind in the area. During that first meeting, Mike took particular note that the quality of the varied merchandise was of higher quality than the other shops, including his friend Sonny's.

The man even sold dinnerware; crystal stemware, some jewelry and what Mike thought were a good quality of knock off oriental type rugs.

Mike fondly remembered their first meeting his second day in the post. He had responded to a disorderly man call. After he escorted the offender from the store, the owner, Shlomo Yohasim, was genuinely appreciative, thanked him repeatedly, and did not try to force "a gift" on him.

That day was the first time the Italian, Mike Romano, had ever met anyone with the name Sholmo and it must have showed on his face. Shlomo looked Romano in the eye and without any prompting said, "Sholmo, it comes from shalom, meaning peace. It's an old Sephardic Jewish name. As a matter of fact," he continued, "King David named his son Sholmo. My parents so honored me also."

Mike liked the man at once. Despite a heavy accent, Sholmo had an extensive English vocabulary; he must have been an educated man.

Shlomo smiled, extending his hand as he approached Mike, "Shalom."

Mike shook his hand, answered in kind and got right to the business at hand. "Listen Sholmo," he liked saying the name, "You may or may not know that there is a merchants association on The Apple. Another store owner and I organized it, well actually he did. I helped by convincing shop owners to join. Anyway, now that I'm permanently assigned to this post, I'm going to ask all the other store owners between here and 6th Avenue if they would like to fill out an application and join. The bigger the association gets could mean formidable political muscle."

"Sure Romano," Sholmo always used Mikes' last name, "I would be happy to join. I believe you are correct. Perhaps with more members comes more power and we store owners will have a bigger voice in the area. Give me an application. Come back and pick it up whenever you want to. Thank you for including me."

Mike continued down the block. He visited all the businesses except the fortune teller and the sex shops. If he had to go inside those places in the future, it would be strictly business, cold and professional. The rest of his day was uneventful. He signed off duty at 1800 hours and drove directly to Staten Island to enjoy his wife and children in their new home. They had been in their own home several months, but Mike still felt giddy as he pulled into the driveway.

The following day, the first half of his tour was rather dull. The only job he had to respond to was to adjudicate an argument in one of the shoe stores.

At his assigned time, Mike took his meal in the chicken restaurant. While inside, shooting the breeze with Gene, the manager, Mike glanced out the windows. He could not believe his eyes. Across the street someone set up a Monty game. The game was operating on the sidewalk against a tiled retaining wall that was part of the phone company's property. Midway along the wall was a stairway leading up from the sidewalk. At the top was a sitting area maintained by the phone company as a mini-park.

Mike immediately removed his uniform hat, leaving it with Gene and walked out of the restaurant. He hoped that by being hatless, he would be less noticeable to the game's lookouts. Mike did not look at the game as he headed across the avenue to Bryant Park. His intention was, if spotted, the games' operators would think that he was unaware of their presence and not run off. Once adjacent to the park, Mike continued south on 6th Avenue to 41st Street. He crossed back over and went directly into the phone building's main entrance. Once in the lobby, he approached two building security guards dressed in their natty blue blazers and enlisted their assistance.

"Afternoon guys. Would you men give me a hand with something?"

By their enthusiastic response Mike knew they were police buffs. Both men were younger than Mike and gave him the respectful, "Yes Sir, how can we help you Officer?"

"Well, there's a Three Card Monty game going full tilt on the 42nd Street side of your building, just below the rear sitting area. I'd like to arrest the dealer and grab as many of the game's operators as I can. There are usually at least two lookouts watching for cops. One is probably up on your wall as we speak. Do the street people run from you guys?"

"No, not at all. When we patrol outside, they completely ignore us."

The second man added, "I've even been standing in the sitting area and watched people smoking a joint. They don't drop it or snuff it out. It's almost like we're invisible.

But we have never seen anyone selling pot in the plaza. Maybe they think that's where we draw the line. If we did see a sale we would grab them and call for you guys. What do you need us to do?"

"Well, at least, I want to get the dealer. If you men have the time and are willing to help out, I would like you guys to walk around the corner and hopefully get the attention of the men running the game. Then, I'll drop off the wall and get the dealer if possible. If you can grab any others involved in the game like the lookouts, hold on to them and I'll take them too. I'm sure you men will recognize them by their actions once they see me. Before they try to run off, someone will probably yell, "Slide 'em up. Are you game for it?"

The response was as expected, "Sure. How do you want to work this?"

"As I said, you men walk around the corner, on the sidewalk towards the game. Don't hurry. Act as if you're outside of your building just killing time. Everyone involved in the game should watch you. As I told you, I'm going to drop down from the wall on the dealer. This is going to sound funny but like in the movies, take three minutes to get near the game. I should be ready by then. I'll drop down and grab the dealer. You guys grab the lookouts. Ok?"

One of the men asked, "What if they fight? Can we clock (hit) them?"

"They shouldn't. These guys will run like hell, they're not fighters. Grab anyone who you think is part of the game if you can. It should be pretty easy. The general public usually stays put to watch the show. Only the bad guys try to run. Just be careful and please try not to get hurt. If anyone fights, let them go."

As the two men left the building to begin their walk, Mike moved close to the door leading to the plaza. He could barely see the stairway leading to the sidewalk. What he could see was a man who was probably midway down the steps. Mike felt that he was a lookout and that concerned him. If the man was part of the game, an alert would be given before he could get into position. Three minutes had passed. Mike moved out on to the plaza. The man on the stairs paid him no mind. *I'm lucky,* he thought. As he drew nearer to the game, Mike was able to hear the usual banter of the dealer. He was not able to see the game.

"Pick the red queen folks. It's easy. Put down twenty. Find the queen and I pay you forty." He moved towards the sound. Luckily as he got to the edge of the wall, he was directly over the dealer.

As the man manipulated his cards, Mike jumped down behind him, putting his arm around the man's head as he landed on the sidewalk. Shocked, the dealer shouted, "What the fuck….," as his legs buckled beneath him.

There was pandemonium as people watching the game, one of two potential victims of the game and two lookouts, all broke in different directions.

One of the lookouts ran right into the two security guards and had his arms twisted behind him as the second guard shouted, "You're under arrest."

It was like a scene from a grade B movie, but Mike had two arrests. He always carried two sets of handcuffs, even in uniform. He handed one set off to the security guards. "Here you go. Have fun. Don't make them too tight."

The larger of the two guards looked at the nameplate on Mike's chest, and replied, "Thanks Romano. That was fun. Do you need our names and stuff?"

"Yes, as soon as I get transportation here, I'll get all your info." Mike withdrew his portable radio from its case and called for transportation, informing the dispatcher that he had two men under arrest and gave his location.

Mike was surprised to see the big green van belonging to the Conditions Unit pull to a stop where he was standing. Alan jumped out and laughing said, "Mike, I see they can't keep a good man down. Good going. Don't let the bosses get to you."

Mike put his defendants into the rear of the van. Between congratulations and teasing from his former team mates, he recorded the names and contact information of the two guards that assisted him. One of them could not contain his enthusiasm and asked, "Romano, Officer Romano, when can we do this again? We never had such fun."

Later, after processing his prisoners, Mike phoned Betty to tell her he had collared up and expected to be home before morning. The courts weren't crowded, he was home by midnight

***

On his way to post the next day, Mike made his usual stop at Sonny's finding his friend anxious to see him.

"I'm happy you stopped in early Mike. I have something you might be interested in. My contact in the mayors' office filtered some information down to me. The Department is about to make promotions and Dennis Bryan is not on the list." Sonny paused for effect before continuing. "I thought you'd like to know."

"Sonny, are you sure? That's great. Now I can use the info to harass the fat bastard."

"Yes. I'm sure you will Mike, knowing how much you love the guy. But be careful. Oh, my man also said that he would notify me each time future promotions are coming up and if Bryan is going to be on the list."

Mike was like a kid at Christmas. He gave Sonny a hug and thanked him two more times. The information had made his day. He could hardly wait to use his new weapon.

As Romano walked the block midway between Broadway and 6th Avenue, his portable radio crackled, "In the South, ten-thirty, assault in progress in front of 340 6th Avenue. Acknowledge, K"

Mike was still keyed up from his visit with Sonny and had excess energy to disperse. "South post ten will respond Central. Will check and advise, K"

He sprinted around the corner to find a small cheering crowd. They were watching two men who were fighting. Mike waded through the throng to reach the combatants. Before he reached the men, he was grabbed from behind by someone shouting, "Let them fight. Let them settle it."

Mike tried to shake the person off by swinging his arm as he continued toward the combatants. The man continued in a jeering tone, "The big bad cop is gonna make an arrest and stop our fun." The man would not let go of the back of Mike's jacket. Mike was instantly torn between giving his attention to the man behind him or continuing to reach the two fighting men. The wrong decision could get him hurt.

Suddenly, Mike felt his assailant's arm rise upward as if the man was being lifted off his feet. From somewhere behind Mike came, "Don't worry Romano, I got your back." It was Herman. The big man left his shop to assist.

Mike was still attempting to separate the combatants as a patrol car team screeched to the curb. As the men were separated with the assistance of the two additional cops, Mike turned to see Herman. He was holding his man by the back of his neck with his large right hand and with his left hand slipped under the man's pants belt, lifting the antagonist slightly off the ground and keeping him on his toes. The guy looked like a reluctant ballerina. He also looked very uncomfortable. Herman wasn't even breathing hard.

When all was sorted out, the two combatants filed complaint reports against each other for assault. They never told any of the officers why they were fighting. The patrol car team took their reports and closed each one out with "Complainant wishes no summary arrest at this time. 'Referred to court."

Mike, still enjoying the fruit of his earlier conversation with Sonny, had no desire to arrest the man Herman held. After some quick conversation, Mike filled out a "Stop and Frisk" report, a procedure required when detaining someone and no further action was taken. Mike noted the fight as a sidewalk argument and the reports subject as interfering with the adjudication. The report would also cover Mike's butt in case the civilian later filed an abuse complaint against him.

When everything was more or less back to normal, Mike entered the restaurant to thank Herman for his assistance.

"Herman, you may have saved my ass. Thanks. That guy looked like a little kid in your hands. Thanks again. Those sidewalk fights can get messy. Even without weapons."

"No problem. I told you Mike, I like cops in general and you have treated me better than most of them. You have a friend in me. I'd like you to know that I could always put in a good word for you with my Fire Island friend. He's an Assistant Chief. Some people in the job don't like him because he's tough. They gave him the nickname of Terrible Terri. Terri is his last name."

"Thanks Herman. Maybe someday I'll take you up on the offer." *Fire Island is for the very rich and a secluded homosexual hangout reachable only by ferry. Wonder if the Chief and Herman are a couple?*

After the early sidewalk incident, the balance of Mikes' patrol tour went easily, but to Mike, it seemed to last forever. He was anxious to visit Bryan and use his new information to upset the man.

When the end of Mike's work day finally arrived, the first thing he did was to look for Dennis Bryan. Finding his office empty, Mike checked with the desk officer and was assured that Bryan was present and somewhere in the building.

Before continuing to look for Bryan, Mike went to his locker and changed out of his uniform. Leaving the locker room, he began to slowly walk through the hallways of all three floors of the station house, hoping to run into Bryan. He had no luck and resigned himself to the possibility that he could not harass his CO until the following day. Mike knew that there was one last chance to see Bryan that day. If he left the building thru the front doors, he had to pass the Pumpkin's office and he might get lucky.

As Mike crossed the lobby in front of the Desk, he became elated. The door to Bryan's office was open and he heard the man inside on the telephone. Mike stopped as if he was reading some notices posted on the wall near the office door and waited for the Great Pumpkin to get off the phone. The wait was short.

Walking up to the doorway, Mike rapped on the doorjamb, "Inspector, are you in there?"

"Romano. What brings you here? Make another bribery arrest?" he asked sarcastically.

"No. I just wanted to tell you that some bosses are getting promoted next week."

The Pumpkin responded, "Oh. You came to wish me luck. That's nice of you considering our situation." Once again he was twisting Mike's shorts.

Mike now moved in for the kill. "No Inspector, not at all. I'm here to tell you that you are not getting promoted. Thought you should know. Have a good day." He flamboyantly spun on his heel and left the doorway.

From inside the office came an irritated, "What the hell are you talking about. Come back here. That's an order."

Mike returned. Careful not to actually enter the office, he remained in the doorway. "Just telling you that I know you are not getting promoted in the next group. That's all."

"First of all how would you know that? Secondly, why come in here to tell me?"

"I'll tell you why, because, I can. You put me, a good cop, someone who did you a personal favor, who worked the conditions unit so well that it got a write up in New York Magazine, through changes. So I figure that when I could, I would return the favor, and now I could." Mike's angel wings were fluttering like mad at that point.

"Be careful Romano. I'll remind you again that I command this precinct. I'm your boss and I can transfer you out of here in a heartbeat or keep you here and make your life here a living hell." Bryan was bright red and beginning to shake now.

The big man continued with spittle flying out of his mouth, "When I go to those cursed merchant association meetings, there is nothing but praise given to you. That store owner, Sonny something or other, says that forming the association was your idea. Thanks for giving me another pain in the ass. You're beginning to push too hard Romano."

Mike continued, "Do what you think is best." He couldn't resist the urge to twist the verbal knife, "Just remember the garage incident. My records of that fiasco are terrific, if I say so myself. How could you explain it?"

I'm going over the edge now. Gotta get out of here before it gets out of hand, he thought. Mike knew he said enough. It was time to leave the building.

"Have a nice day."

Bryan bellowed, "Careful Romano. Don't screw up. I'm watching you."

Mike left the building a happy man. He had twisted the Great Pumpkin's balls to the point that he was probably spitting seeds on his desk.

***

It was three weeks after Mike's tit for tat with Bryan before he received the news that most of the store owners on his new posts had officially joined the existing merchants association. Mike continued to make arrests for possession of marijuana and promoting gambling (Three Card Monty). He was racking up many hours of overtime.

Once again, he was summoned to Bryan's office. Mike thought, *its open warfare now. It was only a matter of time before he called me in. Here we go.* Casually approaching the office door, he asked, "Inspector, you sent for me?" as he crossed the threshold.

The conversation was not what Mike expected. Bryan began with, "You have been making too many misdemeanor arrests on your post. You have been racking up too much overtime and the Borough Command has noticed it. From now on you are to only make felony arrests. Do you understand?"

Mike wished he had a tape recorder running. "Are you telling me not to make arrests for minor crimes? You're telling me not to do my job? Did I hear you correctly? You're telling me to disregard my oath of office? You, Deputy Inspector Dennis Bryan, the Precinct Commander, is telling me to ignore crimes committed in my presence. Did I hear you correctly?"

Without waiting for a response, Mike decided to shift gears and tried to soften the questions he just spewed at Bryan. Softly he continued, "You claim that you gave me those three posts because I could do the job. Well, how do you expect me to keep the merchants happy and to keep order, if I don't make minor quality of life arrests? That's the only kind of crimes that usually occur out there. Didn't the Conditions Unit start because the Mayor wanted to rid the area of those types of crimes? Correct me if I'm wrong."

Bryan cautiously answered, "Romano, don't be a smart ass with me. I'm not telling you not to do your job or make arrests. I'm telling you that when you call for transportation and bring the man in, a sergeant will assign another officer to the collar. He will process it and bring the man downtown. That will cut your overtime and lower my budget a little. That is how you will work from now on. Got it?"

"Sure Inspector." Mike was already planning a way around Dennis' latest order. Mike would carefully elevate each crime committed to a felony if at all possible. Of course he could always use the catch all phrase, "Defendant made statements to arresting officer", to get to the District Attorney's complaint room. With that statement, another officer could not bring the arrest downtown because the writing Assistant District Attorney would need to hear the statement directly from the arresting officer and record it on the initial affidavit. If the assigned officer told him it was second hand, the statement was considered hearsay, and could not be admitted as viable evidence.

Mike was ready to leave and thought the conversation was over. It wasn't.

"Oh, Romano. You have gained more admirers. Besides the merchants on the Apple, those on your new post also joined that damn association you started."

"Yes Inspector, I know all about it. Pretty cool isn't it? Can I go to work now?" Wanting to tie yet another knot in Bryan's shorts, Mike smiled and added, "My people await me."

Mike's last remark must have twisted Bryan's shorts around his gonads because his next remark was clearly threatening. "Remember Romano. I'm watching you, closely. Right now I can't transfer you because it might cause too much trouble from the Association, but some day you're going to make a mistake. I'll be there to kick you in the ass. Now get the hell out of my office."

Mike was grinning like the Cheshire cat in Alice in Wonderland, as he turned away to leave. The Great Pumpkin was unnerved.

***

On his way out to post, Mike made his usual stop at Sonny's store. It had become routine. Sonny, always interested in any exchanges between Mike and Dennis Bryan, chuckled at commander.

After Mike finished, Sonny said, "By the way Mike, there will be promotions again at the end of this month. Dennis is not included."

Mike, more curious than ever about his friend's source asked, "Sonny, how can you keep such close tabs on Bryan? Is your hook (connection) in the Mayor's Office that good?"

Sonny smiled, "Well Mike, when you get an award and you're on the Mayoral Advisory Committee, you can check these things." He did not elaborate. "It's enough to say that I can."

"Yeah, thank you for the info. Now I can break his balls again in a couple of days while he's still shaking from this morning's conversation."

Sonny added, "Mike, I might have a surprise for you in a week or so. You're going to enjoy it."

"What kind of surprise Sonny. You know I won't take any gifts. No disrespect meant"

"None taken. You are going to like this one. I'll give you a hint. Dennis Bryan is sure not to like it. How's that? Is that kind of gift OK?"

"I love it. I'm looking forward to it. Let me go now. Have to see the shop owners on my posts and thank them for joining the association. Thanks"

Mike left Sonny's and went directly to his foot post. He had made quick stops in each store, thanking it's proprietor for joining the association. As he approached midblock, he saw a tow truck hooking up a small refrigerated delivery truck in front of the chicken restaurant. The restaurant manager, Gene, was on the sidewalk with paperwork in his hand. He spotted Mike and waved for him to hurry over. The driver had just been inside making a delivery and was having an argument with the tow truck operator, who in turn, was asking a meter maid to call the police to arrest the deliveryman for interfering with his tow.

Mike approached and said, "Now folks, let's just calm down, and one at a time explain what this is all about." He pointed to the meter maid and said, "You first Miss."

"Well you see officer; I'm assigned to 42nd Street between Broadway and 5th Avenue. This truck is parked in a no parking zone. I wrote him a summons and ordered a tow. The driver is threatening us."

"Ok, now let's hear from the deliveryman please," pointing to the driver.

While this conversation was going on, the tow driver had finished hooking up the truck. Slowly, Mike maneuvered himself in front of the tow truck. The delivery driver began to smile as he said, "Listen. I just made a delivery inside. There's the manager. He can verify that. I was here less than ten minutes. Writing a ticket is one thing, but towing the truck is crazy. There's food in the back to boot. By the time I get the truck back, the stuff inside will be worthless."

Mike walked over to the tow driver and shook his head. "You will put that truck back on its wheels please. Now!"

The driver was shocked. "You can't tell me that. She wrote a summons and called for the tow."

"First of all, I can tell you. This driver is working and a Police Officer supersedes the posted signs and any traffic regulations that exist when he is on the scene. Now if you don't unhook the truck, I will lock you up for disregarding a lawful order of a police officer. Do I make myself clear?"

The meter maid chimed in, "You can't do that. This is my post."

Mike was getting annoyed, "Now listen little lady, I am a police officer, you are a traffic agent. My powers go beyond yours and I don't get a kickback from the tow driver when I write a summons so he can hook a tow and get paid. Do you understand me? Do you have anything else to say?"

Mike was referring to an unproven rumor that the private tow company contracted by the City to work in midtown Manhattan, paid a bounty to the drivers for each vehicle brought in. The drivers in turn gave a piece of their money to the meter maids for writing a summons, thus authorizing a tow. Mike had even observed a traffic agent get out of a tow truck to write a summons. In his mind that was all the proof he needed to believe the rumor because he knew that the meter maids were not assigned to a specific truck nor authorized to ride in tow trucks.

In response to Mike's chastising remarks, the meter maid began to pace the pavement and mutter.

Mike stood in front of her to stop her movement and tore into her, "You will not come on this block and write summonses when you see me here. This is my block. If you have any problems with that, go and tell your supervisor to come and see me. Now please leave my post and take the hook with you."

Gene began the cadence of a slow applause. Several onlookers had gathered during that exchange and joined in. In New York City, everyone disliked meter maids.

The next couple of hours progressed rather slowly until an employee of Adult Show; a peep show shop located next to the office supply store, came running across the street to Mike, shouting as he ran.

"Listen officer, there's going to be trouble inside the show in a minute. You have to come right away."

Mike responded, "Easy man. Let's go I'm right behind you", and sprinted thru traffic with the man. As he mounted the sidewalk, Mike notified the radio dispatcher, "Apple post sixteen to Central, K".

"Post sixteen, what's your message? K".

"Post sixteen is responding to a pickup (called into service by civilian on the scene) dispute inside 154 West 42nd Street. Will check and advise. K."

"Post sixteen, ten-four, K."

Once inside the premises, Romano saw two men arguing. One of the men, obviously a customer, had his adversary by the shirt sleeve and was threatening to punch him in the face.

Mike stepped up to the two men. Upon seeing the police officer, the man being held spoke, “Officer, I know you. You’re the steady foot man. Please tell this guy to let me go. He stole from us and I want him arrested.”

Mike spoke, “Sir, let go of the man or I will arrest you. For emphasis he added in a stern loud voice, “Now.”

The “customer” was quick to respond and instantly released his grip. The man was well groomed and in casual business attire. He looked like an office worker.

“Now. You first,” Mike said pointing to the shop employee.

“Well, this guy comes in here sometimes. I’ve seen him before. He gets tokens and goes into one of the booths to look at the girls. You know how it works. Put the coin in and the shade goes up. She does her thing and if you want to see more, you gotta put more coins in. We also have a slot that the people can use to tip the girls. The slot is for bills. It doesn’t work the shade. Anything put into the tip slot drops directly into a box on the girls’ side.”

The customer started shouting, “I tip the girl, always. Just ask her. I don’t cheat. I’ll kick your ass in front of the cop. I don’t care that he’s here.”

Mike turned his attention to the loudmouth. “Shut up or I’ll kick your ass.”

Quickly the man held his hands up and replied, “Okay, okay.”

Mike then addressed the employee, “So, now tell me what the problem is.”

"Officer, whenever this guy comes in, at the end of the day, we find slugs in the box where the tokens go. It's inside the girls' side of the booth next to their tip slot. We don't know what's there until the end of the day when we empty the boxes. Today, the girl saw him put slugs into the window slot."

The customer shouted, "I did not. That was someone else. She's full of crap because she pulled her G-string off and expected a bigger tip. She's lying."

Mike was getting annoyed at the guy, "Listen, I'm not going to tell you again. Shut up. You'll get your turn to tell your side of the story."

"Now, what's your name anyway?" he asked the employee.

"Tim, Tim Johnson."

"Ok Tim. Now explain how the girl saw him put slugs into the slot. Then I want to see it for myself."

"Well, they usually can't see what goes into the token box, but in his booth, the one he was in, on the inside where she is, the cover of the catch box is missing. She saw the slugs fall and used the phone to call me. We have phones hooked up to call for help and stuff. Not really a phone, more like an intercom."

Mike answered, "Ok. Just as soon as I get another cop here, I want to see the booth and the token box. Everybody remain calm."

Romano called the dispatcher, "Apple post sixteen to Central. Please send one car to the location for assistance. No emergency, K."

"Post sixteen, what's the condition? K"

"Just need some help finding something in this location. No emergency, K"

Mike's call was heard by sector Edward. Before the dispatcher officially put the call out, there was a response, "South Edward heard and will respond to the location Central. Advise as to the location, K"

Mike responded with, "Edward, South post sixteen is

requesting assistance is 154 W.42nd Street and present on the scene. No emergency"

The responding team answered, "Central, put South Edward out at that location. We will advise, K"

When the accused customer heard the radio conversation, he became belligerent. "What the hell is going on? Are you going to arrest me for something?"

He began to sway back and forth as he spoke, "The big tough cop wants to go in the back and look at the token box. Bullshit. Are you sure that's the only box you want to look at? You want to see the girls for free? Is that how you get your kicks?"

Mike was getting more and more annoyed. In his mind, he was formulating a reason to arrest the man. *This shithead is going downtown. I could care less about the girls. Betty makes them look like little boys. Right now all I have him on is "Theft of Services" for using the slugs. Bryan will make me assign the collar. Screw him too, the guy is making statements.*

Turning to the irate man, Mike asked, "Do you want to be arrested? What's your name anyway? Keep breaking my balls and I'll arrest you just for the fun of running you down to court and through the system. You're probably on your lunch hour and you'll lose your job when you don't go back to work. Is that what you want?"

Mike was still admonishing the man, when Joe Pinto and Lowery walked in, "Hey, Mike, long time no see. What do you have here?"

Romano quickly related the incident as he understood it and asked Pinto if one or both of them would detain the customer while he went to the rear of the show area with the employee. He wanted to see the broken token box in question.

"Sure Mike, will do," Lowery answered as he and Pinto moved the man into a corner.

Pinto shouted to Mike, "Hey, the guy's name is John Skipper; he works at the phone company."

Mike and the complainant went to the rear of the premises. There was a large, wall enclosed area that acted as a dressing room for the girls. Within the confines of the room were several small desks that served as dressing tables, or undressing tables for that matter. There were three girls present, all naked except for G-strings.

Mike asked, "Which one of you girls saw the man put slugs into the token slot?"

"I'm the one officer", said a small chesty blonde. *She was probably cute at one time,* thought Mike*; she looks a little shop worn now. Maybe the poor kid is on drugs. Well, at least she's not on the street hooking for a living.*

"Which window were you working? I would like to see the broken token box and the slugs. Did you remove them?"

"No officer. Tim told me he would call for a cop and to leave them in the box. Come, I'll show you". She started to walk to the far side of the room. Pushing a curtain aside, Mike and Tim followed the girl into the center working area. It was heavily perfumed and had two bistro chairs and a sofa in the center.

Around the perimeter were eight windows separated by partitions alongside each of the viewing area windows, allowing the girls some privacy as they earned their tips. Every cubicle allowed a full view of the center. The center stage area, if one could call it that, was painted a lime green.

Attached to the perimeter wall, just under each viewing window were two small black wooden boxes. One box was marked TIPS with a slot above it. On the opposite side of the window the boxes were not marked, they were for the tokens and controlled the screen. Mike followed the girl to cubicle number 4 and saw that the token box had no top on it.

Mike peered into the open top and saw what looked like slugs on top of several of the shops' tokens. He asked Tim to reach in and remove the slugs.

Once back in the main shop area, Mike informed the customer, "Listen, I believe everything that this man says and you are going to be arrested for Theft of Services.

The customer was about to object. Mike waved him off and continued, "You received services, viewing pleasure and did not pay for it. You used slugs and not store bought tokens to watch the girl."

Mike further explained that the charge was a misdemeanor and if he qualified after investigation, he could be given a Vera Summons (a desk appearance ticket) at the station house. Skipper would be allowed to go to court on his own in twenty eight days.

Pinto turned to Mike, "Mike we'll transport you and this guy soon as you're ready."

"Thanks, cuff him for me, will you?"

From the time Pinto and Lower y walked in until that instant, the customer had remained silent except to give his name when asked for it. Now his mouth began to run.

He had not yet been secured and approached Romano while speaking rapidly, "What the hell are you guys doing? Hey, Mr. Tough guy, Mike is it? " Did you get a hand job while you were back there and you're paying for it by arresting me?"

Romano did not answer him. He reached out, snatching Skipper's right arm and twisted it behind his back. At that point, the highly agitated John Skipper turned his head around and spit right into Mike's face, simultaneously reaching back with his right leg and catching Mike in the groin with his foot.

Mike could only grunt and twist his assailant to face him head on. He then punched Skipper square in the mouth drawing blood. Pinto and Lowery quickly grabbed the man as Mike shook off the pain he felt between his legs. Handcuffs were applied quickly and with great vigor. Skipper whimpered and whined.

"Now, Mr. Smartass, felony assault on a police officer will be added to your charges. Now you go thru the system. Mike turned to his cousin, "Pinto could you take him out to the car and wait for me? I need some information from Tim before we go in."

"Sure Mike. We'll go when you're ready. We'll notify Central that you have one under. Take your time." They took Skipper outside.

Mike recorded the girl's information as witness to the crime and all other pertinent information he could obtain from Tim, listing both parties as witness to the assault against him. He also took the slugs and one token giving Tim a hand written receipt for the items. They would be evidence to substantiate the crime.

Once in the arrest processing room, Mike scratched his initials into the slugs and the token for identification purposes. He prepared vouchers, an arrest report and had Emergency Medical Services respond to the station house for the injury to Skipper. After he was cleaned up, Skipper chose to refuse further treatment. Mike would notify the booking officer downtown of the injury with the appropriate paper work.

On the arrest report, Mike entered the following in the circumstances of arrest section, "The defendant did assault the arresting officer by kneeing him in the groin and while attempting to bite officer's hand did cause injury to his own mouth. Justifiable force used."

Mike then phoned Betty to tell her he would be home late. He was going on overtime with a new arrest. He had just beaten Dennis again.

***

After processing Skipper thru the court system, Mike returned home for only four hours. It was enough time for only a quick nap and an even quicker shower. There was no time to spend with his family.

Mike returned to work the following day tired and grumpy and could not wait to get to post, find a corner in Herman's restaurant and relax. When roll call was completed, he headed directly for the exit door. He was just about to push it open when he heard, "Romano, get in here. That's an order." It was Dennis Bryan.

Mike cringed and thought, *Not now you moron. I'm not in the mood to play games with you.* "Yes Inspector. I'm on my way."

As he walked into Bryan's office, Mike was greeted with, "You think you're cute Romano, don't you? I've been informed that you made another arrest yesterday. You charged an assault against your person. Was it? You took a simple dispute and elevated it into a felony arrest. You think you can compete with me? Think that you can disregard my orders, do you? Well, I'm letting you know, that I'm watching you closely. You have no idea how closely. I have no idea why you insist on bucking me. I was good to you. You screwed up your cushy detail yourself because you think you're smarter than the next guy. But, I'll tell you this, someday I'm going to nail you if you keep busting my balls. My experience and rank far surpass yours. Walk with caution. One day you're going to make an error, like break a Department regulation. On that day, I'm going to have you. If I only transfer you, you'll be lucky. Have anything to say, you arrogant shit?"

Mike was no longer weary. The sound of angel wings fluttered in his head. "Yes Inspector, I do have something to say.

"The next promotions will be announced soon. You're not on the list again. Have a good day."

With a snappy improper salute, Mike spun on his heal and walked out. He expected to hear Bryan bellow again. There was only silence. Mike left the building feeling better and proceeded to his foot post with a spring in his step.

***

Once on post, Mike had made his one full round of his post, then crossed over to Bryant Park on the South East side of 42nd Street. He was bored and thought he would try his hand at issuing a summons or two for marijuana smoking in the park. Bryant Park is located directly behind the famed Fifth Avenue Library. It covers the entire block from 42nd Street to 41st Street and halfway up to 5th Avenue. There was always some kind of action there.

As he entered the park, Mike spotted a few members of his old Conditions Unit working the park. Out of courtesy, he did an about face and left the park walking back across 42nd and into the Lobby of 55 West, a large office building. He had decided that he would remain out of sight for at least fifteen minutes to allow his old friends to do what they do.

To relieve his boredom, Mike was peering out of the glass front of the building watching the world pass by and saw one of his old team mates, Danny Glen, chasing a black man coming from the direction of the front of the library. The guy's flowing dread locks were flapping in the wind. Danny was running behind the man and favoring his left leg. It was apparent he would never catch the man without some help. Both men were coming in his direction.

It appeared that they would probably cross the street in close proximity to him. From his vantage point, Mike saw no other men assisting Danny and doubted that they were even aware of the foot race. Mike quickly exited the lobby and secreted himself alongside a concrete pillar under the entrance overhang. He peered around at the street, determining the proper time to intercept Mr. Dread Locks. Mike came out of hiding too soon. The man spotted him, spun an about face and headed back into traffic.

Mike lost his hat as he launched himself into the street in hot pursuit and attempted to cut around two cars to get ahead of the man. The guy anticipated Mike's move and headed back towards 55 West. The runner obviously knew that if he could get into the building lobby, he could run thru the doors that opened onto w. 43rd Street and hopefully lose his pursuers. Mike spun about, bumped off a taxi cab and continued chasing the man. Romano did not know that Danny had stopped running to nurse his left leg.

As the man's stride brought him to the sidewalk, Mike accelerated, determined to stop him before he gained access to the building. He was now within a few feet of the man. Just as the runner was about to reach a small door alongside the lobby's revolving door, Mike gave it all he had and lunged at the man.

Mike grabbed the man's flowing locks with his left hand and the guy's flailing right arm with his right hand. Both men were off balance at that point. Mike was trying to steer the man away from the doorway. Their forward momentum added force to Mike's maneuver. He saw a concrete wall coming at them yet did not let go of his man.

The sound of Dread Locks face hitting the wall made Mike cringe. The man slid down the wall as if he was made out of hot wax. Mike quickly dropped down next to him and applied handcuffs. With a thick West Indian accent, the man shouted every foul word known to mankind.

As Mike began to lift the arrestee to his feet, he saw the large crescent shaped cut on the left side of the man's face. There would be one hell of a scar. He also recognized the man and was especially pleased he did not get away.

Several months before, when Romano was still in his beloved plainclothes detail, the Conditions Unit was engaged in a big push to rid Bryant Park of drug dealers. Mike had grabbed a couple selling pills to the lunchtime crowd. The woman was pushing an infant in a carriage and secreted the contraband under the baby's mattress.

When he brought the couple over to the van for detention, Sergeant Castro, who was present supervising the operation, told him to only formerly arrest one of the couple and make a Stop and Frisk Report on the other. Castro felt it was not in the interest of the unit to have to worry about placing the infant in the system while the parents went to jail.

Mike could not believe his ears when the woman volunteered that she would make the trip downtown and that her husband should go home with the baby and arrange for an attorney. It upset Mike that a man would allow his wife to go thru the system while he went home. At the time, Mike told her husband, identified as Stanley Livingston, that he would get him again someday and put him thru the court system.

Today was that day.

Danny was now hobbling up to Mike, and another prisoner was being escorted by Barry and Wendell. Barry was carrying three shopping bags. Wendell was holding Danny up.

Danny spoke first, "Mike thanks for catching him. I got hurt jumping down off the plaza in front of the library. When I told him he was under arrest, he slapped me in the face and took off running before I could cuff him. He jumped down off the plaza, so I thought, 'what the hell, I can do it too.' Well, I obviously didn't do it as well as he did."

As he spoke he turned to look at Stanley and saw the now crimson flow oozing from the cut, "Wow, he ran into something. What did you hit him with Mike?"

"I hit him with the building. Actually he hit himself. We were going so fast when I caught him, he struck the building. Anyway, he's all yours. What's in the bags?"

Wendell answered, "Must be ten or fifteen pounds of marijuana in here. I think this guy is going to jail."

Mike could not resist the impulse to turn to Stanley and ask, "Hey Stanley, do you remember when you sent your wife to court and you went home? Look at me, I promised to get you again and send you to jail. Have a nice time."

Stanley only looked wide eyed at Mike, obviously remembering, and said, "Man, take me to a hospital. I'm bleeding bad."

Mike replied, "Talk to your arresting officer Stanley, I only caught you. You belong to one of these guys. They'll take care of you."

Danny thanked Mike again and said, "Mike, you're still a team player. I'll put you down for the assist. Thanks again."

The Conditions men took Stanley away and Mike went back to his post.

Chapter Sixteen

Just before his meal hour, Mike was visited on post by Lieutenant Armini and he was driving alone in a marked patrol car. Romano knew something unusual was about to happen because Bryan insisted that Armini always walk the command. Mike saw Armini in a patrol car only twice since he had been assigned to The South.

Remaining seated in the auto, slightly excited, Armini began, "Mike, I came across something unusual and want a good, trustworthy uniform man with me. Are you up for going to Brooklyn?"

"Go with you Lou? Sure. What's going on?"

"You know Larry Frend in the Pussy Posse (Prostitute Unit). He needs help arresting some people in Brooklyn. The complainant, one of the girls he regularly locks up, plies her trade in our command and says she was raped and held prisoner by four cops at gun point in Brooklyn. She claims that the bad guys are in the Brooklyn apartment now and might have other women there as we speak. Larry came to me, I came to you. I'll fill you in on the way over."

"Ready. Let's go. Will you cover me for leaving post? You know Bryan wants my ass."

Armini responded with, "South day Lieutenant to Central, K"

"Day Lieutenant, what's your message? K"

"South Lieutenant and South foot post 16 will be 10-62 out of service for the balance of the tour on special assignment. Acknowledge? K"

"Central acknowledges your message and will take you and foot post out of service, K"

"Get in Mike. You're going to like this. We'll pick up some men from Larry's unit at the station house before we head out. Here's what's going on."

As he put the car into gear, Armani began, "Larry knows many of the prostitutes by their first names. He's got the most collars in the unit. The regular girls, the repeat collars, have come to sort of trust him. They feel he's fair and doesn't abuse them by asking for favors, if you know what I mean. Anyway, a prostitute came up to him earlier today and told him that she was tortured by four white plainclothes cops in Brooklyn. She says that she and other girls were picked up, sometimes two at a time here in the South, transported to Brooklyn, to an apartment and kept there for the cops' sexual pleasure."

Mike couldn't believe his ears. The Lieutenant continued,

"She also claims they're being tortured. The girl states that they are kept naked and chained to a bed for a week or more until the men tire of them. They are then replaced with new girls and the guys threaten them to keep quiet about their abduction before letting them go. She says she was burned with cigarettes on her breasts and other body parts. Apparently, she felt comfortable enough with Larry to flip her boobs out and show him the marks. He said they sure looked like cigarette burns and believes her story."

Mike only said, "Holy crap. Do you think it's really cops doing this? Brooklyn cops, taking girls from Manhattan and keeping them in Brooklyn? They probably think if someone hears about it from whores, they won't believe the story."

"Don't know Mike, but Larry sure does and is waiting for us. Her name is Sandra Lewis. I spoke to her only to verify what she told Larry and to confirm her identity. She adamantly swears the story is true and she would go thru the entire court process to nail the guys. You know from your time in plainclothes that the street girls are a fountain of information if they like you. They apparently like Larry."

The lieutenant parked on the street behind the station house several doors away from the actual rear of the station. To Mike it appeared that his boss wanted to keep their possible excursion to Brooklyn quiet. Romano had not said a word during the ride to the station house. In response to Mike's silence, Armini tapped Mike's arm to get his attention, smiled and said, "By the way, I did not ask to see the burn marks."

"Mike, stay in the car and wait for me. I'm going inside to get Larry and his guys and have them meet us on Tenth Avenue behind the bus terminals. Then we go to Brooklyn."

Romano was keyed up the whole time his lieutenant was gone. He wanted to get the men that he believed were bad cops. Mike tried to imagine the women's pain and humiliation. Angel wings fluttered inside his head. His heart pounded. It was ten minutes before Armini returned to the car.

"Ok Mike. We'll follow Larry with one man and the girl, another team in another unmarked car will follow us. The girl didn't know the address so, she has to come along. She says that she took a taxi from somewhere near the Brooklyn piers to the Apple, went directly to the substation and asked for Larry. This kind of thing usually goes to IAD, but because it is supposed to be happening now, as we speak, I'm not waiting. I want these criminals, especially if they are cops. There will be no notifications to dispatch until collars are made. Not a word. Got that? Complete radio silence. You can keep your radios' volume on low, but no transmissions unless your own life is in danger. Understand? Sandra claims they have a police radio in their car and one in the apartment."

"10-4 Boss, will comply. Thanks for taking me along."

Armini called the dispatcher, "South Lieutenant is still 10-62 out of service, K"

"10-4 South Lieutenant. Out of service, K"

Larry led them thru the Brooklyn Battery Tunnel, exiting the highway in Brooklyn Heights near the piers. The area was mostly brownstones and small apartment buildings and was becoming gentrified with many buildings undergoing restorations. The ethnicity of the neighborhood was seventy percent white and the balance racially mixed. Four rogue cops could easily get lost in the mixture.

Once on the local streets, Armini waved the two unmarked cars over to a gas station. "Listen, Larry, you and the girl cruise the neighborhood and locate the apartment. When you find it, come back and get us. Also let us know the proper address and make sure you have the right apartment. Then, we'll all go back and take the place. Remember, no radios. Now take off."

For fifteen minutes Armini and his men sat in the gas station anxiously waiting for Larry to return.

Mike asked, "Hey Lou, do you think we're in the right neighborhood?"

As if in response to the question, Larry's car rocketed into the driveway and bounced to a stop. Larry popped out of the vehicle and ran up to the lieutenant, "We got it Lou. Sandra is sure of it. She even said that the car they used to transport her is parked on the block. We looked inside and there is a police scanner and a CB Set. Boss, that CB set makes me think that they might be police impersonators. Sandra says the apartment is on the top floor. She remembers red curtains on the windows. We saw the curtains. It's a small five story apartment house."

Armini asked, "Approaching the apartment, do we pass the car first?"

"Yeah Loo we will. It's about one hundred feet before the building as we drive down the block. The street is one way. Why, planning something?"

"Yes, one of you will give the car two flats by letting the air out of the front tires. I don't want it to disappear any time soon." Before they left the gas station, Armini formulated a tactical plan and instructed everyone as to what was expected of them.

Larry led the little caravan to the apartment building, first stopping at the subject's auto to indicate which one was the subject car. He continued to the building. The suspect's auto was a black four door Chevy Impala and to an untrained eye could pass for an unmarked police car. The lieutenant slowed his auto to a crawl to get a good look at the car.

While they were still moving, Mike jumped out and bled the air out of the two front tires. He was itching to begin the action and didn't wait for orders. Romano caught up as Armini parked at a hydrant about fifty feet from the target building. The unmarked cars were double parked; the public would pay them no mind because double parking was a common occurrence on Brooklyn streets.

Once in front of the apartment house, Armini noted the address 425 Nelson Street, and description of the building in his memo book.

It was a small five story brick apartment building. The building entrance was slightly above sidewalk level and had an ornate grill covering a large glass panel in the center of the door.

Four steps led to a small landing in front of the entrance door. The building looked as if it was once a fine place to live. Whoever owned the property kept it in good repair. Armini signaled for everyone to gather at the entrance. Sandra would be useful to get someone to open the apartment door once they got inside.

The building's entrance door was locked; however, it appeared to have a slam type lock on it. Slam locks are designed to allow a door to close and deny access to anyone without a key. Armini was prepared with a stainless steel tool used for slipping slam locks, a process called loiding. Most active, experienced cops can open those types of doors after a little effort. Armini did it in three seconds. One man, Tom Delaney, was instructed to remain outside under the apartment's windows.

Once inside the building, the group quietly climbed the four flights of stairs to the top floor. Sandy pointed to the apartment door that the "Cops" occupied. Muffled sounds of conversation could be heard.

Armini took a position just to the left of the doorway, on the hinged side, and motioned for Sandy to stand behind him. Mike and Larry were on the right side of the doorway, just out of sight. The last man, Doug, stood next Armini.

Once everyone was positioned, Armini signaled Sandy to knock on the door and announce herself. She knocked and called out, "Hey, it's me Sandy. Let me in I left something inside that I need. My mother gave it to me."

From inside a male voice shouted, "Shut up", to person or persons within the apartment. The same voice spoke again, "Who the hell is Sandy and what do you want?"

Armini was studying the lock on the door. It had slam lock and a deadbolt. The deadbolt clicked. Hearing the click, Armini moved Sandy aside and motioned for her to crouch down and remain where she was. He then crashed into the door with his shoulder. It almost buckled. He hit it again and it flew open. Guns drawn, the four cops rushed thru the doorway and into the apartment. They were standing in, what should have been a living room or the like. Two men in their underwear stood with their eyes wide open in disbelief.

Both of them began to chatter unintelligibly and threw their hands over their heads. Across the room, to the left was a double bed with a naked girl spread eagled on top, apparently tied in some manner. Next to her, propped against the bed, was a single barreled shotgun. Larry lunged for it. Later, the cops found out that it was not loaded.

In addition to the bed, there was a kitchen table, three chairs, and a small sofa. To the right was a small kitchen.

It took seconds for Doug and Mike to handcuff the two men. They almost knocked Armini over as they raced to the men.

Sandy, unable to remain outside, rushed in and ran to the girl on the bed. “Alice, we’re here. You’re safe now.” Stroking her face she continued, “These cops are gonna lock up the bad cops, put them in jail and throw away the key.”

Sandy then yanked the pillow from under the girl’s head, startling her, and threw the bed pillow over the naked girl’s torso in an effort to ease her emotional pain. Without turning around, she shouted, “Will someone get her off this bed so she can get dressed.”

The young woman on the bed appeared to be only nineteen or twenty years old. Her arms and legs were fastened to the four corners of the bed with handcuffs. There were some visible signs of physical abuse on her body.

Only about five seconds had passed since the team entered the apartment and both men were already in handcuffs and standing against a wall. Sandy turned around, saw them secured and ran up to one of them kneeing him in the groin. She was headed to the second one when Mike grabbed her in a bear hug, lifting her off her feet and pulling her away from the moaning deviate.

After securing a promise that she would remain calm, Armini ordered Mike to release her.

From behind a closed door a female shouted, “Help. Help, don’t leave me here. I’m in here, in the bedroom.”

Larry, after checking the shotgun, handed it to Mike and cautiously opened the door to where the girl was. Sitting on the edge of yet another bed, in a slouched position, was a beautiful blonde girl. Her right hand was handcuffed to the left bed frame, causing her to be most comfortable only while laying belly down on the bed. She too was stark naked. Realizing she was about to be rescued, her nakedness embarrassed her and she tried to hide her womanhood by twisting herself in an attempt to lay face down. There was nothing on the bed that she could use to cover herself with.

Larry, while trying not to stare, spoke, "Easy miss, we're here to help you. Where are your clothes?"

"They keep the clothes that we wore when they took us in one of the dresser drawers. The one painted red in the corner. Please give me something to put on."

Larry retrieved some articles of clothing from the dresser and spread them across her much too attractive backside to hide her shame. With his arms fully extended, as if he didn't trust himself, Larry began removing her handcuffs as Armini came into the room.

The Lieutenant tried to break the tension with, "Stop shaking Larry, she won't bite", then keyed the radio that he was holding, "South Lieutenant to Central, K."

"Central here Lieutenant. What's your condition? Still out on special assignment?"

Armini then gave their location and status. "Central, this unit is at 425 Nelson Street in Brooklyn. Top floor apartment number two. Acknowledge? K"

"South Lieutenant. Did I hear correctly? You're in Brooklyn? K"

"South Lieutenant to Central. That is correct. Please send an ambulance to treat aided victims and two local sector cars for transportation of prisoners. We have two under arrest. No emergency. I repeat no emergency, K"

"Central to South Lieutenant, acknowledged. Will have bus (ambulance) and two local sectors respond, K"

Once the call for assistance was made, Armini directed his men to look around the apartment for anything that could be used as evidence. Tom, who had been covering the windows, heard the call and came up into the apartment.

"LT, I heard the call to Central and came up." His eyes were everywhere; the girls, who were getting dressed with their backs to the men, the shotgun, the two prisoners. "What can I do?"

"Help Mike cuff these men to the bed so we can move around while we wait for backup. Make sure they can't leave the bed either."

With the prisoners basically immobilized, Armini and his men looked around the apartment. The three women remained in the bedroom and sat down on the other bed, clinging to each other. All were sobbing.

What looked like a police shield was on top of the kitchen table. It was in fact a fairly decent imitation. Only a police officer might be able to spot it as false if shown quickly. The women obviously could not. There were also several Polaroid photographs. The cops could not believe their eyes. The two fools they had in custody were in several of the photos. The pictures were photographic records of the debased acts described by Sandy as they were being performed. Also depicted in that depraved array of photos were many other perversions not initially described by her.

There were close-up photos showing cigarette burning of arms, legs, breasts buttocks and genitals. Included were several photos of revolvers being held against the girls' heads as they were performing fellatio on their captors. There were photographs of the recovered shotgun being inserted into various women. In short, every debased, sexually perverted act imagined that could be performed by a man on a woman and girl on girl was represented. In almost every photo, a firearm or the threat of its use was present.

The faces of the three women in the apartment were clearly visible in some of the pictures. So were the faces of many other women. Unbelievably, the faces of the men involved were also visible in some of the photos. Many of the photos included the faces of all four of the men involved. It seemed the crew liked group shots; those photos especially would assist in their prosecution, conviction and subsequent length of their incarceration.

Armini asked the two prisoners for the names of the other men in the photos. "Who are these other two men? What are your names?"

"Sol Levine", the dark haired man answered. The light haired guy answered, John MacNally. "We go to college. We're engineering students."

MacNally also answered the first question, "We don't know. We only partied with them." The twitching of his right eye and the sweat running down his face were obvious clues that he was lying.

Armini spoke again, "Whose apartment is this? If you don't tell us who the men are, you are going to take all the charges that come with everything here, all by yourselves. Don't you want a chance at bail and if convicted, a lighter sentence?"

The response showed how scared the two men were, "You mean, if we cooperate, we can go home? We don't want our families to know." The man speaking was showing his lack of common sense. It was Levine. He admitted to renting the apartment.

Armini had them right where he wanted them. He turned to Romano, "Mike read them their rights. Mike was happy to do so even though the collars belonged to Larry.

The lieutenant continued when Mike was finished, "Listen, as a help in your case, can we look around the apartment, in drawers and closets and stuff?"

"In unison, they both answered, "Yes."

Armini turned to his men, "Gentlemen, go thru the place slowly and thoroughly, recording everything you find. Before picking it up, call me to witness it. But first let me go thru the kitchen and look for some plastic bags or something we can use for holding evidence." Armini found a box of small plastic bags.

As evidence was gathered, Mike found school books belonging to two other men, not Levine and McNally. "These sick bastards are college students at Brooklyn College. They're screwed now. We got 'em Lou."

From a closet, Larry's partners recovered two unloaded Smith and Wesson .38 caliber revolvers and two more phony shields in a brief case.

Five minutes had passed since Armini called the Manhattan Dispatcher. Delaney, who had just glanced out the window excitedly announced, "Two Seven Two sector cars and a bus just pulled up now Lieutenant."

It got crowded in the small apartment rather quickly. Armini directed the two EMS attendants to the women. The girls who had stopped sobbing, started again as the attendants approached them.

Armini gave orders, "Check them out, if they are able to walk under their own power, take them to the local hospital for physicals. Delaney, you follow in your car and after the ladies are checked out, if they're up to it, bring them to the Seven Two, otherwise stay with them until they are."

Delaney answered, "ten-four Boss."

As the women came into the main room with EMS trailing them, Sandy walked over to Larry who was standing next to the two prisoners. She reached up and wrapped her arms around his neck and said, Thank you for believing me. We all thank you. Put them away forever."

The display of affection embarrassed Larry. His guard was down. Sandy took full advantage of it and grabbed one of the men by the groin as he sat on the bed. She was so quick that he never had time to react as she squeezed his genitals with one hand and brought her other hand down hard, with clenched fist into his male equipment as she opened her palm. Her timing was perfect. She got him good. His eyes rolled back in his head as he lunged forward in pain trying in vain to hit her with his free hand. She anticipated the action and quickly ducked away.

Mike thought, *Holy shit, she has the reflexes of a cat.* He shouted, "Damn, Sandy, remind me never to piss you off," and chuckled.

The lieutenant placed himself between Sandy and the prisoners and was gently pushing Sandy toward the exit. He was laughing as he spoke, "Tom get them out of here and hold on to Sandy. She might go off again. But first get these idiots dressed."

Armini threw some men's clothing that was found strewn about the place at the two prisoners and instructed them to dress. He made sure that a team of Seven Two officers stayed with each man. He then ordered the prisoners transported to the Seven Two in separate cars.

When the apartment was void of civilians, a final tally of evidence was taken. The team would voucher: one shotgun, two revolvers, eight sets of handcuffs and keys, 252 Polaroid photos and one reel of 8mm film. The team was unable to find any cameras or movie projector. In addition there were four bogus police shields and a police scanner. The keys to their "police car" were previously found in McNally's pants pocket. The cops also tallied twenty three pair of panties. They were placed into a paper sack to preserve any biological evidence. The plastic bags were used to transport the other confiscated items. There were no rounds of ammunition for the weapons recovered.

With the apartment search completed, Armini assembled the rest of his men in front of the building and called for a Department tow truck to hook up the Impala and bring it to the Seven Two as soon as possible. One man was to remain with the car and wait for the tow while the others left for the Seven Two.

***

As soon as the Manhattan cops arrived at the Seven Two, the desk officer, Sergeant Cullin, informed Armini that his command had been notified as to his whereabouts and was given the names of the men who were with him. The Midtown XO (executive officer), upon being notified that his men had been en route to the Seven Two had ordered that Lieutenant Armini telephone him immediately as soon as he arrived.

Armini spoke to his men first, "Men find the arrest processing room, bring these prisoners in there, if they have a cage; throw them in. Leave the cuffs on. Then start vouchering all the evidence. I'll notify Sex Crimes and tell them what we have."

Armini first called Sex Crimes and brought them up to speed and then he phoned the desk at his own command. The desk officer, after hearing Armini identify himself said, "Good going Lou, we all heard what you guys did. Hold while I transfer you."

Captain Collins, the second in command picked up the telephone. He wasn't pleased.

After the Captain said his piece, Armini could be heard saying, "Captain, once Larry Frend got the info and his informant stated there were crimes in progress I made a decision to gather some good men and go immediately to apprehend the perps if at all possible. Larry's informant stated that they had police scanners, so we could not notify Central and maintained radio silence until we made the arrests. I'll make a complete report when we get back."

Collins responded, "You know Louie, we know each other for years before being assigned to MTS, this one is unusual, even for you. It's good police work, but you disregarded several Department regulations."

"Yes, I'm aware of that. But my oath of office comes first. People were in danger, and I'm sworn to protect them."

"Yeah. You're morally correct, but Bryan is going to try to take a piece of your ass. By the way, please tell me that I was misinformed and you don't have Romano with you. You know how Dennis feels about him. That will put fat into the fire."

Armini chuckled and answered, "OK, I don't have Mike with me."

Collins let out a deep sigh on the other end of the phone. "Listen, Louie, just do everything else today by the book. Notifying Bryan can wait until he comes in tomorrow. At least by then we'll have all the proper paperwork completed. Good luck." After another sigh, the phone went dead.

In the arrest processing room, it was like a circus. Word about the collars spread quickly thru the command causing both uniform and non-uniform personnel to come in to see the two idiots who photographed themselves committing crimes. Sexual crimes at that, considered the worst kind after crimes against children. Everyone wanted to see the photos too.

Armini was forced to order all onlookers to leave the room. Getting too slow a response, he shouted, "Charges and specs to all those not directly involved in the case."

Cops scattered like their asses were on fire. With order restored, Mike and the other men sorted out the photos and other evidence, carefully marking each one as to where it was recovered and by whom. The arrest reports would be completed last.

Larry and two responding Sex Crime detectives questioned the two men in custody. After being questioned for over an hour, the two subjects finally gave up the identity of the other two men involved in the crimes. The sex crimes detectives left to find them and bring them in.

Armini and his men were four hours into the morass of paper work. Just before they were finished, Sex Crimes brought the other two men into the arrest processing room. They too, were students at Brooklyn College. One was an engineering student and the other studying pre-law. Jerry Hall and Barry Fisher, respectively.

When Mike heard that one of the men were studying to become an attorney, he felt compelled to announce to all persons in the room, "Some people think attorneys are all dirt bags, that guy certainly is. His career is over before it starts. They're going to love him extra special in Rikers."

Barry began sobbing and whimpering, repeatedly saying, "Oh no!" when he heard Mike's statement.

Auto Crime had been over the car that was confiscated in the case. It would be held in evidence at the Brooklyn Auto Pound. As suspected, the vehicle was registered to McNally's parents. The kid was a poor little rich boy. He and the Levine boy lived in Sands Point Long Island, a rather upscale neighborhood.

All the boys were given an opportunity to notify their parents or attorneys. Three of the men called their parents. McNally did not. He was still hoping that his folks would not find out about his little hobby and elected to take his chances in court.

It took almost five hours to complete the arrest processing before the prisoners were ready to go Downtown. Larry, Delaney and two Sex Crimes detectives took the men down to Central Booking. The rest of the Midtown men returned to their command.

As usual, Mike related the entire day's events to Betty when he arrived home. She sat silent thru the entire narration then only remarked, "Those poor girls. I hope those guys get life."

Chapter Seventeen

After reading all reports regarding the prior day's incident in Brooklyn, Deputy Inspector Bryan ordered Lieutenant Armini to his office. The lieutenant first finished roll call then went to Bryan.

Bryan began, "Lieutenant, please explain to me why you journeyed to Brooklyn without authorization. You certainly have enough time on the job to know not to make that kind of breach of regulations. Let's hear your explanation."

Armini started with, "Well Inspector, Larry Frend received information about several men taking, kidnapping if you will, women from within our command, transporting them to Brooklyn and using them as sex slaves. The men were reported to be cops and possess police radios. The informant, a released victim herself, explained that while she was speaking to Frend, at least one other girl was being abused."

"Officer Frend believed the girl. After I interviewed her, I believed her too and gathered some men and went to Brooklyn. We did not notify Central because the perpetrators might have heard us on what we believed, at the time, to be police radios. That's about it. We caught two of them in the act of abusing a girl. There was a second girl present also. It's all in the reports. One girl was a prostitute and the other, was seeking directions after leaving the Port Authority Bus Terminal and was conned into their car."

Observing a displeased expression on Bryan's face, Armini added, "I understand that Borough Command is quite pleased with the result."

Bryan knew that his lieutenant was rubbing salt into an open wound and felt the need to get personal, "And you decided to take that other Italian, Mike Romano, with you. You know he is to always be on post and my standing orders are for all supervisors within this command to monitor him?"

Dennis was about to step over the line. "What is it with you macho Italians? Do you all think you're invincible?"

Armini could not control himself at the ethnic attack. "No Inspector. We're not invincible, just sober." Without realizing it, he had just joined Mike's ranks and declared war against Bryan.

Bryan's face got very red as he tried not to lose his temper,

"That's a good one Lou. Thanks be to God you men don't drink. Especially while working. You would really be a problem."

"Anything else, Boss? I have to get out to my men."

Bryan realized he might have a problem with his last comment about Italians. He wanted Armini out of his office quickly. In a feeble effort to lessen the sting about the lieutenant's ethnicity, he responded "No Lou. Thanks for your time. Although it was not procedure, your actions showed good police work. We're done."

The lieutenant turned and left Bryan's office.

***

Mike, as usual, stopped at Sonny's store for his morning visit on the way to his post. He was anxious to tell his friend all about the previous day's Brooklyn arrests.

"Good morning Mike. Glad to see you here today." Sonny also had something to tell him. "I have some interesting news."

Mike was hooked at once. "What is it? Don't hang me out like this. Tell me."

"Well, I spoke to someone in the Mayor's Office about you. They already knew you were instrumental in forming the 42nd Street Merchants Association and about the robbery investigation that took you to China Town. I've told them that you handle a three man post by yourself and do a great job of it. The Mayor himself asked for a report on what's happening on 42nd Street and your part in it. Next Tuesday, someone named James Brown will speak with you while you're working. Is there somewhere on your post where you two can meet and get to know each other?"

"Wow, Sonny. I didn't think you had so much weight. This could be awesome for me. Let me talk to some of my shopkeepers. Can I call you later and give you a location?"

Sonny was pleased with Mike's enthusiasm, "Sure Mike.

Whenever you get it lined up, call me. I'll be here all day."

"Great, now I have to tell you about yesterday." Mike then spent half an hour in Sonny's office telling him about his trip to Brooklyn and the resulting arrests.

Just as Mike was getting out of his chair to leave, the radio crackled, "South Day Lieutenant to Central, K"

"Day Lieutenant, go."

"Central please determine the location of South Foot Post 16 and have him acknowledge, K"

"Ten Four, South Lieutenant. South Post 16, what is your location at this time? Please acknowledge for your Lieutenant, K"

Mike felt it was about the previous day's escapade. He responded quickly. "South post sixteen to Central. This post will be in front of Popeye's Chicken at 135 West Forty Second in ten minutes, K"

Lieutenant Armini heard Mike's transmission and responded, "South Lieutenant read direct Central. Stand by post sixteen, please acknowledge, K"

"Ten four, Lieutenant. Post sixteen will stand by, K" He turned to Sonny, "Sonny, gotta go quickly. It's probably about yesterday. I'll call you later about the meeting location. Thanks" He almost ran to Popeye's.

To keep busy while waiting for his lieutenant, Romano kept glancing off to his left and watched the gypsy fortune teller standing in the doorway of her little business. She was a reasonably attractive woman. Mike thought she looked like the stereotypical gypsy, the usual dark eyes, flowing black hair and large ornate earrings and colorful clothing. He had heard rumors the last two weeks that she would stand in front of her place of business and waited for men as they passed her location. She would then gently touch them in an effort to get them inside, purportedly to read their palms and tell their fortune but actually lifting their wallets. The victims would not know until hours later.

Mike took note that she had touched two passersby while he waited for his lieutenant. Mike promised himself that he would check the complaint reports for any Grand Larcenies that fit that particular action.

Lieutenant Armini finally showed up fifteen minutes after the radio transmissions. "Mike where can we go for a quiet conversation?"

Romano was slightly surprised at the question. "Inside or outside Boss?"

Armini looked like he had something important on his mind. "It doesn't matter. Mike, it's your call. As long as we're undisturbed."

"Well Lou, if you don't mind, we can go inside here and I'm sure Gene, the manager, would let us use his office or we can go into the back room of one of the shoe stores."

"This restaurant is on the corruption prone location list for giving out free meals. Let's go to a shoe store."

Mike led the way to the Knapp shoe store a few doors back towards Broadway. He introduced the lieutenant to the manager and asked if they could use his little office area for a private conversation.

Once in the back, out of earshot of anyone, Armini related his earlier conversation with Bryan. Mike became visibly agitated and began tapping on the desk they were sitting at.

"That bigoted bastard. Bad enough he's always screwing with me Lou, but now he's playing with you too." The angel wings were beating in his head again.

"Easy, Mike. I'm a big boy. We got some good press from Downtown for yesterday. Bryan's probably pissed because he wasn't with us and he never got to see the photos. I just wanted you to hear it directly from me that he definitely has something against you. Do you know what's up his ass?"

"Sure do Boss. Remember that collar I made at the garage almost nine months ago? You remember it was voided? Well, he caught some shit about it from various people. But you know that, don't you?"

"Yeah, Mike I heard. But tell me, the way you're talking makes me think that you know something. What are you not telling me?"

Mike wanted to tell his lieutenant all he knew about Bryan, from his taking money for protecting his brother-in-law, to taking $8,000 to void the arrest they were discussing. He let a little out, "Well Lou, let's just say that the voided arrest was done to accommodate some people not on the job. Bryan is no saint."

"Mike, what are you telling me? Do you have something on Bryan? Is he corrupt? Internal Affairs should be told. What do you have? Let's talk about it."

"Lieutenant, I consider you a friend in addition to being my boss. The best I can tell you is that I have heard stories from various people, both on and off the job." He looked his lieutenant in the eye and lied, "But I have nothing concrete. There's nobody that admits to firsthand knowledge. Nobody can confirm any of the stories."

Mike continued, "You know of course, that he lost his slot as Staten Island Borough Commander because he got caught in the middle of a tour in the home of a civilian member of the Department. That's how he was sent to The South. That little escapade made the local newspaper even though the job tried to keep it quiet."

Armini was aware of the circumstances surrounding Dennis' assignment to the South. What he didn't understand was how come Bryan retained his rank and still got command of a unit. He expressed his puzzlement to Mike. Romano had no theory either. Of course, Bryan lost Borough Commander's pay scale and use of a Department Auto. Maybe that was punishment enough.

After some small talk regarding the quirks in the Pumpkin's personality, Armini got back to business. "Mike, we go back to the old three two. I remember the day you were shot at in your car while going home and I responded. Remember when I patted you on the back and told you that you were a real three two cop at that minute?"

"Yeah Lou. We became instant friends at that moment. I still feel that way."

"So do I Mike. That's why I'm here to caution you. I agree with you about the fact that Bryan is a bigot and doesn't like Italians. He would have some trouble hurting me because of my rank and time on the job, but you're low man on the totem pole with short time on the job. Be careful. He is out to hurt you. You must have really put a knot in his shorts over the garage incident."

"Boss, I mean no disrespect by not elaborating on my next comment, But, I sure did. P.S., there's more to come. You'll know when the results are in."

Armini's face took on a look of genuine concern as he spoke, "Mike, from a friend, please be careful, don't break any Department rules and cover your ass at all times."

"Don't worry Lou, I always do. If I can't, I go dormant and do nothing. Thanks for your friendship and concern."

The two friends shook hands, went out into the business area, thanked the manager, parted and left the store, going off in opposite directions. Mike went directly to Herman's restaurant. Once inside the restaurant, Mike quickly asked Herman if he could sit at a corner table with him, he had a favor to ask. Herman quickly responded by grabbing two cups of coffee and bringing them to a table in the far corner of the place, away from the main eating area.

"What's up Mike? You look stressed. Anything I can do to help?"

"Yes, there is", Mike quickly responded. Do you know Sonny Levine; he's on the merchant's association board? Anyway, he arranged for someone from the Mayor's Office to meet me and do a study on post conditions here on 42nd Street and the story is that Dennis Bryan doesn't know about it. I need someplace on post to meet with him and would like to see him here since it's not right on the block. Can I use your place for the meeting?"

"Sure Mike, just try not to have your meetings at lunch time. My place is small and I need all my tables at lunch time. Otherwise the place is yours."

Thanks Herman. I'll have him here no later than ten in the morning or after two in the afternoon next Tuesday. That's our first meeting. There may be others. Thanks."

"No problem Mike. Always ready to help a cop, especially a straight shooter like you."

"Herman, I have one more favor. Can I use your phone to call Sonny and tell him next Tuesday is good and let him know the meet is here?"

"Sure, make as many calls as you need."

Mike made the call and went back on foot patrol. After his meal hour, Romano went across the street to the elevated plaza behind the telephone building. He wanted to watch the gypsy woman with no distractions. He sat down on the end of a bench that faced her doorway, after removing his police hat in the hope that she would not notice him and continue doing whatever it was that she did.

During the next twenty minutes Mike observed the woman across the street as she "touched" six men. None of the men appeared distressed after the incidents.

All but one of them continued walking after contact. The last pedestrian she engaged went into the doorway with her. He emerged just as Mike was about to leave, spent a few minutes in an apparent friendly conversation. The man even gave her a parting handshake as he left. Mike filed the incident into his memory and left the plaza.

One hour before his tour ended, Mike stopped at the Police Sub Station to check for any Grand Larceny reports that named the fortune teller. The officer in charge explained to him that he would have to check for any report that was more than a day old back at the station house. Paul Oscar, the officer in charge of crime coding was the person who could help him.

***

Back home, Mike excitedly related the day's events to Betty and the children over dinner. Annie and Danny were not able to understand what was about to happen, but Betty did.

"Michael, just what do you hope to accomplish by meeting this Brown person and having a conversation with him? I know that he is from the Mayor's Office and all, but please explain why you think his report will help you."

"Well, first Betty, he will see that your husband, Mike Romano, is working three posts, alone. That's kind of unheard of in the Department. Second, his report will probably include the fact that I helped start the 42nd Street Merchants Association, another feather in my cap you can say. Third, hopefully it will unnerve Dennis Bryan so much he'll explode."

"I knew your war with that man was the reason for the meeting. Why can't you just do your job and leave him alone? One day, he'll get his without you getting hurt."

"Betty, this is all legit. I can only reap the benefits of this report. Maybe the mayor will even talk to me. Maybe I'll get back in plainclothes after this. We'll see. So please stop worrying. If the report is good, at least Dennis will never be able to screw with me again."

Realizing that if she continued the conversation, they might end up arguing, Betty dropped it.

***

After roll call the next day, Mike sought out Paul Oscar. He explained to Oscar that he was trying to secure copies of any Grand Larceny complaints on 42nd Street within the past year. To Romano's surprise there was only fifteen.

After pulling copies, Paul handed them to Mike. Further review showed that only one of them mentioned a loss as a result of pick pocketing. The location was recorded as somewhere between Broadway and Fifth Avenue on the north side of 42nd Street. The complainant reported that he was bumped into several times by various people while walking there. Also noted in the complaint was the fact that as the complainant passed a doorway, he was touched on the arm and invited in to have his fortune told by an attractive woman. He suspected that she was the pickpocket, but the complainant could not say if she lifted his wallet. There was no other supporting evidence. The complaint was marked closed.

Mike decided that if given the opportunity, he would bring the gypsy woman to the attention of James Brown from the Mayor's Office when they met, if all went well, maybe they could send undercover officers to tempt her and arrest her on the spot.

Before he left the command, Mike ran into Larry Frend and asked for an update on the Brooklyn sex abuse collars. Larry was happy to fill him in.

"Mike, first, let me say thanks for the help. Second, the DA's office recommended that all officers involved get recognition for excellent police work. I thought that was really cool."

"Yeah, Larry, it's terrific that the DA's Office compliments police officers like that. Usually they are telling us, 'Go back and get me a better case'. Did Sex Crimes get any other evidence?"

"Yes Mike, they did. Those guys are up to their eyeballs in crap. Crime scene went over the guys' car and lifted prints from the interior. They identified three known prostitutes from latent fingerprints. That made three more complainants."

Larry excitedly continued, "In the car, under the spare, was an address book belonging to Barry Fisher, the law student. Inside the pages, he was stupid enough to record the identity of every girl they had in the apartment at one time or another. That gave us fifty five potential complainants. Some lawyer he would have been. The DA also ran the 8MM film we recovered yesterday and saw all four of the idiots in the film. They're screwed. Each man was arraigned for Impersonating a Police Officer, various weapons charges, kidnapping, unlawful imprisonment, sexual abuse, rape, sodomy and a bunch of charges that I can't even remember now. They all were held in two hundred fifty thousand dollars bail each. No cash alternative. I almost feel sorry for them."

With a sardonic smile he continued, "You know how inmates treat rapists in jail. They get the favor returned."

Mike was almost giddy when he heard all that Larry had to say. "It was fun getting those guys and I'm happy to know that they'll get what they deserve, both in the courtroom and in the cells on Riker's Island."

As the conversation ended, the men exchanged pleasantries and parted. Mike went out to his post.

The balance of Romano's work week was rather uneventful when compared to the last few days. He made a drug possession arrest and issued some parking summonses.

His drug arrest however, was cause for Mike to once again be summoned to Bryan's office.

"Romano, you just got another arrest under your belt, didn't you. I understand you made a possession collar. Drug possession is a misdemeanor charge. I told you that you were to make only felony arrests. Just what the hell do you think you're doing disobeying my orders?"

Mike's blood pressure was rising as he answered. "Well, I'll tell you inspector. The man I arrested had five glassines of cocaine, ten dime bags of marijuana and fifteen black beauties on him. As far as I'm concerned, that's possession with intent to sell, a felony. He could not have had that much on him for personal use. If you have a problem with that, write me up for a bad collar and report me to Internal Affairs. I'm sure they would love to talk with me."

Bryan's face took on an almost iridescent glow. He was getting more irritated with Romano each time they had a conversation.

"Listen Romano, you're going to step on your dick someday and I'm going to be there. I don't know who the hell you think you are or what makes you think that you're strong enough to take me on, but you had better back off or get hurt. Your career is in jeopardy. Now get the hell out of my office."

"Gee Inspector. Seems that every conversation we have ends with those words. Oh, and by the way, do you think you'll ever make full inspector? Have a nice day."

Bryan was mumbling to himself as Mike exited the office.

***

Tuesday morning finally rolled around and with it, the meeting with James Brown. After roll call, Mike went directly to Herman's restaurant, arriving at 9:40 a.m.

Brown arrived at 10:00 a.m., walked over to Mike, the only uniformed officer in the place and introduced himself. "Good morning Officer Romano, I'm James Brown from the Mayor's Office. It is a pleasure to actually meet you. Our mutual friend, Sonny Levine, has told me about you and the fine job you're doing here."

Mike took the man's extended hand, "Sir, it's my pleasure. I hope we can be of a mutual assistance to each other. I'm at your service. Please have a seat. We can sit here, away from the rest of the tables," Mike said as he indicated the table in a little alcove.

"Would you like something before we get started?"

Brown smiled at Mike's easy friendliness and asked for black coffee.

Mike turned in Herman's direction and ordered "Two black, please."

"Ok Mike, let's get down to business. The Mayor's Office is aware that you personally assisted in organizing the Forty Second Street Merchants Association. That was fine work. What I'm interested in is the fact that you alone patrol three foot posts. Can you explain why you don't have a partner or another officer on an adjoining post?" Sipping his coffee, Brown continued, "It seems to me that besides being pressured to cover three posts, there is a safety issue here. What if you need assistance?"

"Well, Mr. Brown, first of all, it's not all that dangerous."

Before Mike could continue, Brown interrupted, "Please Mike, Call me Jim. For the purpose of my research and report, I consider us sort of partners. Please continue."

Mike went back to his previous answer, "As I said before, it is not really dangerous. I'm here during daylight hours for the most part. I work 10x6 tours. Some time ago, deciding I needed assistance, I made multiple arrests with the assistance of two security officers from the phone company across the street. The crime, a Three Card Monty game, was in progress alongside their building. It was advantageous for me to use the phone company's men. I knew from experience that most security personnel are police buffs so I asked the two men if they would assist me. They jumped at the chance. The guys loved it and the Association gave them a letter of recognition for their help. In addition, I gave them each a PBA card. As a result of that incident, they are always looking out for me. The owner of this place has helped me during a sidewalk scuffle. Basically, I'm fine. I always have a radio to call for assistance if necessary. The local street people know me and I usually receive lots of cooperation from the store owners. It's not bad."

Brown smiled, "You're very modest in downplaying what you do. Sonny has had many nice things to say about you. Is there anything you would like to do that we can help with?"

Mike jumped at the chance to tell Brown about the Gypsy woman.

"Jim, recently I've taken an interest in a fortune teller, a woman, around the corner from here on 42nd Street. She stands in the doorway of her loft and attempts to get people, usually men into her establishment. She actually 'touches them' to stop them as they walk past her. I thought about arresting her for disorderly conduct, you know, impeding pedestrian traffic, or something, but never did. There have been a few complaints filed for lost wallets. Some of the complainants think she may have picked their pockets. We have nothing concrete. Is there anything that can be done? Can we get an undercover officer here?"

Jim answered with a question, "Have you brought this to the attention of the Association or your command?"

"No, because, I want to handle the problem without Bryan's knowledge. The Association would probably send someone out here, maybe to speak to me, maybe also to the gypsy woman and I don't want her alerted to my interest, and I certainly do not want Bryan to hear what I'm trying to do. I'm sure Sonny has told you that Dennis Bryan and I do not like each other."

Jim opened his note pad and asked Mike to repeat his statements about the gypsy woman again so he could take some notes.

When finished, Jim spoke," Mike, I think we can get something going here. It will be a week or two before a decision is made and we'll have to do a sting type operation to get her. My office will try to use an undercover operative. By the way, I forgot to ask, is she offering sex for money?"

"I have no idea Jim. I've never been upstairs in her work area. I've also never observed her coming to or leaving the premises. Maybe she lives there. I have seen a younger woman with her at times. The younger woman looks to be in her late teens or very early twenties, possibly a daughter."

"Ok Mike, we'll talk about that later. First give me a good feel for your post, or should I say posts. Can we walk them and you note the boundaries for me and particular conditions on each one?"

"Sure Jim. That will give Herman a chance to handle his lunchtime crowd with us out of the way. We'll start right here on post 18." Mike stood up, thanked Herman and motioned to the door. "After you Jim, Let's go."

Once outside the two men walked side by side to the corner of W. 43rd Street, remaining on the west side of 6th Avenue. Romano explained that 43rd to 42nd, only on the west side of the street, where they were walking, was all there was of post 18. It was very small. Jim asked why it was so small. Mike had no idea.

The duo crossed to the south side of 42nd Street, to the corner of the telephone company building. Mike stated that they were now on foot post sixteen, and began detailing the circumstances of the Three Card Monty arrest he had made with the help of two security guards. Slowly Romano led his new friend westward along the block.

The first storefront they passed was an employment agency whose main clientele were local area businesses. Mike mentioned that they were members of the 42nd Street association. As the two men walked past the next business, the office supply and furniture store, Mike, spotted the fortune teller's reflection in the shop's display window. The large windows of the store containing dark office furniture, acted almost like a mirror. Mike could clearly see the Gypsy was standing in front of her business doorway.

Without thinking, Mike turned to Jim, "There she is."

"There who is, Mike? Who's she?" Jim asked.

"The fortune teller I've been watching. You can see her reflection in the window. She's the woman I told you about. I'm sure she supplements her income by being a pick pocket. We can go inside and watch her if you want."

"Yeah, I see her reflection Mike. Good idea. Let's go in and watch her so I can say that I personally observed what appears to be criminal behavior in my report. It would also be helpful in securing approval from the Mayor's Office to launch an investigation as to why you are alone out here. If crime is present, you should have help. You can't patrol and watch the likes of her too."

Once inside the store, Mike sought out the manager and introduced Jim, explaining that he was on a special assignment from the Mayor's Office, adding that they would like to remain in his store for several minutes to observe someone across the street.

The manager cheerfully answered, "The place is yours."

Romano and Brown took a position behind a large furniture display positioned in the center of the window. They positioned themselves to afford the best possible view of the gypsy. As it was a bright sunny day, the sidewalks and street outside was much brighter than the store's interior. Mike knew from his daily patrol that it was almost impossible to see beyond the window's displays and into the store's interior. Mike pulled out his small collapsible telescope and handed it to Brown "Here Jim, this little tool has helped me on many occasions. At this short distance, you should be able to see the whites of her eyes and especially what she does with her hands."

At seeing the small instrument, Brown, actually surprised at Mike's preparedness, said so, "Wow, Mike, you sure are prepared for anything. You must have been a Boy Scout. No wonder the shop owners and the Association love you so much. I can't understand why your Commanding Officer breaks your shoes by putting you alone out here and giving you three posts to cover. You're probably his best man."

Slightly embarrassed by the compliment, Mike responded, "Thanks Jim, just doing my job."

Brown took the little spyglass and peered thru it. It took several seconds for him to find the woman because the lens was small and had a narrow field of vision, but at ten power, the little scope, once focused on the subject was adequate.

Brown was impressed with the instrument, "Mike, this is terrific. I should get one for myself. I can see her quite well, hands, facial features and all. By the way, she's very attractive you know."

"Yes, Jim, I know. I think that's how she can manipulate her marks, her victims, so well. They're flattered that such a good looking woman would kind of paw them."

Mike spotted a man in a business suit approaching the gypsy from the west.

"Jim, here comes someone that looks like a successful kind of guy. Keep a close eye on her as he passes and see if you can spot anything." As the man approached, Mike spoke, "Get ready, he's on her……now!"

"Holy crap Mike, she's good. I tried to catch her as she put her hands on the man, but could see nothing. The telescope is hard to use if you move it, maybe the guy will go into a store and we can go across and ask him if he's missing anything. What do you think?"

"I just recorded the time on the palm of my hand. Let's go."

The two men abandoned their observation point and jogged out of the store. By the time they hit the sidewalk, they could not see the gypsy. They surmised that she must have gone into her building. However, they were able to see the business man go into the luncheonette on the corner.

Upon entering the luncheonette, Mike went right up to the man who was now perched on a stool and ordering a BLT and coffee.

He didn't see Mike approach and was startled as Mike spoke to him and almost slipped off his seat, "Sir, my friend and I were across the street and saw a woman, dressed like a gypsy, step out of a doorway and put her hands on you. Did anything happen?"

The man looked at Mike with a puzzled expression. Defensively he replied, "I don't understand. Is it against the law for a man and a woman to have a conversation on the street? What did I do wrong?"

Mike answered quickly. "Sir, you did nothing wrong, but we, Mr. Brown, from the Mayor's Office, and I, believe that the woman did something wrong."

Before Mike could continue, the man answered, "She didn't proposition me or anything. She just asked if I wanted my palm read and if I would like to know what the future held for me. I told her that I didn't believe in that stuff, thanked her and kept walking. I don't know if I even lost a step."

Mike continued, "You are correct Sir, you never lost a step. We were watching, however, we believe that you lost your wallet, or more accurately, lost it to her. Mr. Brown and I believe that she took it from your person without your knowledge. We believe you were pick pocketed. Please check if you will."

The business man's face flushed with disbelief as he patted the left side of his suit jacket with his right hand. "My God, my billfold is gone. How did you know?"

Jim now spoke, "My friend, Officer Romano here, has been kind enough to notify my office of the antics of that woman. We observed her from across the street. We have been watching her. Please give Officer Romano some contact information for you. My office would like to arrest her. Once that is done, we will need you to hopefully identify your billfold should we recover it and press a complaint. Here is my card. You can call me in a couple of days if you don't hear from someone before that."

Mike recorded the man's name, address, business address and telephone contact numbers into his memo book as quickly as he could.

He then turned to Jim and asked, "What do you want to do now. Should I call Headquarters and ask our Legal Division to try and obtain a verbal search warrant? Once we get that, we can request backup before we try to enter her place. Even if we catch her holding the guy's wallet, the arrest is no good if we force our way in without a warrant. First I should call my boss."

Jim quickly responded with, "No, Mike. I'll call my boss."

The beat of wings began in Mike's head. *Oh boy. Gonna get some action here. Right now.*

After returning to the office supply store to make use of their phone, Jim explained to Mike that his office would have an answer soon. "Mike, I'll call them back in about an hour. We should know by that time, what, if anything, we can do today." It was 10:40 a.m.

With his usual confidence Mike answered, "Great, Jim. Let's hope we get into the gypsy's place while she still has the guy's billfold."

Mike and Jim continued their tour of the south side of the block. As they approached the gaudy windows of the "sex show", Jim asked, "Mike, do you have any trouble with those kinds of places? I would think that they must be nothing but trouble."

Mike smiled as he answered, "Well, not really. They keep to themselves and they didn't join the association, not a single one of them. Neither did the gypsy. Birds of a feather I guess." He chuckled.

Brown asked if they could go inside as he stopped in front of the doorway.

"Sure we can, it's open to the public."

Once inside, the attendant remembered Romano from their previous interaction. "Officer Romano, it's me Tim, Tim Johnson. How have you been? Thanks for the help on your last visit. Since you were here, we haven't had anyone put slugs into the windows' coin slots. What can I do for you? Does your friend want some coins?"

Jim remained silent. Mike assumed that he would want to see the operation of the shop and answered accordingly. "My friend here is from the Mayor's Office doing a report on the Apple. You'll have to ask him if he wants some coins." Mike was not about to accept a favor from somebody who ran a porn parlor. It went against his principals. Jim Brown was a grown man and could answer for himself.

Tim turned to Jim and asked, "Sir, do you want some coins to see our operation first hand. It's strictly legitimate and we have all our permits and business licenses. I can show them to you if you want to see them."

Jim quickly answered, "Thank you, but a walk around the store and only one coin will be sufficient. You have nothing to hide. Do you?" Jim was enjoying the feeling of power.

He had never been involved in a field investigation of any kind before. Now he will experience two, first the gypsy pickpocket and checking out a porn parlor.

Tim almost ran to his station near the entrance to retrieve some coins. He offered three to Jim, "Here you go. Check any booth you want."

Jim, true to his word, only took one coin. He walked around the shop, looking at the magazine racks and the display case with sex toys in it. After a complete tour of the shop, he entered a booth and dropped the coin into the slot as the background music played.

Mike waited while his new friend visited the booth. He knew the wait would be short. Typically, a window shade would go up for approximately thirty to forty seconds with the girls teasing the customers. Just as a girl was about to remove an article of clothing, the time would run out and the window shade would come down. If the customer was quick, he could raise the shade and continue the show before the girl could tidy herself up. If he was too slow, he would have to start over. Mike, to satisfy his curiosity, timed Jim's sojourn into sleaze.

Jim Brown stepped out of the booth in thirty-two seconds. "It's very interesting and somewhat intoxicating, Mike. These people must make plenty of money."

Grinning like a Cheshire cat he added, "I can see why someone would want to feed the coin slots." Embarrassed by his obvious enjoyment of the experience, he quickly ushered Mike toward the door.

Once outside, the conversation went back to the gypsy. "Mike, let's continue our little tour of this block. When we reach the corner, we should be just in time to use the substation's telephone to call my office and see what they suggest about that fortuneteller." Jim Brown, a mayoral aide, was bitten by the police investigator bug. He was buffing out.

The two men reached the police substation by 11:20AM. Brown's instructions had been to call back in one hour. Jim wanted to wait the full hour and use the time to record what he had seen. He also asked Mike some questions regarding his police experiences to include in his future report. As usual, Romano down played his experiences, going into depth only on his bribery arrests. He was particularly proud of them. As far as Mike could tell, Jim appeared appropriately impressed.

At 11:40 a.m., Jim telephoned his office. Mike could see him writing furiously as he listened, occasionally saying "Yes" and "I understand" with, "We'll do it", thrown in from time to time.

When the call was completed, Jim turned to Mike, "Ok Mike, we have instructions. Do you think that we can get some plainclothes men from your old Conditions Unit here now?"

Romano almost leaped with joy. "I'm sure we can. Let me call my Lieutenant first. He's in charge of the entire day squad."

"Fine. I'll fill you in while we wait for him. When he gets here we'll let your boss plan the details."

Mike used the telephone to call the station house. He asked for Lieutenant Armini and was informed that he was out on patrol. Giving the desk officer no information, he added that it was not important and he would see the lieutenant after the tour was over. Romano then called the radio dispatcher directly. He informed the dispatcher to please have the Midtown Day Tour Lieutenant telephone the substation. The call went over the radio seconds later.

When his lieutenant called back, Mike excitedly told his supervisor, "Lou, I have a guy here from the Mayor's Office, he saw the gypsy woman, you know, the fortune teller on the "Deuce" up near Sixth Avenue, pick some guys pocket. We have his contact info. He, the guy from the Mayor's Office, called his office and we're going to try to collar her. He wants some Conditions guys and you here too. We're gonna do it now, today.

We don't want Bryan to know until it's over. Can you meet us at the substation?"

On the other end of the phone, Armini listened intently, not being able to get a word in between Mike's fusillade of words.

He finally was able to say, "Mike, once again you're about to stir up a hornets nest. But I'm backing you all the way, especially with the Mayor involved. Don't do anything until I get there. That's an order."

"Thanks" Mike quickly turned to Jim and said, "He's on his way. Fill us all in when everyone gets here. And, thank you for your interest. This should be great fun, we're gonna have a ball."

"No. Thank you, Mike. I've never done anything like this before. You know, my office told me that technically, because I'm assisting the police at their request, I'm temporally deputized. My God, I'm a cop for a few minutes. It's crazy and exciting."

When the lieutenant arrived, Jim Brown explained what his office had told him. He, Jim, was to remove any personal information from his wallet and count his cash and record the serial numbers of any bills he had. Brown should then walk past the woman's location and engage the gypsy in light conversation perhaps asking for information. If she should lift his wallet, the cops would move in and take her into custody.

Brown's office would have a judge on call to issue a verbal search warrant based on the information at hand. They would also need the name of the earlier complainant, the exact time of Romano's observation of Jim's physical contact with the subject, and the time of Jim's loss, should it occur. The search warrant would be for the premises occupied by the fortune teller and any persons therein. The exact street address and description of perpetrator(s) would also be necessary when the request is called in.

Once the warrant is issued a number and approved by a judge, all officers at the location may assist in the execution of that warrant. It was recommended by Brown's office to have a ranking police supervisor there. Lieutenant Armini would fill that requirement.

With the arrival of three men from the conditions unit, all the police officers and Jim Brown began walking to the north side of the block between Broadway and Sixth Avenue. Brown was nervous. Feeling comfortable with Romano he asked, "Mike, what do I do? You've worked plainclothes before. I never acted like an undercover cop before. It sure is an adrenalin rush and I don't want to blow it. Should I stop and talk with her or just ask directions?"

Mike answered, "Just appear to be looking for something. Try to act like you're preoccupied with your own thoughts as you pass her. The lieutenant and I will be across the street watching from our earlier vantage point. We'll see everything. Take your time walking. It will give our plainclothes people time to set up. Once you've made contact, walk around the corner to Herman's place, the vegetarian restaurant where we met today. Assuming she gets your wallet, we'll meet there and use his phone to get the warrant. Our plainclothes men will remain on the block to make sure she remains at her place and doesn't leave."

Brown turned to Lieutenant Armini, "Lieutenant, you have some cop here. Let's do it. I'm all keyed up."

Armini answered, Thank you Mr. Brown, I know. Mike is one of the best men I ever had the pleasure to work with. Let's do it."

As Mike crossed over to the furniture shop with his lieutenant, his heart was pounding, it was almost audible. Maybe it was the beat of angel wings. He wasn't sure.

***

Armini and Romano were stationed inside the furniture store and ready as Brown approached the doorway of the gypsy's business. The younger woman was also outside with her.

Brown was a natural. He stopped just before reaching her doorway and clumsily opened the briefcase he carried, pulled out a paper, looked at it and continued walking, returning it to the case as he passed his target, acting as if the sheet refused to go back into the case, allowing him to hesitate directly in front of his target. The intended target, the older woman, stepped ever so lightly towards her mark, gently nudged him and apologized just as he returned the sheet of paper into its carrier.

"That's quite alright Miss. It's entirely my fault. I wasn't looking where I was going," Brown replied and continued walking towards the corner, anxiously wanting to check to see if he still had his wallet.

Brown had not taken three steps away from the women when Mike and Armini exited their observation point and quickly headed up the street to cross over and meet Brown in the restaurant. It had worked like a well-oiled Swiss watch. The plainclothes conditions men remained at their stations.

As the two uniformed cops approached Herman's restaurant, Brown was excitedly waving to them and giving the thumbs up sign. He almost ran to them as they drew closer.

"It's gone. She's got my wallet. Quick, let's call it in to get the warrant number and get her. Now I know why you guys love this work. This is so exciting. I haven't felt this way since I unhooked my first bra in high school"

Armini spoke first, Ok Mr. Brown. You call your office and when you get the clerk on the phone, please explain who I am then hand me the phone. OK?"

"Lieutenant, call me Jim, please. We're all in this together, no need for formalities now. Give me a few minutes."

Once inside the restaurant, Mike asked Herman if they could use his rear office to keep the prying eyes and ears of the general public away. Once inside, Brown contacted his people downtown.

"Yes sir, it's Jim Brown. We're ready to go into the woman's business. Yes sir, she's got my wallet. I'm here with Lieutenant Armini of Midtown South and his men. They observed the woman's actions when it happened. Yes sir, the lieutenant will give you the information needed for the warrant. Here he is." Brown handed the telephone to Armini.

"Lieutenant Armini here," speaking as he unfolded his notes, reached for Romano's memo book that Mike held out to him.

Armini continued, "Please give me your name and title sir," he stated as he spread his notes and anchored Mike's memo book open with a large coffee cup.

"Yes sir, your Honor, excuse me for being so dull." Armini was embarrassed that he did not know he would speak directly with a judge. Of course, Brown should have told him that he had a judge on the line.

Mike could hear his lieutenant's answers only. "Yes sir, one of my foot patrolmen, Officer Mike Romano, shield number 11755 and I observed the female put her hands on Mr. Brown as he passed her location." After a slight pause, Armini continued, "The address of her business is 184 West 42nd Street. No sir, we do not have her in the precinct business index. That location is entered as a massage parlor. Yes sir, Female white, approximately thirty to forty years old, long dark hair, black shawl, multi colored blouse and skirt. There is a second female, younger, maybe late teens, also long dark hair dressed in similar manner. She did not approach Mr. Brown."

"Yes Judge, the earlier complaint has been recorded and given complaint number 014-65213…."Yes, we have all the contact information for that complainant and will call him at once if we recover his billfold."

"We have several men from our Conditions Unit to assist in a search and recording of any items we may confiscate."

There were several seconds of silence before Armini said, "Thank you Judge for caring and taking time out from your busy schedule. Please extend our thanks to the Mayor also. Our command thanks him for his interest in this matter. Yes, Sir, here's Mr. Brown again." He handed the phone back to Jim.

Armini's eyes widened as Jim spoke, "Yes sir, Mr. Mayor, we will make every effort to keep this incident under wraps. Yes sir, I'll get copies of everything for my report. Thank you sir."

The lieutenant made some additional notes including the name of the issuing judge, William Kalin, before looking up.

"Gentlemen, we have our warrant. Let's go execute it."

As all three men turned the corner to approach the target location, Mike smiled as he saw Wendell Sloan and Danny Glen sitting on the sidewalk with paper cups and smoking cigarettes. They were within spitting distance of the woman. She was alone. The trio advanced towards their target. Brown was excitedly leading with Armini and Mike about two steps to his rear.

The woman spotted Brown with two uniformed officers in tow. Moving slowly, she began a casual attempt to retreat into the building with the intent to close the door behind her. Glen and Sloan sprang off the ground and grabbed her as she opened the door. Glen moved the woman away from the doorway to prevent her from shouting upstairs, while Sloan prevented the door from closing. The approaching trio arrived at the same time. Just inside the entrance was a small vestibule. It was only as wide as the stairway and about five feet deep.

Armini ordered, "Cuff her and do not let her out of your sight. Watch her hands at all times until she is properly searched by a female officer.

The lieutenant checked the working of the door knob. It was a slam lock type with a dead bolt. Once closed, the doorway was locked from the outside.

Turning again to Glen and Sloan, Armini said, 'She must have a key on her person for the front door. "Once we reach the top of the stairs, call for a sector car and a female officer. After the woman is checked by a lady cop, bring her back inside the vestibule and wait for instructions. Keep the door closed. Mike and I are going up"

His men acknowledged by nodding their heads.

"When the other team gets here, you guys can bring Jim up. Keep the woman in the vestibule until I tell you different."

Looking directly into Jim Brown's eyes, Armini spoke, "Jim, when you do get upstairs, follow orders and touch nothing. Got it?"

Not waiting for an answer, Armini and Mike got moving. The stairway went straight up to the top landing. There was only one doorway. The door was devoid of any markings. In the center of the door was a translucent glass panel approximately a foot square.

The lieutenant motioned for Mike to stand to the side of the door as he reached for the doorknob with his right hand. It was not locked. It swung in to the right, exposing Mike who had his revolver in his hand. The men were now looking down a long corridor with a solid wall on the right side, three doors on the left and a window on the far end that appeared to face a shaft way or alley. The corridor was without pictures, furniture or decorations of any kind.

As Armini was about to attempt to open the first doorway, he used hand signals to remind Mike to stay alert. The lieutenant's experience told him that there should not be any violence from con artists like this fortune teller, but it's always better to be cautious. He opened the door and quickly slid in. Mike remained at the doorway, one foot on either side of the threshold, to back up his boss and watch the corridor. With no activity in the corridor, Mike followed his lieutenant into the room.

The room's interior was a cornucopia of colors. The walls were covered with deep maroon toned velvet drapes. Several tapestries hung suspended against the drapes. Scattered among the tapestries were several ornate framed pictures of towered castles and colorful ornate horse drawn travel wagons, the kind that are depicted by movie producers as "Gypsy Wagons".

The center piece of the room was a large round intricately carved dark wooden table, partially covered by a lace tablecloth. In the center of the table sat a golden colored bowl, darkened inside by what must have been burned incense judging by the lingering odor in the room. Also on the table was a rather large set of Tarot Cards. Directly above the center of the table was a three light chandelier adorned with tasseled shades covering the light bulbs. Surrounding the table were four ornately carved chairs whose seat cushions were covered with well-worn maroon velvet.

Covering most of the wooden planked floor was a rug covered with mystical designs that included unicorns, fairies, zodiac symbols and the like. It too appeared to be very worn or old. The corners of the room that butted against the corridor had floor lamps, their light bulbs also covered with tasseled shades. The windows that faced 42nd Street were painted black, on top of which were painted gold colored stars. Clouds were expertly air brushed on to the black background. There was a large armoire in the far left corner of the room. The doors were covered with some kind of European country scene that scene appeared to be hand painted.

Armini drew close to Mike and softly said, "We'll come back in later to search the room. Let's move on and be quiet. We still don't know if there is someone else here."

Sloan and Glen were now at the corridor doorway. Slightly behind them, standing one step below the landing was a wide eyed Jim Brown.

Exiting the first room, the lieutenant motioned for them to come forward and indicated they should remain silent by putting his finger to his lips. He gently moved Jim into the room they had just left and reminded him not to touch anything. Officer Glen remained with him. Brown moved about the room looking at everything. Glen stationed himself in the doorway.

Now at the second doorway, Armini and Mike, accompanied by Sloan, tactfully positioned themselves. Once set and finding the door unlocked, they quickly entered the room. Again there was no occupant.

The décor of that room was much like the first one except the basic color scheme was dark green, giving a slightly depressing and ominous cast to the room. Once again there was a large table in the center of the room, similar in design to the first one, but this time, dominating the table was the predictable crystal ball. It was huge, about twelve inches in diameter and quite hypnotic as it picked up the rooms colors.

Another noticeable difference from the first room other than color was the placement of various framed pictures placed around the room on tables and walls. Mike thought they had a distinctive religious flavor.

After determining that there was nobody secreted within the room, Lieutenant Armini motioned for the team to move down the hallway to the last doorway. Once positioned properly, Mike peered thru the window at the end of the corridor to gather any further information that might help secure their safety. It faced an apparent blind alleyway. Satisfied that the position of the window presented no threat, Armini tried the door knob. It was locked.

Sloan showed the lieutenant two keys on a lanyard given to him by the responding female officer. The lanyard was removed from the Gypsy's neck when the officer conducted the usual procedural search of an arrested person. Holding one key, he pointed to the front of the corridor and down, indicating the front door. Sloan then took the second key and pointed to the doorway in front of them while shrugging his shoulders. Armini understood there was no guarantee, but took the keys.

Gently he inserted the indicated key into the door lock. It turned easily without much sound. Slowly he opened the door. Noting that the only light in the room came from two glass panels adjacent to the hallway Armini quickly swung the door inward as Mike slid past him and went left, gun in hand and hugging the wall.

When Armini attempted to push the door completely open it had stopped, bouncing back at him. From behind the door came a startled, "What, Momma, what?"

Armini and Sloan quickly moved around the door. There, flat on her back on a daybed, was the younger woman, they had seen earlier. She had apparently been asleep. Sloan and Armini were standing in front of her as she brought her eyes into focus. Sloan had his revolver pointed at her. The young woman looked at it wide eyed and began to shake, speaking in a language that was not understood by the cops.

Armini spoke, "Easy miss, English please. We are not going to hurt you."

Getting some composure back, she looked directly at Mike and spoke without any hint of an accent, "You, I know you. You're the patrol officer on the block. I see you every day. You've never spoken to me. Why are you here? What is this about?"

Armini spoke, "Please stand up slowly. We need to take you to your mother. She's down the hall with another officer. Please keep your hands in sight."

"Is she hurt or something? No, we did nothing wrong. I'm learning my trade. My mother only helps people. We are not doing anything wrong. You, Block Policeman, you see us all the time. We don't bother anyone."

Armini sensed that the young woman was about to become overly agitated and turned to Mike, "Officer, please put her in cuffs, have everyone brought into the first room including her mother, then will you please return here.. Sloan, go with him. First check that doorway over there. Make sure nobody is behind it."

As Romano put her into cuffs, she said, "I thought you were nice. You will now be cursed, now and for future generations."

Sloan reported that the doorway led to a small restroom and it was empty.

Mike thought, *well, she's certainly learning her trade. Complete with curses.* He smiled at her and said, "That's nice. Please come with me" and guided her down the hallway followed by Sloan and Armini.

As Romano and Sloan put the young woman into the first room, she asked, "Who is this other man? Is he police too? I think I saw him before."

Mike could not resist a smart ass answer, "Ask your mother. She's coming right up."

At that instant, the lieutenant called downstairs, "Bring the gypsy woman up stairs."

Seeing her daughter in handcuffs as she was led into the room, the Gypsy shouted, "My daughter did nothing. She is innocent. Release her at once or I put gypsy curse on everyone." Even shouting, her throaty voice and slight European accent was pleasing to the ear.

Mike turned to his lieutenant, "Hey Boss, even pissed off, she sounds sexy. No wonder people find her attractive."

Spotting Jim standing in the far corner of the room she continued, "You!" Her eyes shot daggers at Brown as she spoke again, "You, most of all" and began chanting in some unknown language. She pulled a chair out from the table with her foot and sat down.

Armini turned to the female officer and ordered, "Officer, search the young one, then read them their rights, record the answers and attempt to get their names and residences if possible."

Lieutenant Armini stepped into the corridor and instructed Sloan and Glen to return to their own duties. The patrol car officers were instructed to remain. "Mike, you and Mr. Brown come with me. We're going to begin our search in the room where we found the girl," and lead the way.

When the trio was alone, Armini returned to a less formal demeanor. "Jim, you are here because we owe it to you. You acted as an undercover cop would, allowing her to lift your wallet and helped secure the warrant. Please just observe and once again, I must ask you to refrain from touching anything."

He addressed Mike, "You will search, I will record what and where any contraband is found. Let's begin at that desk in the far side, after I make a quick sketch of the area. Mike, check on the girl and her mother while I make my drawing."

Armini found a yellow legal pad on top of a small table. Using it, he began to record the layout of the room. He recorded everything.

Starting at the doorway and moving to the left were, two rather ornate arm chairs with a floor lamp standing between them on one wall. On the south wall there was a small sofa and another floor lamp. Next to the lamp stood an overstuffed arm chair and a small table. On the west side of the room was a roll top desk with a chair and a light fixture hanging above it suspended from the ceiling and plugged into a wall socket. Continuing around the room there were two windows on the back wall and the bathroom. Back around just adjacent to the doorway was a free standing closet and the daybed. The floor was covered with maroon colored commercial grade carpet. The room was functional and obviously not opened to her customers.

Mike returned as Armini completed his sketch and ordered, “Mike, open the roll top first and look for something that might identify our two detainees.”

Fascinated by everything as it unfolded, Jim Brown followed Mike around like a young puppy.

Rolling back the top of the desk, Mike found nothing of consequence except various names and addresses hand written on scraps of papers and another set of Tarot Cards.

Next he opened a last drawer on the right side of the desk. Inside was a draw string leather purse. The purse contained drivers’ licenses identifying both gypsy women. The older woman was identified as Anasztazia Meszaros and the younger woman as Erzsebet Meszaros. They were thirty five and nineteen years old respectively. Their residence was in Brooklyn, New York. There was also $180 in cash.

In the drawer above, were only a sewing kit and some spools of thread. The top drawer on the same side contained electric bills for the business location in the name of Meszaros Inc. It was in the bottom drawer on the left side of the desk that Mike recovered items that he and Armini hoped to find. There were several empty billfolds and at least four with identification still in them. One of them contained the items that Jim Brown left in his wallet and another billfold contained documents belonging to the complainant from earlier in the day. Jim was so excited that he actually clapped his hands and shouted, “Eureka”.

Mike was ecstatic, “Lou, we got her. Here’s Jim’s stuff and the wallet belonging to the guy from earlier today. We got her.”

It took two hours before the search of the fortune teller’s business was completed and all involved were present at the Midtown South Station House.

Lieutenant Armini signed off on all paperwork and again thanked Jim Brown for his assistance. He even had an opportunity to speak to the Mayor by telephone and lauded the contribution of Jim Brown. The Mayor assured Armini that the police officers involved would be remembered.

Mike asked his lieutenant if Dennis Bryan could remain in the dark as to the circumstances of the arrest. He further explained that as far as he knew, Jim was there without Bryan's knowledge and he wanted to keep it that way.

Armini saw the gleam in Mike's eyes when he asked for secrecy and replied, "I don't quite know what you and Brown have going, but it's fine with me. The fat bastard earned whatever it is. There will be no unusual report on this one. We'll just process it as a regular felony arrest."

All of Jim Brown's personal items were Xeroxed and returned to him. The photocopies were vouchered as evidence.

Before Jim left the station house, he gave Romano his personal phone number, "Mike, I'll meet you at Herman's tomorrow at 2:00 p.m. Please call if you can't make it. I still have my report to do and want your help. And by the way, if you need an undercover man again, call me. I'm your guy. I loved it. Thanks."

Mike called home to tell his wife that once again he would be home very late. He added that the arrests he would be processing resulted from the meeting with Jim Brown.

Chapter Eighteen

After filing the appropriate complaint against the two Meszaros women, Mike was notified that they had a private attorney and would be in court as soon as their finger print results returned from Albany. He was looking forward to a reasonable nights' sleep and was pleased to know that he would not be in the courthouse all night. He expected to be on his way home by midnight the latest. He finished an hour earlier.

The following day, immediately after roll call, Lieutenant Armini took Mike aside. Armini wanted to know what happened with the two gypsy women.

"Lou, it was something. The Assistant District Attorney in the complaint room already had a hard copy of our warrant. All I had to do was give her copies of our paperwork to substantiate the charges. They even listed Jim Brown as a confidential police informant to keep his name out of it. His name was redacted wherever it was written. It's really nice to have the weight of the mayor's office behind a collar."

Before Romano could continue, Armini asked, "What about bail? Was any set, we don't want them back in operation today or tomorrow."

"Yeah, there was bail set. The judge set $50,000 on each of them. That must have come from the Mayor's Office too. Nobody gets that much bail for a larceny. I don't think the ladies will be back too soon. Do you?"

"Guess not Mike. It all worked out well. Was the other complainant happy to come down?"

"He was pleased as hell and said he would write a letter to the Police Commissioner and City Hall about us and how quickly his property was recovered. I never told him that the Mayor already knew what happened. Anyway, he thanked us about a thousand times."

"Are you still meeting with Jim Brown again? Is he still going to write a report as he originally planned?"

"Yes Boss. As a matter of fact he'll meet me at Herman's today at 1400 hours, so I'm not going to get involved in anything today. If there's a collar on post, with your approval, I would like to have it assigned to someone else. I can go down on the arrest report as informing the arresting officer of this and that. OK?"

"Sure Mike. You have my blessing. Just make certain you call me to the scene. Neither one of us wants Dennis on our asses."

"Not to worry. I intend to go to post and keep a low profile today, at least until I see Jim. Thanks again for all you did yesterday."

The two cops shook hands and Mike walked out of the station just as Dennis Bryan entered. As they passed each other, Dennis scowled at Mike. Romano returned a huge grin as he nodded his head in a gesture of acknowledgment and waved. In Mike's head he hummed a happy tune accompanied by the beat of wings. He knew that Dennis Bryan would eventually burst a blood vessel when he heard about yesterday's collars. Thinking about the report that Jim Brown was generating, and the effect it would have on Bryan, Mike almost skipped out onto the sidewalk.

Once out on the street, Mike went directly to Sonny's store on the Apple. He wanted to tell his friend of the meeting with Jim Brown and what happened after the initial meeting. As Romano walked into Sonny's, he saw his friend standing behind the counter, serving an early morning customer.

When Sonny spotted Mike, he quickly passed his customer over to an employee and said, "Officer, will you please come into my office, I would like to speak with you."

Once inside, Mike chuckled and asked, "Sonny, why the formality? Everybody in your place knows me and our relationship."

Sonny answered with a smile and said, "The man I was talking to was recommended to me through the Association. He's a friend of a friend and I don't know him. Let's leave it at that. With Jim Brown in the area, I don't want to give anyone any reason to say that I'm too close to the local cops and bring any heat down on my friends."

Mike acknowledged the comment and brought up the previous day's adventure. "Wait until I tell you about my meeting with Jim Brown, Sonny, it was terrific."

Sonny spoke again before Mike could continue," I got a call from him last night. He gave me a quick recap of the day's events. Are the two women still in jail?"

"Boy, Sonny, once you're on something, you don't miss much do you? Yes, they were in the detention cells when I left court. The judge put 50K bail on each of them. Wonder what prompted that unusual move. Got any ideas?"

Smiling broadly, Sonny answered, "Probably some little bird from City Hall suggested it. By the way, Jim now wants to become an investigator and work with the police. Mike, you created a monster."

"Come on Sonny, he called his office after watching the gypsy woman and they told him to go for it. It wasn't any of my doing."

Sonny knew his friend, "Sure Mike, you had nothing to do with it. I'm sure he asked to watch the woman thru your little blue telescope that he saw in your pocket with his x-ray vision."

Mike laughed as he answered, "Oh, that's how he knew that I had one. I wondered about that."

After they both had a good laugh, Sonny continued, "Mike, Jim is going to do one hell of a report on the post conditions and the cop that handles it all. He likes you. Stay with it, don't drop the ball, you will have a friend in the right place."

After the two of them shared small talk and some coffee, Mike continued to his post. During the first half of his tour, Mike made sure he visited all the shops that belonged to the Association. He chatted with the owners and managers in an attempt to keep off the street. His 2:00 p.m. meeting with Jim was too important to him and was planning to get to Herman's just before the meeting.

Fifteen minutes before the scheduled meeting, Mike was sitting in Herman's eating a Waldorf salad and chatting with his large friend. Herman had heard that the fortune teller and her daughter were arrested and wanted the details. Mike told Herman about his personal observation of the gypsy picking a man's pocket and what happened upstairs in the building. He never mentioned the search warrant and the involvement of Jim Brown.

Mike felt that by downplaying the incident, he might prevent Herman from telling his high ranking friend in the Department about the arrest. Mike was worried about the incident filtering down to Dennis. The avenging angel inside Mike's personality wanted Dennis Bryan to learn about Jim's report and everything it contained only after it was completed and was delivered thru the Mayor's Office. Mike knew that it would rock his world.

At 2:05 p.m., Brown walked in. He spotted Mike at the corner table and walked right over. Herman rose, said hello and offered to get Jim something then excused himself.

Jim started the conversation, "Mike, yesterday was great. I enjoyed every minute of it and hope the office will allow me to work on something with police officers again. The rush was extraordinary. Now, back to business. I want you to know that the Mayor himself has offered the full weight of his office to you. If there is an assignment that you have requested or a transfer you would like, just ask. We'll work on it."

As Jim paused, Mike spoke, "Jim, I'm flattered at the offer. Yes, there is a transfer that I would like. Some time ago, I made a Bribery arrest and went before the Bribery Review Board. They normally try to fulfill requests like you just offered. At the time I asked them to put off doing anything for me until I was ready. Sometime has past. I want to go to Staten Island to work. Once your report is complete, I would like that transfer and would also like the same courtesy extended to my Lieutenant should he desire a transfer. Can you do it?"

"We'll speak to your lieutenant and take care of it. But why wait? We can cut the orders to move you by the end of the week."

"Sorry Jim. Please forgive me for not elaborating, but it's a personal thing. I would like to still be here when your report is filed and Bryan learns about it." Mike grinned as he continued, "I'll call you when I know Dennis knows and then you can transfer me at the end of that week. Thanks."

"Will do Mike. Until then, I personally would like to sit with you as often as necessary to review my notes as I formulate them into my report."

Mike responded, "Thank you. I appreciate all you're willing to do. Do you want to know what happened to the gypsies in court?"

Jim smiled, "No need. We received notification from the assigned ADA this morning." Returning to his notes, Jim then became all business.

"Here's what I have so far. I've been working on it last night and this morning."

The two men sat for two hours and exchanged ideas and wording. At 4:00 p.m., Jim excused himself and left, once again thanking Mike for his time.

Mike responded, "No, thank you. I'm only doing my job. I'm here for you and your office."

The two men shook hands and they parted, each going in separate directions. Mike headed for the substation, hoping that Lieutenant Armini was around. The lieutenant wasn't there and after some thought, Mike decided not to reach out for him. He would fill him in about the conversation with Brown the next day, in person, after roll call. Next he telephoned his wife to give her a quick account of the day and inform her that he would definitely be home for dinner.

***

The next morning, just after roll call, Mike took his lieutenant aside. Taking no chances at being overheard, they went out to the street in the rear of the station.

"Mike, just what is so important that you insisted on being away from everybody before you spoke to me? " asked Armini.

"It's like this, Lou. Jim Brown offered to push any request you or I might have for transfer. You know that I have a war with Bryan that I can't seem to win yet and I know that he doesn't treat you with the respect that you deserve, so I asked Jim to contact you and ask you if you wanted to move to a different command. I told him that I wanted to move to a command on Staten Island."

Armini looked surprised as he answered, "That's a very nice offer and I'm sure they can do it quickly too. I'll definitely give some thought to a new assignment. When is this going to take place?"

"He said he could do it by the end of this set of tours, but I asked him to wait until his report is finished and sent on its way. Once the report is complete, I can say goodbye to Bryan in my own way and leave his command. It's something I have to do."

"Mike, even with the Mayor's Office behind you, use caution regarding Bryan. You don't want to be written up for something stupid, don't cuss him out or anything."

"Not to worry Lieutenant, I have it covered. All I can tell you is that he is no saint and if necessary, I can hurt him."

"Mike, what the hell are you talking about? Hurt a Deputy Inspector in the Department? That guy has twenty years more than you in service time. He has friends and connections in high places. I love you kid, but I think you're nuts.

"It's okay Boss. I've learned that other people can have powerful friends too. Jim Brown is a prime example of one. Can't tell you about any others because I don't want to compromise your integrity, but there are others."

"Mike, are you still referring to that garage incident. You know something. Don't you? I always thought that thing smelled."

"Yeah. Let's say there might be a huge pile of crap behind Dennis Bryan. Someday he'll fall backwards into it. There's other stuff too, from the past." Not wanting to give up too much, Mike quickly added, "Gotta go LT and see Sonny to explain that I'm leaving the command soon. I'm going to miss him."

***

Mike met with Jim Brown four times during the next two weeks since he offered to help him enter a new command. Now, on the second day of a new set of tours, the report to the mayor was finished. Mike and Jim met at Herman's for the last time.

Once again inside the restaurant, Brown and Romano sat at their usual corner table. As Mike finished reading the twenty seven page report, Jim eagerly asked, "What do you think? We want you to be happy with it."

"Wow, Jim. This is really something. You even mention me by name. Thank you. Do you think Bryan, a Precinct Commander, will be transferred as a result of this report?"

Jim smiled as he answered, "Maybe not now. But he will be moved eventually and at the same rank. As long as this mayor is in office, he will not advance in rank. You can count of it."

Mike was almost jumping out of his skin. “You have made me a very happy man. Now, when can you get me transferred to Staten Island?”

“My office has contacted the Bribery Review Board. They will issue orders for transfer this week. As far as the job is concerned, you have been transferred as a reward for a bribery arrest. Do you remember Sergeant Conway from Internal Affairs?”

“Yes, I do Jim. Why?”

“Well, he telephoned your precinct commander and gave him a verbal notification about the transfer before the orders are cut and sent to your command thru channels. He rather enjoyed making the call and wishes you well.”

“That’s great. Did my lieutenant ever tell you where he wanted to go? He was rather quiet about it after I told him about your offer. He never told me what he decided.”

“Yes, you both will be transferred at the end of your respective set of tours. Is there anything else Mike? Do you have any other questions?”

“No, Jim. Thank you again from the bottom of my heart. It was a true pleasure working on this with you.”

As they stood up to leave, Jim shook Mike’s extended hand, “No, Officer Mike Romano, it has been my pleasure to work with you. I hope we meet again sometime.”

As they left the corner table, each man thanked Herman for his courtesy and left the restaurant. Mike went to tell Sonny that he would be transferred in four days.

***

“It’s sure going to be dull around here without you Mike”, Sonny said as he and Mike shared a cup of coffee in Sonny’s office.

“Yeah, I owe you. You worked the whole thing for me. You introduced me to Jim Brown and got the Mayor involved. You put together the Association and all.”

"Sonny just smiled at his soon to be departing friend and responded, "No Mike, I only was the catalyst, you did the work and earned the recognition. There have been good cops in this command for years, but you, besides being one of the best, are truly unique. We can still be friends if you want. I never told you where I live. Did I?'

Mike was puzzled. "Where do you live?"

"On Staten Island, Hylan Boulevard, just two blocks south of the expressway. Stop in anytime. I'll write the address down for you along with my phone number. If you wind up in the One Two Two, it will be even better because that's my resident command."

"Absolutely, Sonny, yes absolutely. We'll certainly keep in touch. Thanks." Mike pocketed the paper with Sonny's information on it. Mike left Sonny's store, went right in to the command and submitted a lost time request. He could not wait to get home and tell Betty what had transpired. He would officially be transferred in two days. He would lay low for the next two work days and plan his going away party.

As it was customary at the time, officers who were leaving a command usually threw a going away party in the precinct lounge. Even though it was officially against Department regulations, it was generally overlooked and widely accepted. Most commanders allowed it, even Dennis Bryan. After all when a man threw a party, he could drink for free and didn't have to hide in his office while he did it.

As Mike passed the desk officer on his way out of the building at end of tour, Fondalar called him over and spoke quietly, "Mike, you're going to the One Two Three on the Island. Good luck my friend."

***

Mike drove home as if propelled by the wings of Pegasus. Once home, he took Betty in his arms and swung her around several times almost falling. “Betty, Jim Brown did it. This Friday is my last day under the command of that thieving red faced fat bigot. My transfer is effective on Monday. I’m going to the Tottenville Command, the 123rd Precinct. No more rush hour traffic.”

“Mike, I’m happy for you, for us. No more worries about your war with Bryan. But, we may have to tighten our belts a little. I’m sure there’s not much overtime on Staten Island.”

“Betty,” Mike began, “It’s like getting a raise. The command is nine miles from our house and there is no longer the expense of crossing the Verranzano Narrows Bridge. The toll is $1.50 each way. I’m also saving gas money. The loss of overtime by making collars won’t hurt too much because of reduced expenses and I’ll have more time at home. This is what we wanted. And especially for you Betty, a bonus, no more Dennis Bryan.”

“You convinced me Mike. Let’s celebrate,” Betty said as she led him to their bedroom.

***

There had been many going away parties in Midtown South. Mike was going to have pizzas, beer and soda available at end of tour on his last day. Armini was made aware of it and bought the pies, Mike paid for the drinks. Louie requested that everyone was told, that he alone paid for it all without any contribution from Mike. The two friends figured that Bryan would not try to burn one of his leading officers and Louis Armini was after all, a ranking officer. The party was a cop tradition even though drinking on Department property was forbidden.

Mike spent his entire tour on Thursday saying good bye to all the good people on his post. He made arrangements with Tony to make several pizzas explaining that men from his old unit would be in on Friday to pick them up about 5 p.m. Mike signed out at exactly 1800 hours and arrived home on time.

On Friday, near the end of his last tour, Mike changed into civilian clothes and along with Sloan and Rosenburg from Conditions, loaded the War Wagon with two coolers full of iced beer and soda, and ten pizzas.

Naturally, Tony, the King of Pizza, had supplied everything at a serious discount. The three of them ferried the party goodies to the basement lounge. Already present were about a dozen officers, mostly from the Conditions Unit. The only ranking officers present were Deputy Inspector Dennis Bryan and Lieutenant Armini. The lieutenant was in civilian clothes, Dennis was dressed in as usual, a superior officers white shirt and uniform pants. Mike entered the lounge and found Dennis Bryan sitting, tucked in a corner, on a red vinyl covered bench type seat.

Mike walked up to his former commander, looked him in the eye and said, "Deputy Inspector Bryan," with emphasis on Deputy, "Glad you could stop in, free beer and all."

He instantly turned away before the Great Pumpkin could answer. The gathering got quite large in about fifteen minutes. Mike engaged his lieutenant in conversation in an unproductive attempt to extract Lou Armini's new assignment.

All the lieutenant would answer was, "You know I live upstate, I'm moving closer to home."

Mike accepted the answer. It was fair. After all, he kept secrets from Armini. The room was filling up as more officers, both in and out of uniform filtered into the lounge. Mike spent some time with each of the men that he knew, especially the members of his old unit.

With every man he spoke to, he felt both joy and remorse. The emotional toll was beginning to get to him. After going once around the room, all Mike wanted to do was leave behind what he thought was an appropriate parting remark to Dennis Bryan, one that was pregnant with multiple meanings.

Mike Romano popped open a cold beer and took a swallow. He stared at Bryan and searched his mind for the right words. Mike considered Dennis a bigot and because of that, wanted to leave him with parting words that were ethnic in nature. Some Italian style idiom, he wanted to say something appropriate and remotely threatening. His goal was to completely unnerve the man and he wanted to say something that Bryan would remember for a long time. He wanted to insure the fat man's continued distress. Mike Romano, like Saint Michael, wanted to punish an evil entity.

Mike searched the recesses of his memory; conversations with Rocco Banducci, movie clichés and old family stories. When he finally had formulated in his mind what he considered appropriate parting words to the Pumpkin, Mike went around the room and quietly said goodbye to his close friends, saving Louie Armini for last.

"Well, Lou I'm ready to leave now. It has been a pleasure to know you and work for you. It has been a blast."

Armini saw the twinkle in Mike's eyes during the exchange and asked, "What are you planning now Mike. I know you're saving something for Bryan. You can't possibly leave without a parting shot. Hope it's not too explosive. Maybe I should go."

"Not at all Lou. I think you may even enjoy hearing my parting remarks. Stick around. Here goes."

Mike Romano, with the beat of wings fluttering in his head walked over to Dennis Bryan. The big man was slouched against the back of a padded bench with a six pack of Mike's beer on his ample belly.

He held one in his left hand and used his right hand to balance the rest of them. *What a sight,* thought Mike as he got closer, carefully choosing his words. "Well, Deputy Inspector Bryan, all I can say is that it has been a true experience serving in your command."

Bryan smiled, took a swallow of beer and answered, "Glad to see there's no hard feelings Romano. You're a good cop. A little crazy, but a good cop. By the way, hope you like your new command. Where is it?"

Mike thought, *either he's playing me or he's drunk and can't remember.* "It's the 123 Precinct, Tottenville, on Staten Island, sleepy town, not very busy."

Again the big man asked a question that Mike thought he should know the answer to, "How did you manage that? Got a hook?"

Mike craftily calculated his response, "Well, Boss, you've seen my jacket. Bribery collars, killing a pedophile, I saw you at his funeral, remember? Anyway, Staten Island is slower than Manhattan and you know that I like being active. I've usually had steady tours and haven't worked the clock more than a total of three years in my entire career. In Tottenville there are no steady tours. I'll have to work the clock. The midnights will be boring. I like to fish though. I'll probably carry a fishing pole on the midnight tours and sneak some fishing in. Do you like fish?"

"Sure do Mike, Are you going to come visit and bring me some?"

"No."

Bryan looked puzzled as he asked, "How will I get the fish then?"

Mike smiled and said in a voice loud enough for most of the men to hear, "I'll send the heads to you by way of Department Mail. Enjoy."

Dennis's eyes got wide, his ruddy complexion paled, as he dropped the open can of beer soiling his pants and shirt. The six pack thumped to the floor.

The Pumpkin sputtered, "Just what the hell are you trying to say Romano?"

Mike smiled broadly, "What I'm saying is that you and your bigotry can kiss my fuzzy Italian ass!"

Mike spun around to see Armini smile and make a hasty retreat to the stairway door. Louie turned, grinned and made a thumbs up to Mike as he passed thru it. Mike turned to face the majority of the men in the room, extended both his arms, bowed from the waist and followed the Lieutenant out.

As he walked to his car, Mike began humming to the beat of wings echoing in his head and was happy. As he put his car in gear for the ride home, he began singing the Battle Hymn of The Republic.

Two weeks later Bryan was transferred to a desk job at the Police Academy and still without a promotion.

When Mike heard about the transfer, He mumbled to his new partner, "Another worm has been removed from the apple."

Joe DeCicco is a retired New York City Detective who originally attended college to practice electrical engineering.

After working as a lighting designer for several years, life circumstances decreed that he join the New York City Police Department in 1973. He has spent more than half his service in plainclothes; including over four years as an Organized Crime Control Bureau narcotics investigator, one year with Brooklyn Central Robbery and more than three years with the Brooklyn South Detective Division assigned to the 62nd Squad in Bensonhurst. After spending twenty years on the streets of New York, Joe happily retired with over twenty awards and decorations on July 4th 1993, uniquely celebrating his own independence day and combining it with our Nation Holiday.

Joe explains that his writings come from an inner need to share his experiences with others in a well-defined attempt to show that, "The Job", is not a vocation but an avocation that spans all the nuances of the human spirit. His entertaining works show sometimes complex personalities of those who choose to be the daily guardians of our society, while fulfilling the public's ongoing interest with police work.

Joe has been a featured guest on American Heroes Talk Radio, San Dimas, California and Blue Line Radio, Wilmington North Carolina.

Joe DeCicco now resides in the coastal area of Wilmington North Carolina with his wife and is a licensed private investigator.

www.ingramcontent.com/pod-product-compliance
Lightning Source LLC
Chambersburg PA
CBHW031148270326
41931CB00006B/194
* 9 7 8 0 9 8 9 7 2 2 7 1 1 *